a great book
Mar/ 2007

A MATTER *of*
CHARACTER

ALSO BY RONALD KESSLER

THE CIA AT WAR
Inside the Secret Campaign Against Terror

THE BUREAU
The Secret History of the FBI

THE SEASON
Inside Palm Beach and America's Richest Society

INSIDE CONGRESS
The Shocking Scandals, Corruption, and Abuse of Power
Behind the Scenes on Capitol Hill

THE SINS OF THE FATHER
Joseph P. Kennedy and the Dynasty He Founded

INSIDE THE WHITE HOUSE
The Hidden Lives of the Modern Presidents and the
Secrets of the World's Most Powerful Institution

THE FBI
Inside the World's Most Powerful Law Enforcement Agency

INSIDE THE CIA
Revealing the Secrets of the World's Most Powerful Spy Agency

ESCAPE FROM THE CIA
How the CIA Won and Lost the Most Important KGB Spy
Ever to Defect to the U.S.

THE SPY IN THE RUSSIAN CLUB
How Glenn Souther Stole America's Nuclear War Plans and
Escaped to Moscow

MOSCOW STATION
How the KGB Penetrated the American Embassy

SPY vs. SPY
Stalking Soviet Spies in America

THE RICHEST MAN IN THE WORLD
The Story of Adnan Khashoggi

THE LIFE INSURANCE GAME

A MATTER *of* CHARACTER

INSIDE THE WHITE HOUSE OF GEORGE W. BUSH

RONALD KESSLER

SENTINEL

SENTINEL
Published by the Penguin Group
Penguin Group (USA) Inc., 375 Hudson Street,
New York, New York 10014, U.S.A.
Penguin Books Ltd, 80 Strand,
London WC2R 0RL, England
Penguin Books Australia Ltd, 250 Camberwell Road, Camberwell,
Victoria 3124, Australia
Penguin Books Canada Ltd, 10 Alcorn Avenue,
Toronto, Ontario, Canada M4V 3B2
Penguin Books India (P) Ltd, 11 Community Centre, Panchsheel Park,
New Delhi – 110 017, India
Penguin Group (NZ), Cnr Airborne and Rosedale Roads, Albany,
Auckland 1310, New Zealand
Penguin Books (South Africa) (Pty) Ltd, 24 Sturdee Avenue,
Rosebank, Johannesburg 2196, South Africa

Penguin Books Ltd, Registered Offices:
80 Strand, London WC2R 0RL, England

First published in 2004 by Sentinel,
a member of Penguin Group (USA) Inc.

1   3   5   7   9   10   8   6   4   2

Copyright © Ronald Kessler, 2004
All rights reserved

Library of Congress Cataloging in Publication date available

ISBN: 1–59523–000–9

This book is printed on acid-free paper. ∞

Printed in the United States of America
Set in Sabon
Designed by Leonard Telesca

For Pam,
Rachel, and Greg Kessler

ACKNOWLEDGMENTS

My wife, Pamela Kessler, is both my partner in life and my partner in writing books. A former *Washington Post* reporter and the author of *Undercover Washington: Touring the Sites Where Famous Spies Lived, Worked and Loved*, she preedits my work and contributes her writing talents. Her excellent judgment infuses everything I do.

My grown children, Greg and Rachel Kessler, are sources of love, pride, and support. My stepson Mike Whitehead is a loyal and endearing part of that team.

The hardest part of writing books is coming up with the right subject for the next book. Once again, my agent, Robert Gottlieb, chairman of Trident Media Group, solved the problem by suggesting the idea for this book. For that and for his wise guidance, I am grateful.

Bernadette Malone, my editor, contributed extremely helpful editorial suggestions as well as her enthusiasm. Adrian Zackheim, publisher of Penguin Group's Sentinel imprint, and Will Weisser, Sentinel's marketing manager, applied their skills to bringing out the book at the right time in the right way.

Having written books about the FBI and the CIA, I know how hard it is to obtain cooperation from secret agencies. But that is nothing compared with obtaining access to the Bush White House. Along with President Bush himself, Dan Bartlett was instrumental in making that decision. At crucial points, Clay Johnson III made the path easier, and he lent his wisdom to the project throughout. They have my appreciation.

In addition to interviews with the principals, I relied on the books listed in the bibliography and a wide range of articles. Unless otherwise noted, all photos are from the White House. Those who were interviewed or helped in other ways included:

Michael P. Alexander, M.D., Frederick P. Angst, G.L. Anspach, Jr., Bonner Arrington, Howard Arrington, John Axelrod, Dan Bartlett, Bertram S. Brown, M.D., Beth Ann Bryan, Claire E. Buchan, President George W. Bush, Carl M. Cannon, Andrew "Andy" H. Card, Jr., Cassandra M. "Cassi" Chandler, Margaret Cousley, Rex W. Cowdry, M.D., David Cohen, Robert J. "Rob" Dieter, Joe diGenova, Lawrence "Larry" Di Rita, Donald Etra, David J. Farrell, Walter M. Fiederowicz, Fred F. Fielding, Howard Franklin.

Stephen Friedman, John C. Gannon, Michael J. Gerson, Barbara J. Goergen, Judge Alberto R. Gonzales, Kenneth S. Goodman, Stephen J. Hadley, Sheryl L. Hall, Bill Harlow, Sarah Hayes, Judge David W. Heckler, Elizabeth Hogue, Martha Holton, Emily House, Karen P. Hughes, Clay Johnson III, Collister "Terry" Johnson, Jr., Hollen Johnson, Judy Keen, Richard J. Kerr, John E. Kidde, Barbara Knight, Barnett Alexander "Sandy" Kress, Howard S. Kroop, M.D., Nancy LaFevers, Michael T. Leibig, Flynt L. Leverett, Frederick C. "Ted" Livingston.

Dr. G. Reid Lyon, Carol Martin, Catherine Martin, John L. Martin, Robert D. McCallum, Jr., Franette McCulloch, Wayne Merrill, Harriet Miers, Emily Miller, Robert S. Mueller III, Steven Nehlig, Nelson C. Pierce, Jr., S. Eugene Poteat, Colin Powell, Dina Habib Powell, Lucille B. Price, Hans Raffert, Tomlinson G. Rauscher, Joe R. Reeder, Charles B. "Buddy" Respass, Oliver B "Buck" Revell, Dr. Condoleezza Rice, Krista Ritacco, John F.W. Rogers.

Karl Rove, Donald H. Rumsfeld, Jim Savage, Eleanor Schiff, Robert A. Shaheen, Dr. Nancy R. Shannon, Clifford J. Sharrock, David Sibley, Ashley Snee, Margaret Spellings, Joy Sweet, Robert J. Sweet, Charles E. "Chuck" Taylor, George S. Tenet, Victoria Toensing, Jim Towey, Chase Untermeyer, Peter Vallas, Robert B. Wade, Logan Walters, Judge William H. Webster, Thomas West, Dr. Eric P. Wiertelak, Jim Wilkinson, and Michael M. Wood.

Contents

A section of photographs follows page 146.

A MATTER *of* CHARACTER

PROLOGUE

When Bill and Hillary Rodham Clinton left the White House, the Secret Service and White House residence staff breathed a collective sigh of relief. Both chameleons, the Clintons would charm audiences and speak on television of their compassion for the little people. Only the "little" people around them—the Secret Service, maids, and butlers who helped them in their daily lives—knew what they were really like. Never on time, Bill Clinton alternately ignored the Secret Service and residence staff or flew into rages over imagined failings.

"Many of us thought, 'Why would I want to sacrifice my life for someone who won't even recognize me?'" a Secret Service agent who guarded the president told me.

If Clinton was nasty and temperamental, Hillary Clinton could make Richard Nixon look benign. Everyone on the residence staff recalled what happened when Christopher B. Emery, a White House usher, committed the sin of returning Barbara Bush's call after she left the White House. Emery had helped Barbara learn to use her laptop. Now she was having computer trouble. Twice, Emery helped her out. For that, Hillary Clinton fired him. The father of four, Emery could not find another job for a year. According to W. David Watkins, a presidential assistant in charge of administration, Hillary was also behind the mass firings of White House travel office employees.

When Hillary found a hapless White House electrician changing a lightbulb in the residence, she began screaming at him because she had ordered that all repair work was to be done when the First Family was out.

"She caught the guy on a ladder doing the lightbulb," said Franette McCulloch, the assistant White House pastry chef. "He was a basket case."[1]

Secret Service agents assigned at various points to guard Hillary during her campaign for the Senate were dismayed at how two-faced and unbalanced she was. "During the listening tour, she planned 'impromptu' visits at diners and local hangouts," said a former Secret Service agent. "The events were all staged, and the questions were screened. She would stop off at diners. The campaign would tell them three days ahead that they were coming. They would talk to the owner and tell him to invite everyone and bring his friends. Hillary flew into rages when she thought her campaign staff had not corralled enough onlookers beforehand. Hillary had an explosive temper."[2]

Publicly, Hillary courted law enforcement organizations, but privately she had disdain for police. "She did not want police officers in sight," a former agent said. "How do you explain that to the police? She did not want Secret Service protection near. She wanted state troopers and local police to wear suits and stay in unmarked cars. If there were an incident, that could pose a big problem. People don't know police are in the area unless officers wear uniforms and drive police cars. If they are unaware of a police presence, people are more likely to get out of control."

In Syracuse, a bearded man who aggressively sought autographs accosted Hillary as she went for a walk outside her hotel during her Senate race.

"He grabbed her," an agent said. "She was livid. But she had insisted she did not want us near her."

For her Senate campaign, the Secret Service purchased three Cadillac De Villes.

"She decided they were not compatible with her down-home image. They were used once or twice," an agent said. "She wanted a conversion van with picture windows and two captain chairs. So we purchased three of them, each outfitted with armor, bulletproof glass, and a system to supply clean air. Each was positioned around New York State to help reduce travel time."

Like her husband and his White House staff, Hillary and her staff were disorganized and habitually late. "She had children running her campaign," an agent said. "She had a lack of organization and a lack of maturity. She could not keep a schedule." When she stayed at the houses of Democratic supporters, "We would show up at their homes at 2 A.M., and she would sleep in the master bedroom," he said.

During her "listening tour," Hillary's campaign staff planned a visit to a 4-H Club in dairy farm country in upstate New York. As they approached the outdoor event and she saw people dressed in jeans and surrounded by cows, Hillary flew into a rage.

"She turned to a staffer and said, 'What the [expletive] did we come here for? There's no money here,'" a former Secret Service agent said.[3]

As the Secret Service and residence staff saw it, Hillary and Bill Clinton had a business relationship, not a marriage. At night, their screaming arguments could be heard throughout the White House residence.

"They would talk on an encrypted phone," an agent said. "He would give her advice. It was a political alliance. My impression was they didn't have sex. She portrayed herself as devastated by the revelations of Monica [Lewinsky]. I doubt she cared."

The Clintons' home in Chappaqua allowed Hillary to establish a residence in New York State and run for the Senate. They kept an apartment in New York, but Hillary lived mainly in Georgetown, according to a Secret Service source. They used the Chappaqua home for fund-raisers. More recently, the source said, Bill has been seeing a blonde mistress there.*

"Chappaqua was because she had to be a resident of New York," an agent said. "That was the main reason for taking it. The only reason she ran for the Senate is to be president."

In her book *Living History*, Hillary Clinton wrote of her gratitude to the White House staff. The truth was, said a Secret Service agent, "Hillary did not speak to us. We spent years with her. She never said thank you."

---

* Clinton's office did not respond to a request for comment.

1

NEITHER FISH NOR FOWL

After the 2000 presidential election, George W. Bush was "neither fish nor fowl," as Andrew H. Card, Jr., who would become his chief of staff, put it. As the battle over the results raged on, Bush and Card met for hours on end to discuss the kind of White House and presidency Bush wanted.

Card, a fifty-three-year-old former Massachusetts state representative and General Motors director of government affairs, never got over his first encounter with Bush. Card was driving Bush's father, then ambassador to the United Nations, from Logan International Airport in Boston to Kennebunkport, where the younger Bush was staying with his family.

"I thought I'd see a close replica of George H.W. Bush," Card said. "I expected a Connecticut Yankee. What I got was a real West Texan. He was chewing tobacco. He had a red flannel shirt on. It was buttoned wrong, the way a two-year-old would button his shirt. He was wearing jeans. There was a tear in the left knee of his jeans. He had a Styrofoam cup. There was a little bit of drool coming out of the corner of his mouth. He proceeded to spit into the cup."[4]

"What are you doing?!" Barbara Bush yelled at the thirty-three-year-old future president of the United States.

Andy Card retained his Boston accent and never could acclimate himself to the dry heat of Crawford, Texas, where Bush had his 1,583-acre, $1.8 million ranch. But Card was uniquely suited to carry out the task of managing the White House on behalf of the president. Card had worked in the White Houses of both

Ronald Reagan and George H.W. Bush. He could be tough as nails—he once personally demanded the White House passes of several Reagan staffers who had been fired—but he had a dulcet manner.

"I learned an awful lot about how they vetted decisions and made them," Card told me in his spacious corner office with a beige carpet on the first floor of the West Wing. "I also learned a lot from those who served those presidents: Jim Baker, chief of staff for Reagan, then Don Regan, Howard Baker, Ken Duberstein. Then under Bush, John Sununu, Sam Skinner."

If Card had learned from experience how to operate in the White House, he also had learned from Sununu how not to operate. Sununu was known for his arrogance, symbolized by his use of military planes to go on skiing trips. He ultimately had to reimburse the government $5,665, the total of what these and other trips would have cost at commercial rates.

In retrospect, Card said, the interregnum between the election and Bush's certification as president was a blessing. During that time, Card met with Bush at the Governor's Mansion in Austin and at the Crawford ranch.

"We would spend hours talking," he said. "Sometimes it was while clearing brush. Other times it was eating ice cream. We talked about the kind of White House he wanted and how it would run and about the rules of the road in Washington as opposed to Austin. That luxury would not have been there if he had won the election outright on election night. We would have started discussing policy, seeing members of Congress, starting to select candidates for the Cabinet, working with the Inaugural Committee. I think it allowed him to give thought to the mundane details of the organization of the White House and the presidency."

Since his first meeting with him, Bush had "matured," as Card put it, but he had not given up his Texas roots.

"You don't find a lot of nuance in what he says," Card said. "He's a tell-it-like-it-is person. He does not pick his words to obfuscate. A lot of diplomats will choose words to obfuscate. I think it goes back to Texas and Texas oilmen. He's from the rough-and-tumble world of Midland, Texas. Your word means more than the contract there. In Midland, when you shake hands, that means more than your signature on the contract. So they speak plainly. It's yes or no. It's, 'We have a deal' or, 'We don't have a deal.' He accepts people who can be with him or against him, but it's the people who are with him *and* against him at the same time that he has trouble with."

Card knew that there was nothing Bush hated more than people who were snobbish, full of themselves, given to pretense. "George Bush knows that his feet touch the ground," Card would say. Card would make sure that no one in the Bush White House ever forgot they worked for a man whose idea of having fun was clearing underbrush on his ranch.

Bush's Texas mannerisms fed caricatures created by liberal critics and the media. They ridiculed his speech and intellect, saying that the man who graduated from Phillips Academy at Andover, from Yale, and from Harvard Business School was a dimwit. When he mangled his speech, as he did when trying to say too many things at once, they heaped scorn on him. Gail Sheehy, in an article in *Vanity Fair*, even suggested that Bush was dyslexic, forgetting that Bush had no problem with reading. Reading difficulty is by definition a component of dyslexia. In fact, Nancy LaFevers, one of the two experts Sheehy quoted to support her conclusion, told me she had told Sheehy that Bush was *not* dyslexic.

"She initially asked me if I had noticed some of the words or expressions Mr. Bush mangled in his speech," LaFevers, a speech language pathologist, said. "I told her I had not noticed them. She then quoted some of them to me and asked if these could indicate that he was dyslexic. I told her that these oral language characteristics were consistent with dyslexia."[5]

"Oh, I like that," LaFevers quoted Sheehy as saying. "Consistent with dyslexia."

"However," LaFevers continued, "I also told her that I was unaware of any history that Mr. Bush had of difficulty learning to read, and that dyslexia, first and foremost, is a reading disability. She then told me that Mr. Bush's mother had worked with him after school with flash cards, and I pointed out that flash cards did not necessarily mean that he was working on reading words."

In fact, Barbara Bush, like many supportive parents, used flash cards with her son to expand his vocabulary. She wanted him to learn at least twenty-five new words a week.

"I then told her [Sheehy] that I did not think she could make the leap to dyslexia on the basis of his difficulties with oral language alone," LaFevers said. "He has syntactical difficulty. When he's under the gun, that's how it comes out. He's a plain speaker. He is not dyslexic. She was out to do a hatchet job. I threw *Vanity Fair* in the trash."

Susan Horn, the second expert quoted by Sheehy, claimed that Bush was "probably dyslexic." She based that on the fact that, when Bush was at Andover, he used the word "lacerates" as a synonym for "tears" in a paper describing his reaction at the age of seven to his sister Robin's death from leukemia. Along with Bush's scrambled words, his improper choice of a word meant that Bush "really didn't understand the language," Horn was quoted as saying.

Apparently, Sheehy did not tell Horn that Bush had merely chosen the wrong word from the Roget's *Thesaurus* his mother gave him as a going-away present when he left Texas for Andover. For their twentieth Andover reunion, Bush and Clay Johnson III, an Andover classmate and lifelong close friend, flew up to Massachusetts with their wives. Bush told Johnson how devastated he was when his teacher gave him a zero and wrote on his paper "See me immediately" because he had mistakenly chosen "lacerates" as a synonym for "tears" in the essay about the death of Robin.

"His mother had said, 'Here's a thesaurus,' " Johnson told me. " 'Don't use the same word all the time. Just go here and look up another word.' So he looked up 'tears' and mistakenly used the word 'lacerates,' as in 'to rip.' "[6]

Asked twice whether Sheehy had quoted her accurately and whether she actually thought that Bush had dyslexia based on the incorrect choice of a word when Bush was in high school, Horn declined to comment.

"If choosing a wrong word once meant that someone has dyslexia, we would all have it," LaFevers said.

If the liberal elite hated him, the people who knew Bush loved him.

"With Bush, there was an instant change," a former Secret Service agent told me. "He was punctual. Clinton was never on time for anything. It was embarrassing. Bush and his wife treated you normally, decently. They had conversations with us. The Clintons were arrogant, standoffish, and paranoid. Everyone got a morale boost with Bush. He was the complete opposite of Clinton."

"If he was in a hurry, Clinton would literally push staff out of his way," a former Secret Service agent said. "He could turn on you instantly. Bush stays focused," he said. "Clinton couldn't stay focused if he tried."

"With the Clintons, you heard salty language all the time," a third former Secret Service agent said. "I never heard either Bush or his father swear," he said. "With Bush, his religious beliefs are for real . . . Bush is down-to-earth, caring. He and Laura offer food to agents. They are always thinking of people around them." The difference, compared with the Clintons, "is striking."

To generations brought up to judge presidents by the image they convey on television, such differences in character and competence are often brushed aside. But there is a direct correlation between those traits and the long-term success of a president. Because of the secrecy the White House residence staff and Secret Service agents are sworn to maintain, voters usually do not know what presidents and presidential candidates are really like. If they did, said a former Secret Service agent, "They would scream."

Charles E. "Chuck" Taylor, a former Secret Service agent, recalled driving Lyndon Johnson, who was then vice president, with another agent from the Capitol to the White House for a 4:00 P.M. appointment with President John F. Kennedy. Johnson was not ready to leave until 3:45 P.M. and, because of traffic along Pennsylvania Avenue, they were going to be late.

"Johnson said to jump the curb and drive on the sidewalk," Taylor said. "There were people on the sidewalk getting out of work. I told him, 'No.' He said, 'I told you to jump the curb.' He took a newspaper and hit the other agent, who was driving, on the head. He said, 'You're both fired.' We got to the White House, and I told Evelyn Lincoln, Kennedy's secretary, 'I've been fired.' She shook her head. I was not fired."[7]

"We were serving roast beef one time," Robert M. MacMillan,

a former *Air Force One* steward, said. "He [Johnson] came back in the cabin. Jack Valenti [Johnson's aide] was sitting there. He had just gotten his dinner tray. On it was a beautiful slice of rare roast beef. Johnson grabbed that tray and said, 'You dumb [jerk]. You are eating raw meat.' He brought it back to the galley and said, 'You two [jerks], look at this. This is raw. You gotta cook the meat on my airplane. Don't you serve my people raw meat. If you two boys serve raw meat on my airplane again, you'll both end up in Vietnam.' He threw it upside down on the floor. He stormed off."[8]

If Johnson was unbalanced, Richard Nixon was two-faced and vicious. He had a well-known history of questionable behavior going back to his secret acceptance from private donors of $18,000 when he ran for vice president in 1952, an issue he addressed in what became known as his Checkers speech.

One former Secret Service agent will never forget a reunion for Vietnam prisoners of war held outside Nixon's San Clemente home.

"This POW did a series of paintings of Hanoi camp scenes," the former agent said. "He was quite good. He presented Nixon with a big painting of POWs. Later that evening, after everyone had left, Nixon was going back to his home. It was a warm night. His assistant turned to Nixon and said, 'What do you want me to do with the picture? Should I bring it in the house?'"

"Take that damned thing in the garage," Nixon said. "I don't want to see that."

"I shook my head and thought, 'You smiled and shook hands with these guys, and you could care less. It was all show,'" the former agent told me.

The poor personal character of presidents like Nixon and Johnson translated into the kind of flawed judgment that led to Watergate and the continuing fruitless prosecution of the Vietnam War. Voters tend to forget that presidents are, first and foremost, people. If they are unbalanced, nasty, and hypocritical, that will be reflected in their judgment and job performance. If a friend, an electrician, a plumber, or a job applicant had a track record of acting unethically, being habitually late, or displaying the kind of unbalanced personality of a Johnson or a Nixon, few would want to deal with him. Yet in the case of presidents and other politicians, voters overlook the signs of poor character and focus instead on their acting ability on TV.

"You just shake your head when you think of all the things you've heard and seen and the faith that people have in these celebrity-type people," a former Secret Service agent said. "They are probably worse than most average individuals." He added, "Americans have such an idealized notion of the presidency and the virtues that go with it, honesty and so forth. In most cases, that's the furthest thing from the truth . . . If we would pay attention to their track records, it's all there. We seem to put blinders on ourselves and overlook these frailties."

No one can imagine the kind of pressure that being president of the United States imposes on an individual and how easily a president can be corrupted by power. To be in command of the most powerful country on Earth, to be able to fly anywhere at a moment's notice on *Air Force One*, to be able to grant almost any wish, to take action that affects the lives of millions, is such a heady, intoxicating experience that only people with the most stable personalities and well-developed value systems can handle it. Simply inviting a friend to a White House party or having a secretary place a call and announce that "the White House is calling" has such a profound effect on people that presidents and White House aides must constantly remind themselves that they are mortal.

"The White House is a character crucible," Bertram S. Brown, M.D., a psychiatrist who formerly headed the National Institute of Mental Health and was an aide to President John F. Kennedy, told me. "It either creates or distorts character. Few decent people want to subject themselves to the kind of grueling abuse candidates take when they run in the first place," said Dr. Brown, who has seen in his practice many top Washington politicians and White House aides. "Many of those who run crave superficial celebrity. They are hollow people who have no principles and simply want to be elected. Even if an individual is balanced, once someone becomes president, how does one solve the conundrum of staying real and somewhat humble when one is surrounded by the most powerful office in the land and from becoming overwhelmed by an at times pathological environment that treats you every day as an emperor? Here is where the true strength of the character of the person, not his past accomplishments, will determine whether his presidency ends in accomplishment or failure."[9]

Thus, unless a president comes to the office with good character and competence, the crushing force of the office and the adulation the chief executive receives will inevitably lead to disaster. Those personal qualities, in turn, shape the conduct and culture of the White House and its staff. In the case of George W. Bush and his ultrasecretive White House, the question was: What was behind the caricature?

2

THE SKY'S THE LIMIT

George W. Bush's character was formed in Midland, Texas, an idyllic Ozzie and Harriet town of brick homes, schools, and churches. Midland reflected Texas values squared. It was the heart of oil country, the county seat for the Permian Basin, the source of twenty-two percent of the nation's oil reserves. Named in 1880 for its location halfway between El Paso and Fort Worth on the Texas Pacific railway, the town had wide streets laid out in an orderly grid. It was a place where anyone who didn't respond to "How ya dewin?" with a dissertation on the weather was considered a stuffed shirt.

When Bush lived there from the age of four until he was thirteen, Midland had a population of just 30,000. He returned in 1975 and lived there until 1988. By then, Midland had grown to almost 100,000.

Midland attracted risk-takers. Anyone could buy a stake, drill for oil, and become a millionaire. Just as quickly, they could hit a dry well and lose everything.

What people don't understand about the oil business, observed Robert McCleskey, a Midland accountant and a friend of Bush's from childhood, is that you can do everything right and still wind up broke.

"The great thing about this place is that you get a chance to get up to the plate," he said.

The limitless horizon and flatness of the land confirmed Midland's motto: The sky is the limit. When Bush returned to Midland, his cocky independence flourished in the dusty boom-or-bust atmosphere, where the sky was not cloudy all day. He realized in Midland that "he would rather be in charge of his destiny than have someone else in charge," said Charles Younger, another childhood friend who is now an orthopedic surgeon. "The life of an independent oilman fit his life pattern and style perfectly."

In Midland, optimism was prized, and helping one's neighbor was expected.

"Texas and particularly Midland are just friendly," said Martha Holton, who lives a block and a half down the street from Laura Bush's parents on Humble Street and ten blocks from where Bush grew up at 1412 West Ohio Street, a modest cottage in a neighborhood of tended lawns. Holton's husband Walter helped Bush get started in the oil business and saw "Little George," as they called him in Midland, grow up.

"Midland goes all out if there is a need for anything," Holton said. "That's how they do here. I don't know if George Bush ever met a stranger. We're all-American people. We have a strong sense of right and wrong. The pace is slow. In ten or fifteen minutes, you can go anywhere in town."[10]

People speak their minds in Midland, and their word is their bond.

"If I tell you I'm going to do something, it's what I'm going to do," Holton said. "We don't have to get a notary. You can set your sights on a goal and, if you have integrity and want to, you can accomplish a lot."

Contrary to popular impression, while Bush's parents came from wealth—Barbara's father was president of McCall Publishing Company and a descendant of Franklin Pierce, fourteenth president of the United States, while George H.W. Bush's father was an investment banker—they themselves had little money. When George W. Bush was born on July 6, 1946, after his impatient grandmother administered castor oil to his mother in an effort to trigger the delivery, his father was finishing Yale. The Bush family lived in a small house at 281 Edwards Street in New Haven.

George H.W. Bush's father had enlisted in the Navy on his eighteenth birthday. At a Christmas dance six months earlier, he met Barbara Pierce, then sixteen. They dated, exchanged letters, and became engaged soon after he became the youngest pilot in the Navy. He shipped out to the South Pacific, where his plane was shot down over enemy waters. He was near death when a submarine rescued him, and the elder Bush came home a hero, with three Air Medals and the Distinguished Flying Cross. George and "Bar" were married in January 1945.

In 1948, the Bush family moved to Odessa, Texas, where Bush hoped to make it in the oil business. They moved into a tiny one-bedroom duplex apartment on a fifty-foot lot at 1519 East Seventh Street. They had the only refrigerator on their block and shared a bathroom with a mother and daughter who moved in later and turned out to be prostitutes.

At first, the senior Bush worked as a $375-a-month oil drilling equipment clerk. Then he became an independent oilman, scouting out land that had potential and negotiating with owners for the mineral rights. He worked from morning until night and traveled the oil patch extensively. By then, George Walker Bush, their first child, was two.

By 1950, they had moved to Midland, where they lived at 405 East Maple and then on West Ohio Drive. It was a three-bedroom home on a slab foundation in a section called Easter Egg Row because the homes were painted bright colors. Midland, unlike roughneck Odessa, was where managers and entrepreneurs lived.

"Raise hell in Odessa, raise a family in Midland," people said.

It was a time when dads worked and moms stayed home. Children respected their elders. Neighbors kept an eye on each others' kids. Divorce was unheard of. Laura Welch, who would later marry Bush, also lived in Midland. With friends, she would sip cherry Cokes at the Rexall drug store and dance in her socks to Buddy Holly and Roy Orbison 45s.

Within a few months of moving to Midland, the senior Bush started his own oil business, buying and developing oil leases. He sent Bush to Sam Houston Elementary School, where he traded baseball cards and was on the safety patrol. His parents taught Sunday school at First Presbyterian Church. Bush's father and his partner brought in high-yield wells. With his family helping to attract funds, he pioneered offshore drilling. Soon, he was a millionaire.

If George Bush were an orange sliced down the middle, one side would reflect his father's traits, the other side his mother's.

His father was decent, fair-minded, tolerant of differences of opinion, and ambitious. His mother was irreverent and had a quick tongue and temper. She instructed Bush not to show off and was the family disciplinarian, or "enforcer," as the children called her.

"I don't think your husband comes home, exhausted from work, and you say, 'Well, go sock Marvin,'" she said.

By now, the family had five children. Pauline Robinson "Robin" Bush was born in 1949; John Ellis "Jeb" Bush, who became Florida governor, was born in 1953; Neil Mallon Bush, who became a Houston businessman, was born in 1955; Marvin Pierce Bush, who became a venture capitalist in Alexandria, Virginia, was born in 1956.

Bush was rambunctious, always pushing the limits.

"He was Huck Finn and Tom Sawyer all in one," Doug Hannah, his friend said. "When you met him, you thought, 'I'd like to be around him.'"

The day after Elvis Presley performed at Odessa's Coliseum, Bush used a ballpoint pen to draw a beard and long sideburns on his face. His fourth grade teacher was not amused, and she hauled him into the office. Principal John Bizilo "swatted him three times on the seat of the pants, and I didn't have any trouble with him after that," he recalled. But Bush already showed leadership qualities of a sort. "Old George was a class clown," Bizilo said. "He was a pretty active boy. He wasn't mean or vicious, but he was the leader of his clan."

Bush's father would later write to a friend, "Georgie annoys the hell out of me talking dirty."

"I don't think I was a difficult child, but I must have been pretty strong-headed," Bush would say. "There were rules. One of them was children are to be seen and not heard, especially around adults. I must have violated that one all the time."

With his mother watching, Bush played Little League baseball. He did not have his father's skill but had the grit to play catcher.

In March 1953, Bush's sister Robin, then three, was diagnosed with leukemia. The local doctor said there was little hope. The senior Bush called his uncle, Dr. John Walker, at Memorial Sloan-Kettering in New York. The hospital offered treatment that might buy time. For six months, Bush's parents shuttled back and forth to New York. On October 11, 1953, Robin died.

Bush's parents had not told him how serious her condition was. They were afraid he might tell her, and they also didn't want to burden him. When they drove to his school to tell him she had died, George, in the second grade, was carrying a Victrola from his classroom back to the principal's office with another student. He spotted them as they pulled into the gravel parking lot.

"My mom and dad and sister are home!" he shouted to a teacher. "Can I go see them?"

He raced to the car and thought he saw Robin.

"I got to the car still certain Robin was there," Bush said later, "but of course, she was not."

"We felt devastated by what we had to tell him," Barbara Bush said in her memoirs. "As I recall, he asked a lot of questions and couldn't understand why we hadn't told him when we had known for a long time."

At night, Bush had nightmares about Robin. He asked his father if "my sister was buried standing up or lying down . . . because the earth rotates, they said so at school, and . . . does that mean Robin is standing on her head?"[11]

Georgie felt an obligation to comfort his mother, who leaned on her son for support while her husband traveled. When he came home from school, he was her constant companion. He would joke and laugh to make her feel better. The loss gave him a sense of how fleeting and arbitrary life can be, contributing to his light-hearted approach.

"You look around and see your parents suffering so deeply and try to be cheerful and funny, and you end up becoming a bit of a clown," said Elsie Walker, a cousin.

Bush was bothered by the fact that, outside their family, no one mentioned Robin and her death. As he would later in life, Bush liked to confront issues. Once, he and his father were sitting in the stands at a football game with friends. As he tells it, the younger Bush wanted to break the ice.

"I wish I were Robin," he said.

"Why?" asked Poppy, as his family called him.

"I bet she can see the game better from where she is than we can here," he said.

A few months later, Barbara overheard Bush tell a friend he couldn't come out to play because he had to be with his grief-stricken mother.

"That started my cure," she wrote later. "I realized I was too much of a burden for a seven-year-old boy to carry."

After Neil was born, the family moved to a larger house with a swimming pool and bought a puppy. Dorothy, their last child, was born in 1959. That year, they moved to 5525 Briar Drive in Houston, where Bush attended Houston's Kincaid School for two years.

Bush's parents decided he would finish his schooling at Phillips Academy at Andover in Massachusetts, where his father had gone. Andover, as it is usually called, billed itself as the oldest incorporated boarding school in the country. Founded in 1778, it consisted of bleak-looking red brick buildings, twenty-one miles north of Boston. It wasn't Bush's idea to go there, he said, but, "I didn't balk."

To Bush, it was a lonely, cold place. He and his classmate Clay Johnson III commiserated with each other. Both Texas boys, Bush and Johnson would establish a lifelong friendship. Johnson would become Bush's roommate at Yale as well. Johnson was from Fort Worth, and his father had a ranch in Oklahoma. He grew up riding horses.

At Andover, Bush was the life of the party; Johnson was the straight man. But under his businesslike, no-nonsense exterior, Johnson harbored a wicked sense of humor.

After Johnson got an M.S. from the Massachusetts Institute of Technology's Sloan School of Management, he became an executive at PepsiCo's Frito Lay, Wilson Sporting Goods, and Citicorp. From 1983 to 1988, he was president of Horchow Mail Order and continued as president to 1991 after Neiman Marcus acquired it.

"I'm an organizer, a systematizer, a bring-method-to-madness, bring-order-from-chaos kind of person," Johnson would say.

In 1994, Johnson was chief operating officer of the Dallas Museum of Art when Bush, as Texas governor, asked him to be his appointments director, then chief of staff. He succeeded Joe Allbaugh, Bush's first chief of staff. Johnson, who had made some money when Horchow was sold to Neiman Marcus, took the job but only on condition he would not be paid.

"I want someone whose primary interest is me—George Bush—and who doesn't hope to parlay this into something and isn't trying to curry favor with this one or that one," Bush told Johnson and his wife, Anne, over lunch at a hamburger place in North Dallas.

Johnson fretted that he didn't know enough about politics.

"I'll take care of the politics," Bush said then. "You go find the best people."

While he was loyal to Bush, Johnson had a remarkable ability to give objective advice and a disturbing tendency to be right about almost everything. Asked how his wife coped with it, Johnson joked, "It's not a strength of our relationship."

According to Bush, after Johnson took the job, he acquired the nicknames "Icebox" and "the Refrigerator" because no one could cozy up to him and convince him to lay aside his standards for a friend. A Texas state legislator once asked Johnson to appoint a few people from his district to some "insignificant" boards, just to "throw my area some bones."

"I am not in the bone-throwing business," the six-foot, four-inch-tall Johnson told him.[12]

Johnson's reserve extended to his response to e-mails, usually limited to "yes," "no," "no opinion," or "I don't know." If he responded "good," it was the equivalent of "fantastic job—let's celebrate at the Palm!"

After his election, Bush named Johnson executive director of the Bush-Cheney Presidential Transition and then assistant to the president for personnel in the White House, in charge of putting together a staff to help the president select four thousand Cabinet and subcabinet officers, executives and middle managers, and part-time board members. In June 2003, Johnson became deputy director of the Office of Management and Budget with the daunting assignment of trying to make the government more effective and efficient. In that job, he was the chief financial officer, chief information officer, and chief procurement officer of the sprawling federal government.

As Bush's friend since 1961, Johnson continued to have a role as an unofficial advisor. He was one of a half dozen administration officials who could see the president without an appointment, subject to Bush's twenty-nine-year-old assistant, Ashley Estes, saying the president was free. Johnson was probably the only person to have spanked Barney, a Scottish terrier who was the presidential dog.

"Barney was on the oval carpet making a nuisance of himself," Clay Johnson told me. "So I spanked him and told him 'No!' I put him on the sofa with me. I think that's the only time he's been spanked."[13]

"That shows what a close friend Clay is," said Logan Walters, Bush's personal assistant, who witnessed the event. "He's the only person I know who could spank the president's dog inside or outside the Oval Office."[14]

Within the government, only Donald L. Evans, a Midland oil and gas executive who became Commerce secretary, was as close a personal friend. Since Johnson had known Bush far longer and had served with Bush both when he was governor and president, no one was in a better position to elucidate Bush's true nature.

"He and I started at Andover together in the tenth grade," Johnson told me in his office at the Eisenhower Executive Office Building next to the White House. The office was decorated with a giant photo of the Cowboy Band, showing dressed-to-the-nines cowboys with musical instruments. "Bush came from Houston. I came from Fort Worth. Andover was a long way from Texas. He had some family history there. I had none. It was like Mars for me. I had never seen wood-sided houses with basements. The weather was different. It was a very foreign land. It was a very hard place. It's a challenging school. He and I really struggled to get caught up when we got there."

While he had little interest in academics, Bush at Andover began to display the leadership skills and gregariousness that would make him a successful politician. He was the leader of the pack, the first to launch the next adventure, the first to come up with a nickname or make a wisecrack. Every kid wanted to be friends with him.

"It's just who I am," Bush would say later. "I can make friends well."

"He's always had a charismatic quality about him," said Robert J. Dieter, who played football with Bush at Andover and roomed with him at Yale. "He has a spark and positive energy that attract people to him. At Yale, he knew everyone from the people who worked in the food line to the president of Yale."[15]

Always teasing, Bush would wear a tie with a T-shirt to challenge Andover's dress code. That earned him the nickname "The Lip." He proclaimed himself the "high commissioner of stickball," an informal game the students played with broomsticks and tennis balls after dinner.

"At Andover, the freshmen stayed together," Johnson said. "The juniors stayed together. You rarely fraternized above or below your class just because they were lowly freshmen or scary seniors. It seemed at every grade at Andover, Bush ran with those older and younger."[16]

When passing others in a hallway, many would hesitate about greeting the other person.

"With George W. Bush, there would be none of that," Johnson said. "He would be anxious to make eye contact and connect."

"George and I played sports, and there are some kids at Andover who are not very outgoing or socially dialed-in—nerds or whatever you want to call them," Bush's roommate John E. Kidde said. "I remember two or three of us would be getting lunch, and there'd be Joe Blow, one of the straight-A students who never talked and nobody socialized with, and we'd sit down and start talking, and George would make a joke or a comment and always bring this guy into the conversation, make him a part of the group."[17]

John Axelrod, one of the self-described nerds, said Bush went out of his way to talk with him. He found it baffling that people would later say that Bush made it through school because of family connections.

"You didn't make it through Andover and not have something on the ball," Axelrod said. "They had no hesitation about throwing people out."[18]

At the time, Bush's father had not been elected to anything. His grandfather, Senator Prescott S. Bush, had been a Connecticut senator. Unless a student were from Connecticut, it was unlikely he would know about Bush's grandfather. Bush never mentioned his grandfather's status.

John Kidde recalled visiting grandfather Bush's home in Connecticut. "There was a photo of his grandfather as a senator," Kidde said. "I had not known he was a senator. Bush said, 'Did I forget to tell you?' "

Johnson said Bush's strengths were the same then as now.

"He's full of energy," Johnson said. "I've heard him described as charming. Nobody would describe a fifteen-year-old as being charming. But he was the fifteen-year-old version of charming. Everyone enjoys being around him. He's funny. He is as quick to make fun of himself as anyone else. It's not negative or caustic humor. He likes people. He doesn't like them as a class. He likes them as individuals. That's why he's so good at recalling names, because he just zeroes in on them. He's not someone who studies names to win votes or curry favor."

At Andover and Yale, he said, "We used to joke that everyone seemed to know who George W. Bush was. He wasn't running for anything, but everyone knew him."

Bush became a cheerleader at the all-boys school. He would wield a megaphone at football games and make barbed remarks about spectators and players. The show he and his cohorts put on overshadowed the game, causing some grumbling. But the school paper came to his defense.

"George's gang has done a commendable job, and now is not the time to throw a wet blanket over cheerleading," an editorial said.

Bush was also the "screamer" for a campus band called the Torques. His job was to inspire the audience with whoops and applause.

"School spirit had never been higher," Johnson said. "Mike Wood, the guy who succeeded him as cheerleader at Andover, thought, 'I have to follow this?' You see those qualities now when Bush meets with foreign leaders and members of Congress. They talk about his genuineness and energy."

3

A PRACTICAL MIND

B ush's father never tried to impose his will on him, but Bush knew the family traditions, and one was to go to Yale, where both his father and grandfather had gone. While he would have preferred to return to Texas, he dutifully applied to Yale and was accepted.

"Bush's father would not have said, 'I want you to go to Yale,' " Clay Johnson said. "I'll bet his parents raised him the way he raises his two girls. If you love them enough, they'll come out okay. They don't direct." [19]

The *New Yorker* would later run Bush's Scholastic Aptitude (SAT) test scores—566 for the verbal test and 640 for math. Because of an adjustment in the way the scores are reported, the total of 1,206 is equivalent to 1,280 today.

Once again, the liberal elite made fun of Bush. Based on the scores, Bush's IQ would be more than 120, placing him in the top ten percent of the population, according to Charles Murray, a leading expert on IQ tests. The latest average of high school graduates is 1,026, 180 points lower than Bush's adjusted score.

On paper, Richard Nixon was one of the smartest presidents, with an IQ of 143, yet he orchestrated the Watergate cover-up, leading to his resignation. Bill Clinton was a Rhodes Scholar yet was dumb enough to engage in an affair with an immature White House intern.

Bush had little interest in learning for its own sake. He was goal-oriented and prized action over words. Only if learning helped him make a decision was he interested. What he wanted, he would say in rare reflective moments, was to "get as much out of life as possible and to do as much as possible." When he retires someday to his ranch, he has said, "I want to turn to my wife and say, 'My dance card was full. I lived life to the fullest.' "

"Some guys went to Yale and studied sixty hours a week," said Robert Dieter, his Yale roommate who also went to Andover with him. "I think George really thrived on people and thrived on the environment. He was the kind of person who knew what was going on; he wasn't the kind of person who was over in the library on Saturday night trying to perfect his term paper. He's not an antiintellectual by any means," said Dieter, who became a clinical professor of law at the University of Colorado School of Law at Boulder. "But he doesn't necessarily believe that all answers are found in books. He doesn't believe that the fact that you've got a degree from an Ivy League school automatically means that you're smarter than anyone else."[20]

Bush played intramural sports but never displayed the athletic prowess of his father, who was voted third best athlete at Yale, as well as third most popular and third most handsome. But Bush later said watching his father helped develop his own competitive spirit. In his sophomore year, Bush pledged Delta Kappa Epsilon (DKE), the jock fraternity that was known for the best parties and the longest bar. The following year, he became its president. Johnson, who also joined, remembered that the fraternity members ordered each pledge to stand and try to name the other pledges.

"The average person stood up and named about eight," Johnson said. "George got up and named all fifty pledges." He added, "He was not the smartest. He was not the most athletic. But people kind of rallied around him."

In his junior year, Bush was one of fifteen students inducted into Skull and Bones, a secret ritualistic society that his father and grandfather also had joined. Skull and Bones prided itself on selecting the best and the brightest who would go on to be leaders in their fields and give back to their community and country. In his 1999 campaign autobiography, *A Charge to Keep*, Bush mentioned Skull and Bones only in passing. He said he "joined Skull and Bones, a secret society, so secret I can't say anything more." But many of his closest friendships would be formed there.

Later, when Bush invited friends to stay over at Camp David, the other fourteen members inducted with him would be among them. Andy Card would be amazed at the diversity of those friends. They included Muhammed Saleh, a Moslem Jordanian who became vice president of Timex; Donald Etra, a liberal Democrat and an orthodox Jew who became a lawyer and at one point was one of Nader's Raiders; Chris Brown, who became a key Democratic operative and was New England coordinator of the Carter presidential campaign; and Roy L. Austin, a black student who became a soccer champion and later director of the Africana Research Center at Pennsylvania State University. Bush named him ambassador to Trinidad and Tobago.

Besides his Skull and Bones friends, Bush invited other friends from Yale like Robert Dieter, a one-time Democrat, and Roland W. Betts, a lifelong Democrat who married Lois Phifer, a black woman whom he met while teaching in Harlem. Betts became a lawyer and one of two principals in Chelsea Piers in New York.

In Skull and Bones' Greco-Egyptian house on High Street in New Haven, the fifteen members inducted with Bush would eat lobster or roast beef dinners twice a week during Bush's senior year. Inside the house were faded portraits of venerable Bonesmen—Rockefellers, Harrimans, Tafts, Whitneys, and Bushes—posing with skull and crossbones. Members called themselves "good men," a term Bush would use to describe people he trusted and admired. As part of their initiation, they were supposed to share their sexual history.

While most Yale students made forays to Vassar or Mount Holyoke on weekends to try to find girls, Bush tended to stay on campus. He didn't have a lot of success until he started dating Cathryn Wolfman, a blond former high school cheerleader who was an economics major at Rice University in her home town of Houston. They began going out together during Christmas break of his sophomore year. Suddenly, in Bush's junior year, they became engaged.

"He came back after Christmas and said, 'Guess what, guys? I got engaged,'" Johnson recalled.

By Bush's senior year, they had broken up. Friends had the impression he was more in love with her than she was with him.

The wedding "was postponed, and then it gradually died," she said. "We weren't in the same city, and we just drifted apart." Within a year, she married a man who had just graduated from Harvard Business School.

Bush drank at fraternity parties and engaged in pranks.

"George was a fraternity guy, but he wasn't Belushi in *Animal House*," recalled Calvin Hill, a DKE with Bush. "He was a good-time guy. But he wasn't the guy hugging the commode at the end of the day."[21]

If Bush wasn't Belushi, he had the misfortune of always getting caught. When he swiped a Christmas wreath for the DKE house, police charged him with disorderly conduct. They later had the charge dismissed. When he helped tear down a goal post on the football field at Princeton, campus police brought him to the college police station for questioning.

They said, "You've got ten minutes to get out of town," Clay Johnson, one of the participants in the incident, recalled.

"I think he was far less wild than the media portrays it," his Skull and Bones friend Donald Etra said. "He drank but not to excess. I never saw any drugs. What struck me about him was he was able to bridge different groups in the class. While he was respected and enjoyed his membership in DKE, he also talked to and befriended many of the other members of our class in the undergraduate dorm who had different backgrounds and interests. The dining halls were very significant at Yale. Often we would sit between meals and chat. He would sit with friends from classes, not just with members of his fraternity."[22]

At Yale, Bush's grade average was C, with B minuses in history, a record that elicited more snickers from liberal critics. Cher called Bush "stupid" and "lazy." Martin Sheen said Bush was a "moron." Actor Larry Hagman called Bush a "sad figure" who was "not too well educated." Yet if Bush was not an outstanding student, he was in good company. Bush's record was identical to Franklin D. Roosevelt's at Harvard. In fact, nine presidents, including George Washington, Abraham Lincoln, and Harry S. Truman, never earned a college degree. Moreover, Cher dropped out of high school; Sheen flunked out of high school, finally finishing with summer courses; and Hagman dropped out of Bard College after a year.

Thomas Edison did so poorly in school he was told by his headmaster he would "never make a success of anything." Albert Einstein could not read until he was seven. He hated school and dropped out at the age of fifteen. "You will never amount to anything," one of his teachers told him. Pablo Picasso never finished secondary school. Christopher Columbus had little education and did not learn to read or write until he was an adult. Peter Jennings dropped out of high school at the age of seventeen. Bill Gates, co-founder of Microsoft, left Harvard after two years. Socichiro Honda, founder of Honda Motor Co., Ltd., left home at fifteen and never got a degree, which he said was "worth less than a movie ticket." Henry Ford dropped out of school at the age of sixteen. Edwin H. Land, who brought the world the Polaroid camera, polarized sunglasses, and 3-D movies, left Harvard University after his freshman year. Lawrence J. Ellison, CEO of Oracle, attended the University of Chicago and the University of Illinois but never graduated. Finally, Michael Dell, who revolutionized the computer industry, dropped out of the University of Texas at the end of his freshman year.

Robert D. McCallum, Jr., one of Bush's close friends from Skull and Bones, went on to graduate from Yale Law School and was a Rhodes Scholar at Oxford University. He said Bush was "extraordinarily intelligent" but was not interested in learning unless it had practical value.

"I am sometimes offended by his portrayal as not being intelligent because his brain works like my brain does," said McCallum, who is associate attorney general under John Ashcroft. "He's not interested in how many levels of meaning you can find in a poem. That's not going to pique his interest for a minute. He would do that kind of intellectual gymnastics if it had any consequence to it. Then he would be all over it because he has a very practical mind."[23]

In the same way, McCallum said, "I was not that intellectually challenged and motivated until I went to law school. The reason was what I was studying in law school had consequences. People went to jail or they didn't. People either paid money or they didn't. The government either acted or it didn't, or you prevented it from acting or got it to act."

"The idea that he is not smart I don't understand," Clay Johnson said. "He went to some of the finest schools in the world, Andover, Yale, and Harvard. You don't get in if you're not smart. Maybe he was in the top five percent instead of the top one percent. Okay, he wasn't Phi Beta Kappa. But I just don't get the 'not smart' thing."[24]

Saying he came from privilege, liberal critics would later suggest that Bush got into Yale and somehow received favorable treatment there because of his father, just as they said he was given breaks at Andover. But at Yale, as at Andover, few students knew Bush as anything other than George Bush from Houston.

"Maybe if you were from Connecticut, you knew that his grandfather had been a senator from that state," Johnson said. "His dad ran for Senate in 1964, but unless you were from Texas, you didn't know that. So it was just George Bush from Houston, Texas. That's what people knew him as."

"We had more famous people than he was," said Frederick P. Angst, Jr., a classmate. As examples, he cited Edward R. Murrow's son and Don Schollander, who won four gold medals as an Olympic swimmer.[25]

Johnson said his grades at Andover and Yale were about the same as Bush's.

"When people say he got gentlemen's Cs in college, I take great offense at that," he said. "I worked my rear end off to get those Cs. There were no gentlemen's Cs. This was pre-Vietnam grade inflation. At Andover and Yale, if you didn't do the work, you got Ds and Fs. It was not like C was the lowest grade you got. We're proud of those marks. We worked hard. He would study and do his work and always cram at the last minute," Johnson said. "He was no different from any other student there."

"Bush is vastly smarter than some folks depict him," said fraternity brother David W. Heckler, who became a judge in Pennsylvania. "But he is not overly intellectual. He doesn't look for ways to complicate things."[26]

At Yale, Bush was neither politically active nor introspective. While unrest over the Vietnam War was beginning to spread, Yale was still relatively untouched by it.

"I don't remember us talking much about the morality of the war," Johnson said.

But Bush's other roommate Robert Dieter said Bush "believed that his father's position was correct—we're involved, so we should support the national effort rather than protest it."

"I told him I was thinking about going to Canada [to avoid the draft], and he said, 'That's irresponsible,' " said Robert R. Birge, a friend from Skull and Bones.

As president, Bush would look back at Vietnam as an example of how not to wage war. In taped diary transcripts, Lyndon Johnson's wife Lady Bird quoted her husband as whining, "I can't get out, I can't finish it with what I've got, and I don't know what the hell to do." Meanwhile, tens of thousands of American soldiers were being killed.

If a war was worth fighting, it had to be to win, Bush would say. He called Vietnam a "politicians' war," one where the politicians made military decisions. But at Yale, even if he had had any criticism of the war, he was acutely aware that anything he did or said could harm his father's political career.

"George didn't have that luxury [of being able to engage in protest]," Laura Bush would later say. "He really didn't. He was absolutely devoted to his father."

As for self-analysis, "He'd much rather laugh and needle people and be funny than try to reveal his inner self," she told a reporter in 1998. "I don't think he actually spends a lot of time thinking about how he thinks."

While Bush was not politically active, he tried to help students in need and would not stand for prejudice. When Frederick C. Livingston, another Yale roommate, had to leave Yale temporarily over his grades, Bush reached out to him and tried to give him support, Livingston recalled.[27]

Classmate Lanny Davis, who went on to become a Democratic loyalist and counsel to President Clinton, said that when talk turned to the problems of a lonely African student, "I remember how sensitive George was in figuring out how to help him." When someone made a hurtful remark about a gay student, Bush said, "Don't do that," Davis said.[28]

Davis considered Bush both smart and unpretentious. "I always was struck by his perceptions about people," Davis said. "He could walk in other people's shoes and look through their eyes better than anybody else."

Bush has an "edge to him, which most people find appealing," said Michael M. Wood, who succeeded him as cheerleader at Andover and then as president of DKE at Yale. "He looks you in the eye, and he says something that's funny and personal and perceptive that tells you he has you figured out."

"If you went to a movie with him, you knew you were going to share some laughs and generally have a good time," his friend Robert Dieter said.

Bush graduated on June 9, 1968, three days after Robert F. Kennedy's assassination. Always busy, Bush's father stayed for two hours. Bush spent that weekend with Clay Johnson and his parents. To Johnson, Bush said, "I wish—it would have been great if my dad could have been there during the whole time."

Looking back, Bush would express distaste for the elitism and snobbery of Yale. He called it a "heaviness." Bush would cite Strobe Talbott, a classmate who later served in the Clinton administration, as an example of the kind of liberal intellectual who engages in constant second-guessing and hand-wringing. At the Yale graduation, Talbott was awarded the Snow Prize for doing "the most for Yale by inspiring in his classmates a love for the traditions of high scholarship." When Talbott was with *Time*, he was a critic of Bush's father and of Ronald Reagan for being nasty to the Soviets.

"Strobe was the kind of person George could not stand," said Robert Birge, his Skull and Bones friend. "He was appalled by people like Strobe."[29]

Bush would never forget his encounter with William Sloane Coffin, a Yale chaplain, after incumbent Democratic Senator Ralph Yarborough defeated Bush's father for the Senate. Bush had traveled the state with his father and had listened as his father and his aides plotted strategy. Even though they were on different sides of the Vietnam War, Bush's father suggested his son look up Coffin, one of his contemporaries.

"Oh, yes, I know your father," Bush remembered Coffin saying to him when he met him as a freshman. "Frankly, he was beaten by a better man."[30]

"You talk about a shattering blow," Barbara Bush said later. "It was a very awful thing for a chaplain to say."

Looking back, Bush would see more clearly what troubled him about Yale.

"What angered me was the way such people at Yale felt so intellectually superior and so righteous," Bush said years later. "They thought they had all the answers. They thought they could create a government that could solve all our problems for us. These are the ones who felt so guilty that they had been given so many blessings in life—like an Andover or Yale education—that they felt they should overcompensate by trying to give everyone else in life the same thing." There's a "west Texas populist streak in me, and it irritates me when these people come out to Midland and look at my friends with just the utmost disdain," Bush said. He wanted to "get away from the snobs."[31]

"There was a liberal orthodoxy that pervaded the place [Yale], and if you challenged that, it wasn't that you had a point of view, but that you were dumb," said Collister "Terry" Johnson, Jr., his friend from DKE who was a roommate.[32]

Bush also became annoyed when Yale didn't acknowledge his father's achievements with an honorary degree until 1991—after he had served as vice president for eight years and president for three.

"My son was at Yale in 1992," Clay Johnson said. "George H. W. was running for president. At a seminar, a teacher said, 'None of you is for Bush, are you?' Two raised their hands and said they were. The teacher jumped all over them."

Bush was not a preppie and was "real proud of the fact he was from Texas," Johnson said. That contributed to the perception of a schism with Yale, he thought. But despite the perceived flaws, Johnson said Bush relished his experience at Yale.

"He had tremendous friendships there," Johnson said. "What does the song say? 'The shortest, gladdest years of life?' Well, they really were for George."

Even the encounter with William Sloane Coffin assumed exaggerated importance when retold later in accounts of Bush's early years. Johnson, his roommate at the time, said he only learned of it later.

"He didn't limp around campus for weeks and complain about it," he said. "Because I wasn't aware of it at all. The academic world is full of pretense and arrogance. But when you're a twenty-year-old at Yale, you don't have a full sense of that."

"The experiences at Andover, Yale, and Harvard allowed him to be comfortable with those we would call elite," Andy Card said. "But his experience in Texas taught him that it's not only the northeast elite that make a difference in this country."[33]

If Bush was not tuned in to the Vietnam War, everyone of his age was concerned about being drafted.

"There was a lot of reality to this," Johnson said. "If you weren't going to get married or go to graduate school or teach, you had to have some kind of plan for what you were going to do with the military. You had to either subject yourself to the draft or go to officers' candidate school or go in the reserves or something. You couldn't just let it happen to you or it would happen to you. At the same time, he wanted to fly."

"Everyone was worried about being drafted. It was all-consuming," said classmate Walter Fiederowicz.[34]

Reporters who had never served in the military in any capacity would later pick apart Bush's decision to join the Texas Air National Guard as a fighter pilot. The National Guard is primarily a domestic military service, but it can be called to active duty. While there was a waiting list to join, there were four openings for pilots, according to retired colonel Rufus G. Martin, then personnel officer in charge of the 147th Fighter Group. Most people who joined did not want to undertake the almost two years of full-time training required to become a pilot. Martin said Bush got the last pilot opening.[35]

Bush denied that family influence was used to get him into the guard. After an exhaustive investigation, the *Los Angeles Times* concluded, "No evidence has surfaced to dispute his statement that neither he nor his father, by then a member of Congress from Houston, sought preferential treatment for him."

But Bush acknowledged the obvious—that he chose the guard rather than the draft and combat. "If I'd wanted to, I guess I would have," he said. "It was in my control."

"He felt that in order not to derail his father's political career, he had to be in military service of some kind," his friend Roland Betts said.[36]

"He didn't dodge the military," said Craig Stapleton, who is married to a Bush cousin. "But he didn't volunteer to go to Vietnam and get killed, either."

Bush flew an F-102 and became a first lieutenant.

The "achievement of learning to fly an unforgiving military jet was all his own," the *Los Angeles Times* said. "The airplanes had no idea who his father was."

4

DIPPING SNUFF

Bush had earned degrees from two of the top schools in the country, but having returned to Houston, he was unsure of his future direction.

"I didn't know what I wanted to do, and I wasn't going to do anything I didn't want to do," Bush said.

He took a job as a trainee at an agricultural company that produced fertilizer from chicken manure, giving Bush ammunition for crude jokes. In the summer, Bush was a roughneck on an oil rig. He gave up the job seven days early when he found the offshore assignment too confining. Hearing that his son had abruptly quit, his father called him into his office in the Houston Club Building.

"In our family and in life, you fulfill your commitments," Bush's father said. "You've disappointed me."[37]

To Bush, the admonishment was chilling.

"Those were the sternest words to me, even though he said them in a very calm way," Bush told a friend. "He wasn't screaming, and he wasn't angry, but he was disappointed. When you love a person and he loves you, those are the harshest words someone can utter."

Bush lived at the Chateau Dijon in Houston, a popular spot for singles. It had six pools filled with secretaries, students, and young businessmen. By coincidence, Laura Bush lived there as well. They didn't meet then.

"He lived in the wild end," Johnson said. "Laura lived in the librarian end."

Bush dated pretty women, including Christina "Tina" Cassini, the daughter of actress Gene Tierney and fashion designer Oleg Cassini. He drove around town in a blue Triumph TR-6.

Over Christmas 1972, Bush took his younger brother Marvin out drinking while visiting their parents in Washington. When returning to his parents' home, his car ran into a neighbor's trash can and dragged it down the street. After the run-in, his father summoned him for a chat in the den.

"I hear you're looking for me," Bush said defiantly. "You wanna go *mano a mano*?"[38]

Much as Bush adored his father, he also felt a trace of competitiveness, a need to measure up to the man who had been Phi Beta Kappa at Yale. As Bush matured and had his own accomplishments, that feeling went away.

"My dad was not happy," Bush's sister Dorothy Bush Koch recalled after the trash can incident. "My dad did not think that was attractive or funny or nice."

Chastened, Bush became a counselor at Professionals United for Leadership for Youth, a mentoring program for inner-city children in Houston.

More than four years later, on September 4, 1976, Bush was arrested in Maine for driving under the influence of alcohol after he left a bar with his sister Dorothy, Australian tennis star John Newcombe and his wife, and Pete Roussel, a family friend and press officer to Bush's father before he became president. At the police station, his blood alcohol level registered at 0.10, the legal limit at the time. Bush pleaded guilty, was fined $150, and had his driving privileges temporarily suspended. The incident would not come out until just before his election as president.

Bush would later say he could pass a background check going back to 1974. The date was chosen because when his father was inaugurated in 1989, background checks of appointees went back fifteen years.

"I'm not going to talk about what I did years ago," Bush said. "This is a game where they float rumors, force a person to fight off a rumor, then they'll float another rumor. And I'm not going to participate. I saw what happened to my dad with rumors in Washington. I made mistakes. I've asked people to not let the rumors get in the way of the facts. I've told people I've learned from my mistakes, and I have."[39]

Yet if he had used illegal drugs, few around him knew about it.

"I don't know why he said all this about drugs," Diane Paul, his girlfriend from 1970 until 1972, said. "He never did anything like that. He was the straightest guy I knew. The most we ever did was go to a party and drink beer."[40]

"I've never known him to take drugs, and he's never talked to me about taking drugs," Johnson said. "I've never been with him when he was taking drugs. He drank in college, and he drank as an adult. I never saw him drink to excess any more than anyone drinks to excess in college."

"I was unmarried and single," Bush would later say. "I deny every accusation," he said jokingly. "But I was a carefree lad."

Having been rejected by the University of Texas Law School, Bush quietly applied to Harvard Business School. In case he wasn't accepted, Bush did not want his parents to know. He still had not decided whether to go when his brother Jeb, on the night of the trash can incident, broke the news that he had been accepted.

"You should think about that, son," his father said.[41]

Bush enrolled at Harvard and, in the fall of 1973, took an apartment in Cambridge, where he slept on a mattress on the floor. He had impressed his parents, but he found life in Boston no more comforting than in New Haven. He told his aunt Nancy Bush Ellis, who lived in suburban Lincoln, Massachusetts, that he despised the "smugness" of Harvard elitists. Ellis pacified him by serving him hot fudge sundaes, his favorite treat.

At Harvard, Bush shocked other students by wearing his National Guard pilot's jacket and cowboy boots, and by chewing tobacco in class.

"One of my first recollections of him," classmate Marty Kahn said, "was sitting in class and hearing the unmistakable sound of someone spitting tobacco. I turned, and there was George sitting in the back of the room in his [National Guard] bomber jacket spitting in a cup. You have to remember this was Harvard Business School. You just didn't see that kind of thing."[42]

"While they were drinking Chivas Regal, he was drinking Wild Turkey," said April Foley, a classmate who dated Bush briefly and remained friends with him. "They were smoking Benson and Hedges, and he's dipping Copenhagen, and while they were going to the opera, he was listening to Jimmy Rodriguez over and over and over."[43]

If Bush didn't fit the Harvard mold, he earned acceptable grades and embraced the school's approach. Harvard taught students to delegate, look at the big picture, and decide. It was an approach he would use as president, Clay Johnson said. Johnson recalled Bush's questions when being briefed by Dr. Condoleezza Rice and other national-security experts as he began his presidential campaign.

"What's the purpose of the Defense Department?" Bush asked. "What is its goal? How does it measure success?"

While Bush's critics might mock them, they were the sorts of questions a good management consultant might ask. Without an eye to the basic questions, people lose sight of the goal and get lost in mundane details, as President Johnson did during the Vietnam War. Johnson micromanaged the war and tried to measure success by the body count—how many of the enemy had been killed. That was a sure way to lose, because without detonating nuclear weapons, the United States would never kill enough Vietcong to wipe them out. Only a complete military victory would end the war.

Similarly, President Carter got bogged down in detail.

"Carter said, 'I'm in charge,'" a Secret Service agent said. "'Everything is my way.' He tried to micromanage everything. You had to go to him about playing on the tennis court."

At a press conference, Carter denied that White House aides had to ask him for permission to use the tennis court. The truth was worse. White House aides had to call Carter to get permission to play on the courts even when he was traveling on *Air Force One*. Because other aides were afraid to give Carter messages asking for permission to play, Charles Palmer, the chief *Air Force One* steward, often wound up doing it.

Carter "approved who played from on the plane," Palmer said. He said Carter enjoyed the power. Carter would say, "I'll let them know," Palmer said. "Other times, he would look at me and smile and say, 'Tell them yes.' I felt he felt it was a big deal. I didn't understand why that had to happen."

One day, Carter noticed water gushing from a grate outside the White House.

"It was the emergency generating system," said William Cuff, an assistant chief of the White House military office. "Carter got interested in that and micromanaged it. He would zoom in on an area and manage the hell out of it. He asked questions of the chief usher every day. 'How much does this cost?' 'Which part is needed?' 'When is it coming?' 'Which bolt ties to which flange?' "

In the same way, Carter micromanaged the Iranian hostage crisis, which began on November 4, 1979, when Iranian militants seized the U.S. embassy in Teheran. They held fifty-two Americans captive for more than a year. Responding to Carter's pressure, the military came up with a foolish, disastrous plan to rescue them. No thought had been given to the fact that sand could foil the helicopters sent to free the hostages. The malfunction of most of the helicopters forced the commander to abort the rescue. During the operation in April 1980, one of the helicopters collided with a transport plane, killing eight servicemen.

While Clinton mastered issues and facts like the Rhodes Scholar he was, he tended to micromanage just as Carter had. A few weeks after he took office, Clinton was returning to the White House from a jog. He saw an engineer from the General Services Administration, the government's housekeeping agency, strolling toward what is now called the Eisenhower Executive Office Building.

"Clinton came over and asked him his name and what he does," recalled Lucille Price, a GSA manager. "He said he was the chief engineer and takes care of heating and air-conditioning. Clinton asked what he was going to do now. He said he was going to check on these chillers."

"Do you mind if I go with you?" the president asked.

For the next half hour, the engineer briefed Clinton on the intricacies of the White House heating and air-conditioning system.

Like Carter, Clinton would endlessly pore over policy material, holding debates over pizza about minute decisions long into the night, then reexamining the issues for weeks. He approved sending Cruise missiles into Osama bin Laden's tents, forgetting the big picture: that such puny attacks only confirmed to bin Laden that the United States was a paper tiger, goading the terrorist into more aggressive actions.

"During the campaign," Clay Johnson noted, "they said Bush didn't read big briefing books the way Clinton did. Well, Clinton was misspending his time. Let others read the briefing books and answer the question about the purpose of the Defense Department."

As for chewing tobacco at Harvard, Johnson said Bush was not trying to make an impression on anyone.

"That's what guys from Midland, Texas did in the 70s," Johnson said. "They chewed tobacco. You weren't going to walk in with a coat and tie and suit and a polished pair of shoes and get anybody to lease you their land."[44]

Bush was one of the few students who posed for his Harvard yearbook photo in a sport shirt. The other prominent photo shows him in long hair, sitting in the back row of class blowing bubble gum.

Clay Johnson said that after Bush announced on June 12, 1999, that he would run for president, a fashion magazine called him.

"They said they were doing a story on how the candidates dress. I couldn't fathom that they were doing a story on his wardrobe. Because in college, his wardrobe was which of these five or six T-shirts—which had not been washed in, not days, but weeks and were lying on the floor—was he going to don that day. He had no interest in it. It wasn't a rebellious thing. It wasn't an affectation. He just had no interest in it. But that works real well in Midland. That's just the way he is. He was not going to transform himself into something else at Harvard Business School."[45]

5

OIL HUSTLING

A fter graduating from Harvard with an M.B.A. in 1975, Bush visited friends in Midland and decided to stay.

"All of a sudden, it dawned on me that this is entrepreneurial heaven," Bush said later. "This is one of the few places in the country where you can go without portfolio and train yourself and become competitive. The barriers to entry were very low in the oil sector. I can't tell you how obvious it was."[46]

Bush observed that he always remained "closely part of the world I grew up in. I was educated in the East, but my heart was always back in Texas . . . I could have chosen to remain in the East, but I love Texas. I have great pride in Texas and everything Texan."

By Clay Johnson's definition, a Texan is "direct, friendly, has big ideas, and is energetic, tells a good tale, has a good sense of humor, a good common touch, keeps his word, and is hardworking."

The 1973 Arab oil embargo had sent prices skyrocketing. From 1973 to 1981, the price of oil rose eight hundred percent. One of every five Midlanders was a millionaire. "I was inebriated by the atmosphere out there," Bush said.

Bush looked up Walter Holton, a friend of his father's who lived ten blocks from where Bush grew up. Holton agreed to teach Bush to be a land man, someone who searches courthouse records to determine who owns property and whether they own the mineral rights. Often, a land man becomes involved in leasing land for drilling wells. Because a land man has the inside track, he also invests in the business himself. Bush's father had given him $15,000 left over from a trust fund he had set up for him for his education. With the money, Bush invested modestly in oil leases and exploration across West Texas and eastern New Mexico. He didn't borrow, and he didn't take big risks.

Johnson called him one day and asked how his oil hustling was going.

"Well," Bush said, "I won $100 in a poker game last night, and that's my income for the week."

Bush lived in a guest house at 2006 Harvard above a cinder block garage. The apartment, which had a tiny window overlooking an alley, was crammed with shucked-off clothing, discarded newspapers, and a bed literally lashed together with neckties. Bush's friend Joe O'Neill III, the son of one of Midland's wealthiest oil men, called it a toxic waste site.

Bush wore jeans and T-shirts. He often wore slippers outside, ones his parents had brought him from China.

"He would bring his dirty clothes over to our house, and my wife would wash them," recalled Don Evans, who was president of Tom Brown Inc., an oil exploration company, and would later become Bush's Commerce secretary.[47] "Material things have never been important to him. If you give him a couple of good books and a pair of running shoes, he's happy."

When friends were about to throw their clothes away, Bush would say, "You gonna throw that out?"

"He's not frugal, he's cheap," said Bob McCleskey.

Much later, after Bush married Laura, Johnson's wife Anne and her sister, a decorator and artist, convinced Laura to buy a decorative pillow that cost $1,000.

"I thought George Bush was going to go nuts," Johnson said. "He's pretty tight."[48]

In his 1970 Oldsmobile Cutlass, Bush listened to the Everly Brothers and country music, which reflected his personality: uncomplicated, emotional, patriotic, bold, and with plenty of twang. Like his father, Bush would tear up at tales of heroism and service to the country.

Back in Midland, Bush once again was the life of the party, the prankster-in-chief. People called him Bombastic Bushkin and ribbed him about his "Phi Beta Kappa years" at Yale and Harvard. He dated attractive women but never got serious.

On July 6, 1977, Democratic Representative George Mahon announced he was retiring after forty-four years in Congress. Bush decided to run for his seat. By then, Bush had worked in three of his father's campaigns and had been on the campaign staffs of two Republican Senate candidates, Edward J. Gurney in Florida and Winton Blount in Alabama.

Going back to Prescott Bush, the family always had a sense of noblesse oblige. Prescott declared that a man's first duty was to secure a fortune and provide for his family. Then he might turn to public service.

Politics was "in his blood," Doug Hannah, his childhood friend, would say. "Once your family's in politics, you see how it works, and you move in that direction."

One thing Bush's father "inculcated into all of us was the sense that, if you feel you can achieve something, go for it. Don't sit around and hem and haw and ask people and try to rationalize everything in life," Marvin Bush said.[49]

Bush staked out moderate positions, but his opponent in the primary election, Odessa Mayor Jim Reese, attacked him as a liberal East Coast Republican aligned with the Rockefeller wing of the party. While Bush said he was personally opposed to abortion, he was against a "prolife" amendment to the Constitution.

Reese called Bush "Junior" and tried to tie him to the Trilateral Commission, of which his father was a member. The Trilateral Commission was a group of international political and corporate leaders viewed by many conservatives as sinister elitists plotting to establish a world government.

Referring to the wild charges and conspiracy theories, Clay Johnson asked his friend, "How can you stand it?"

When he thanked his cheering supporters after beating Reese in the Republican primary, Bush said to Johnson, "That's how I stand it." Bush explained that there were benefits to having people "excited about what you're trying to do."

In the general election against Democrat Kent Hance in 1978, Hance accused Bush of being a "dilettante" who was "riding on his daddy's coattails." He said, "George Bush hasn't earned the living he enjoys. I'm on my own two feet, and I make my own living."

Full of frustration, Bush responded at one point, "Would you like me to run as Sam Smith? The problem is, I can't abandon my background."

Farmers would ask the candidates about the Trilateral Commission, and Hance would reply, "I don't know anything about it. But in 1973, when the Trilateral Commission was formed, what were you getting for corn and wheat? And what are you getting now?"

"I remember going to the American Agricultural Convention in the Lubbock Coliseum," Bush said. "I was surrounded by farmers. They wanted to talk about the Trilateral Commission. And I look over their shoulders, and there was Hance. I take my hat off to him."

When Bush ran television spots showing him jogging, Hance commented that in Lubbock, the district's largest city, the only time a man ran was when someone was chasing him. Bush's advisers begged him to go on the attack, but he refused.

At a Jaycees luncheon in Odessa, talk show host Mel Turner, the moderator, asked Bush, "Are you involved in, or do you know anybody involved in, one-world government or the Trilateral Commission?"

Fuming, Bush said, "I won't be persuaded by anyone, including my father."

On the way out, Bush refused to shake hands with Turner.

"You asshole," Turner heard him hiss as Bush walked away.

Bush lost to Hance, fifty-three percent to forty-seven percent, just after Bush's father resigned from the Trilateral Commission.

"I got out-country'ed, and it's not gonna happen again," Bush said.

Ten days after declaring his candidacy, Bush accepted an invitation from Joe O'Neill and his wife Jan to a cookout at their Midland home. For years, they had been trying to set Bush up with Laura Welch, a childhood friend of Jan's. Laura, thirty, was a pretty Austin librarian and former teacher. A graduate of Southern Methodist University in Texas, she obtained a master's degree in library science from the University of Texas at Austin. Bush and Laura had grown up near each other in Midland but had never met. In contrast to the brash Bush, Laura, an only child, was quiet and calm, a self-contained woman who was happiest curled up with a good book. Laura and George were the last of the O'Neill's single friends.

Finally, Laura agreed to meet Bush. Laura had resisted meeting him because she thought he was "real political," and she was uninterested in politics. But she was feeling lonely and starting to think there weren't many unmarried men left her age. She had been thinking that she would like to have children.

O'Neill knew Bush was interested because he stayed at the cookout until midnight, then walked Laura home to her parents' house, where she was staying while visiting them. Normally, Bush would leave social events by 9 P.M. to go to bed a half-hour later.

Six weeks after the cookout, they were engaged.

"The thing I like about him is that he made me laugh," she told her mother.

When Barbara Bush asked her what she did, Laura said, "I read."

On November 5, 1977, a day after Laura's thirty-first birthday, they were married at First United Methodist Church in Midland. They had met just three months earlier.

"That's a typical George decision," O'Neill said. "He doesn't dawdle."[50]

Johnson, who was one of seventy-five guests at the wedding in Midland, noticed that Bush's father did not give a toast. Having been a congressman from Texas, ambassador to the United Nations, chairman of the Republican National Committee, and chief liaison to China, the elder Bush was now director of Central Intelligence. Johnson thought Bush Senior did not want to draw attention from his son. Years later, he asked Bush about it.

"The reason he wouldn't want to give a toast is that he would end up crying," Bush told his friend. "The Bush men are quick to tears."[51]

Laura had an impact on Bush's wardrobe and living quarters—upgrades in both cases—and how he spent his time. From then on, it was more time at home and less golf. When Bush, lubricated by alcohol, became overly boisterous or made outrageous re-marks at social occasions, she would give him a look and tone him down.

"She really complemented him so much and mellowed him," O'Neill said. "She rounded him out."

"I don't give George advice," Laura would say later. "I know George has plenty of people who want to tell him things. I don't need to be one of them." But Bush said he listened to her advice. "She has a lot of common sense," he said. "I trust her judgment, probably a lot more than she knows."

Before the wedding, Laura made Bush promise she would never have to give a speech. The thought made her stomach churn. But after a honeymoon in Mexico, they spent the next year campaigning for Congress. Barbara Bush gave her advice on being the wife of a candidate: "Don't ever criticize his speeches," Barbara said. But one night late in the campaign, when they were driving home from Lubbock, Bush pestered Laura for her reaction to the speech he had just given. He knew he had not done well.

"I guess I was expecting her to cheer me up, to tell me I had done better than I thought I had," Bush said in *A Charge to Keep*, his campaign autobiography written with communications direc-tor Karen P. Hughes. "As we drove into the garage, I gave it one last try."

Bush said, "I didn't do very well, did I?"

"No, it wasn't very good," Laura replied.

Bush was so shocked, he drove the car into the wall of their house.

6

THE NOMAD

A few months before he met Laura, Bush had started Arbusto Energy and began looking for other investors. *Arbusto* is Spanish for "bush" or "shrub." Family friends invested several hundred thousand dollars, some persuaded by Jonathan Bush, George's money manager uncle in New York. By then, Bush had a net worth of $500,000 from five gas wells and three oil wells.

"I can't tell you that his name and the fact that his father was respected and known didn't maybe get him in some doors that you and I might not get into easily," Charlie Younger said. "But George really struck out on his own."

"The biggest key [to success in Midland] is to get along with folks," said Buzz Mills, another Bush mentor in the oil business. "He had that from the beginning. He got deals made. With George, people know that what you see is what you get," he said. "George was a very good businessman."

In 1981, Bush renamed his company Bush Exploration Company, and he took it public. It was bad timing. The Texas oil industry was collapsing as prices fell. He raised only $1.3 million, a quarter of his goal. His partners lost seventy-five percent of their money due to dry holes.

"I made a bad mistake," Bush said. He joked that he was "all name and no money."

In late 1984, Bush merged his company into Spectrum 7, an oil-drilling firm, and became its chairman. As prices continued to fall, Bush hastily arranged to have Harken Oil and Gas buy Spectrum 7. In the previous six-month period, Spectrum had lost $402,000. It was $3 million in debt. Harken had a strategy of buying distressed oil companies. It assumed the company's crushing debts, made Bush a consultant at $80,000 a year, and gave him $530,380 in stock. Harken hired some of his employees, and Bush made sure the rest were hired by friends.

"One of the reasons Harken was so interested in merging was because of George," Paul Rea, his chief financial officer, said. "Having him with the company would be an asset . . . having George's name there. They wanted him on their board."[52]

Unlike many, Bush did not have to declare bankruptcy.

"He was incredibly successful because he survived it," said Don Evans, who became a friend after both men moved to Midland in 1975 and they separately began exploring for oil. "I know a lot of people who didn't survive it."[53]

"It's a humbling experience to drill a dry well and call up all your investors and tell them that you convinced them to put money into something that was no good," said Ernie Angelo, a leading Republican businessman in Midland. "He became a much more likeable person in a few years after he got here. He had the reputation when he came here of being cocky and arrogant."

The same year he sold to Harken, Bush had a reawakening of his Christian faith. While vacationing at Kennebunkport, the Reverend Billy Graham, a family friend, talked to him about accepting Jesus Christ as his personal savior. Bush had grown up worshiping at Presbyterian and Episcopalian churches, but after he married Laura, he switched to First United Methodist Church, where she went. With Don Evans, a teetotaler whose wife Susie went to grade school with Bush, he began to study the Bible and recommit to his faith.

As his spiritual life evolved, Bush began to reconsider his nightly consumption of beer or bourbon. He knew that drinking sapped his energy. Others noticed that it made him overly feisty and annoying. At a sedate summer cocktail party in Kennebunkport, Bush walked up to a prim woman who was a friend of his parents. She had just turned fifty.

"So, what's sex like after fifty, anyway?" he asked her.

In early April 1986, Bush ran into Al Hunt, Washington bureau chief of the *Wall Street Journal*, at a Mexican restaurant in

Dallas. Hunt was with his wife Judy Woodruff and their four-year-old son. The April edition of *Washingtonian* magazine had just come out. It listed predictions by sixteen pundits on who would lead the 1988 Republican presidential ticket. Hunt had predicted Jack Kemp over Bush's father, who was then vice president. Hunt said Bush approached their table at the restaurant and began cursing at him. There was no doubt he had been drinking.

Hunt said Bush swore at him and said, "I will never forget what you wrote!"[54]

Hunt mentioned the incident to Bill Minutaglio, a *Dallas Morning News* reporter who was writing his 1999 book *First Son*, the only previous serious biography of Bush. Two weeks later, Bush called Hunt to apologize.

Bush admitted later that he frequently drank too much and was unpleasant to be around.

"I was not drinking heavily every day," Bush said. Even at the height of his drinking, "I was always the first one to go to bed," he said. But "I realized that alcohol was beginning to crowd out my energies and could crowd out my affections for other people . . . When you're drinking, it can be an incredibly selfish act."

"Once he got started, he couldn't, didn't shut it off," his friend Don Evans said. "He didn't have the discipline."[55]

In July 1986, Bush and Laura spent a weekend with Evans and his wife Susie; Joe O'Neill and his wife Jan; Penny Royall, a friend; and Bush's brother Neil in Colorado Springs to celebrate Bush's and Evans's fortieth birthdays. They stayed at the Broadmoor Hotel, a grand old resort where Bush golfed with his friends. Despite his drinking, Bush ran three or four days a week, usually for three or four miles, averaging seven-minute miles. But at the Broadmoor, Bush awoke with a hangover after a dinner served with $60 bottles of Silver Oak Cabernet. He felt befuddled and had trouble running.

Laura had been urging him to stop drinking, saying it was "necessary" for him to stop and reminding him that having four bourbons on the rocks at a party wasn't very smart.

"He'd say things over and over again," Laura Bush said of his drinking. "He wasn't an alcoholic in the sense of he had to get up in the morning and have a drink to get things going. But he . . . couldn't hold his liquor, as they say."

Bush had been trying to cut down or stop for a year. At the Broadmoor, he decided to quit entirely. His religious awakening played a role, as did his near disaster in the oil business. He was also aware that he had new responsibilities. He had agreed to serve as a "loyalty enforcer and listening ear" for his father's 1988 presidential race. His role would be to come down hard on leakers and loose cannons, mediate staff disputes, and pass along what he considered useful advice from others.

"To put it in spiritual terms, I accepted Christ," Bush said later. "What influenced me [to stop drinking] was the spirituality, sure, which led me to believe that if you change your heart, you can change your behavior."[56]

When they returned home, Bush told Laura of his decision.

"He just said, 'I'm going to quit,' and he did," she said. "That was it. We joked about it later, saying he got the bar bill, and that's why he quit." Except for his drinking, Bush was always disciplined, she said. "He was a great runner. And when he was able to stop, that gave him a lot of confidence and made him feel better about himself."

Bush did not tell his friends for several weeks.

"The next time I saw him, he said he had stopped drinking," Johnson said.

"He looked in the mirror and said, 'Someday, I might embarrass my father,' " O'Neill said. " 'It might get my dad in trouble.' And boy, that was it."[57]

"I had to make a choice," Bush said later. He had "had enough." Bush never had another drop of alcohol.

Looking back, Bush would say he had led a nomadic life up to that point.

"The act of shedding the most childish behavior has taken awhile," he said. "When you finally make it to the 40s, you're prepared to be an adult." He credited Laura with helping him mature. "She helped me grow up with a sense of responsibility for family," Bush said. "If I am cocky and brash, I'm less cocky and brash because of Laura."

Yet during that nomadic, immature time, Bush started an oil company, ran daily, taught Sunday school, campaigned for Congress, and began a family. On November 25, 1981, his twins Jenna and Barbara were born. For all his swagger, Bush, living under the shadow of his father, had always been a bit insecure. From the perspective of his father and his later ascension to the presidency, Bush may have been a nomad until his 40s. But by traditional American standards, he was a success.

During those years, said his former girlfriend Diane Paul, Bush was casting about for a way to live up to his family's traditions. He spoke of his father and grandfather with awe and saw them as powerful role models.

"The whole way he talked about his father and grandfather, it's no accident that he tried to repeat what his dad did, in the same order," Paul said. "It's what I thought his goal was: to see how he could step into those shoes, how he could live up to that family legacy. It was in his bones."[58]

Bush's comments about being a nomad reflected the fact that he was honest to a fault and had a tendency to downplay his own success. In his book *The Right Man*, Bush's former White House speechwriter David Frum wrote that Bush insisted on accuracy to the point of pedantry.

"If his schedule called for him to read a radio address in Washington to be broadcast during a visit to California the following day, nothing could induce him to say, 'Today, I am in California.' He would look up from the script with exasperation," Frum said. He would say, "But I'm not in California."

Frum learned not to routinely insert idle compliments like, "I'm happy to be with you." If Bush was "not happy to be here with you, he would not pretend that he was," Frum said.

Early on in his presidency, Bush would say that he made decisions based on instinct or a gut feel.

"I went into the Oval Office and said, 'I have a suggestion,'" Clay Johnson said. "'I heard you last night in an interview say you make decisions on gut feel. I don't think you do that at all. I think that's a mischaracterization. To me, someone who goes on instinct is someone who doesn't have a brain. That's not the case. You have the ability to get to the essence of things in nanoseconds.

What's the purpose of the Defense Department? What's the definition of success in Iraq? Posing those questions and insisting on clear answers is not going on gut feel. To me, it's getting at the essence of situations. That's what you're really good at. Maybe to you it's gut feel because it's easy.' "[59]

Johnson encouraged Bush to describe his decision-making process as "getting to the central issues and making sure your advisers never lose sight of the central issues." After that, Bush dropped references to gut feelings.

In the same vein, when Bush said he had led a nomadic, irresponsible life, he was minimizing his success. When it came to the question of whether he had taken drugs before 1974, Bush's honesty impelled him to lean over backward and make a blanket statement that could not be challenged. But in doing so, he opened the door to endless speculation about what, in fact, he had been doing.

"He talked about being wild and crazy," Clay Johnson said. "I never knew him to be any wilder and crazier than anything I was doing or maybe you were doing."

For most of his life, Bush had followed in his father's footsteps, attending the same schools in the east and plunging into the oil business. But no child wants to be considered a clone of his parents. When asked to define the differences between himself and his father, Bush would say that his father "went to Greenwich Country Day School in Connecticut, and I went to San Jacinto Junior High" in Midland. Or he would say, "He grew up in Greenwich. I grew up in West Texas."

Bush would bristle at the suggestion that he was part of a dynasty. Dynasty "implies you inherit something," he would say, adding that "the concept of dynasty just doesn't exist" for his clan. "If you mean political tradition, then yes."

Indeed, Bush's great-grandfather, Samuel P. Bush, was a steel and railroad magnate in Ohio who was a Federal Reserve Bank director and an adviser to Herbert Hoover. His other great-grandfather, George Herbert Walker, cofounded Brown Brothers Harriman and was an adviser to President Roosevelt.

Bush's pattern of following in his father's footsteps would change when he got a call during his father's presidential campaign

from William DeWitt, Jr., a friend who was an owner of oil exploration company Spectrum 7. DeWitt's father had owned major-
league baseball teams. DeWitt told Bush that Eddie Chiles, owner
of the Texas Rangers and another friend of the Bushes, wanted to
sell out. Would Bush be interested in forming a group to buy the
team? Bush jumped at the chance.

As a kid, Bush had dreamed of being Willie Mays, not president. At this point, he had no idea what he would do after his father's campaign ended. If he bought the team, he could meld his
proven business expertise with his love of baseball. Now, besides
his Midland upbringing, he could point to another difference between himself and his father.

After his father became president, Bush put the Rangers deal
together in April 1989. The previous year, he and Laura had
moved to 6029 Northwood in Dallas, a ranch-style home with a
limestone façade.

"He always wanted to carve out his own niche," Charlie
Younger said. "And when your dad has carved out a pretty big
niche of his own, that makes it harder."

"He loves sports, he puts people together and makes things
happen," Clay Johnson said. "That's what the oil business is all
about. You get a lease and a drilling rig and you get some money
and you kind of put it together. Putting people together and making things happen is what he had been doing his entire adult life.
Putting the Rangers deal together was the same idea."

For $75 million, Bush and other investors bought eighty-six
percent of the Rangers. To buy his stake, Bush put up $606,302,
with $500,000 of it borrowed from a bank. He became the man-
aging general partner along with Ed "Rusty" Rose III. To pay off
the loan, Bush sold two-thirds of his interest in Harken for
$848,000. It was just before bad news broke about Harken's fi-
nancial condition. The Securities and Exchange Commission in-
vestigated and found no wrongdoing on Bush's part. The company
recovered, and if Bush had kept the stock another year, he would
have profited even more.

As a son of the president, Bush was a brand name, and he turned
it to the team's advantage. He had baseball cards printed up with

his picture. Instead of sitting in one of the owner's air-conditioned sky boxes, Bush sat in the front row behind the dugout.

Bush eschewed limousines. He wore the same ratty suits and eel-skin boots emblazoned with the flag of Texas. He appeared almost nightly on TV sports news. As if he were a star player, he signed autographs and greeted potential constituents.

With characteristic bluntness, he said, "I want the folks to see me sitting in the same kind of seat they sit in, eating the same popcorn, peeing in the same urinal."[60]

"He had an important father and a nice name, so that gave him some visibility," Johnson said.

Bush wasn't afraid to fire or demote people if he thought it was necessary. When the ax fell on Tom Grieve, general manger of the Rangers, Bush was campaigning. That night, the phone rang at Grieve's home. Bush was "calling to say he was sorry the decision had to be made, that he thought a lot of me personally, and that he hoped things worked out for me," recalled Grieve, who was demoted to assistant to the team president. "He didn't have to do that."

Similarly, the job of telling John Sununu, Bush's father's overbearing chief of staff, that it was time to go fell to Bush. Bush knew his father would have had a difficult time firing his top aide. Sununu resigned the day after they talked.

In managing the team, Bush employed his Harvard Business School training: He delegated and let everyone do their job. But he also made sure employees knew they would be held to account if they didn't produce results.

"George was my boss," said Tom Schieffer, who served as president of the Rangers under Bush. "But he never made me feel that way. He went out of his way to treat me as a partner, not a subordinate."

To attract even more fans to the Rangers' games, Bush pushed for a temporary half-cent increase in the local sales tax to pay for a portion of building a new $135 million stadium. The team kicked in the rest. The new ballpark opened in Arlington, Texas, in 1994. Attendance soared from an average of 18,000 a game to 31,000. The value of the team zoomed as well.

"I like selling tickets," Bush would say. "There are a lot of parallels between baseball and politics."

"The conventional wisdom on George is that the turning point of his life was giving up his drinking," said Roland Betts, his Yale friend who was an investor in the team. "I don't believe that. The turning point of his life was buying the Texas Rangers, succeeding with the Texas Rangers."

The success "solved my biggest political problem in Texas," Bush said. "My problem was, 'What's the boy ever done?'"[61]

By the time the ballpark opened, Bush had plunged into running for governor of Texas against incumbent Ann Richards. Bush had seethed at what he perceived as unfair press treatment of his father during George H.W. Bush's unsuccessful run for reelection as president. Nothing grated on him more than *Newsweek*'s October 1987 cover. It had a picture of his war hero dad with the caption, "Fighting the Wimp Factor." When he was designated to respond to an unfounded claim that his father had had an affair—based conveniently on a statement of a man who had died—Bush told *Newsweek*, "The answer to the Big A question is N-O."

But when Richards created the caricatures of Bush by making fun of his intellect, saying he owed everything to his father, and calling him "jerk" and "Shrub," Bush kept his cool. Bush always acknowledged that his family name and connections had helped him in life.

"Look, I don't deny it. How could I?" he would say.

But few offspring of presidents had achieved as much as he had by dint of hard work and drive. Many inside the Bush camp trace the stereotypes of Bush to Richards's name-calling.

When claims came up during the presidential race that Bush would never have won the nomination if he were not the son of a president, Bush spotted Frank Bruni, a *New York Times* reporter, on his campaign plane.

"Do you think that Sulzberger worked his way to the top?" Bush asked him, referring to *New York Times* publisher Arthur O. Sulzberger, Jr.[62]

"With that question, Bush made a big point: that he was not the only one in the world to benefit from his background, and that the advantages that people like he enjoyed did not mean they were undeserving of their stations and responsibilities," Bruni wrote in his book *Ambling into History*, which focused on Bush's campaign.

Ann Richards's name-calling "didn't bother me in the least," Bush said later. "It gave me credibility. Why would an incumbent governor who was supposedly extremely popular call me a name if she didn't think that I had a chance to beat her?"

It was when his father was a target that Bush's temper flared.

"Say something about his family, and he will bristle," his friend Younger said.

Bush ran a disciplined campaign on four issues: school accountability, limiting civil lawsuits, tightening juvenile justice laws, and welfare reform. He visited one small town after another. When the press grew tired of hearing him talk about the four issues, he announced he had just added a fifth: To concentrate even harder on the other four.

Bush was elected the forty-sixth governor of Texas on November 8, 1994. In his office in Austin, he installed a glass-paneled display of 250 signed baseballs he had collected since he was a child, including one signed by both Ted Williams and Joe DiMaggio.

The Rangers' investors sold the team in 1998 for roughly $250 million. Bush's share of twelve percent was $14.9 million from his $606,000 investment. Not bad for someone who said, "Money has never been a way of keeping score for me."

7

DICK AND JANE

In February 1995, Karl C. Rove was in Bush's office on the second floor of the State Capital in Austin when officials from the Texas Education Agency gave the governor the third grade reading test results from Texas schools. Some 43,000 third graders could not read.

"What happened to those forty-three thousand?" Bush asked.

"Thirty-nine thousand went on to the fourth grade," he was told.[63]

By the spring, the results had gotten worse: Some 52,000 of the state's 230,000 third graders could not read.

After the meeting, Rove had never seen Bush so angry. A former aide to Bush's father, Rove had known Bush since 1973. When they met, Bush was visiting his parents in Washington for Thanksgiving. It was Rove's job to give him the car keys.

The adopted son of a geologist, Rove described himself as a nerd. Going to high school in Salt Lake City, he carried a briefcase, wore a pocket protector, and spent hours in the library preparing for debate club competitions. When he was nine, Rove supported Richard Nixon over John F. Kennedy for president. A neighborhood girl punched him out for his beliefs. But Rove was elected a student government officer in both junior high and high school.

Rove went to the University of Utah for two years but dropped out to move to Washington and become executive director of the national College Republicans. He attended four colleges in all but never graduated. In 1981, Rove set up shop in Austin as a political consultant and direct mailer. After moving to Texas, he and Bush, who is about the same age, would talk for hours, either by phone or in person.

The media would portray Bush as being attracted to the fact that Rove had not graduated from college. In fact, Bush was comfortable with both college graduates and those without degrees. What he loathed was intellectual snobbery, pretension, and elitism.

Besides collecting stamps, one of Rove's passions was hunting quail. In Austin and later in Washington, Rove would serve what he called "the wily bobwhite" to an appreciative George Bush.

"Thanks so much for the wonderful dinner," Bush wrote to Rove after one such supper. "Good eats, good friendship. There are few places I can relax. Yours is one."

Rove was a brilliant tactician and student of American history, surpassing the most erudite history professors. The press dubbed him "Bush's Brain," suggesting that Bush had none.

"Karl Rove thinks it, and George W. Bush does it," James Moore and Wayne Slater said flatly in *Bush's Brain*. But it was Bush who decided how to meld Rove's political advice with his own principles and advice from policy aides about the content of programs.

Rove was the architect of Bush's 1994 and 1998 campaigns for governor. As a political strategist, Rove's job was to advise Bush what programs, policies, and campaign promises would sell well. He admired Bush's discipline and focus and his "centered" character. While they were friends, it was always clear who was boss. Occasionally, Bush would bring him up short. Seeing reporters gathered around Rove on the presidential campaign plane, Bush said sarcastically, "Is the Karl Rove press conference over yet?" But when Bush discussed ideas with other aides, he would ask, "What does Karl think?"

"Rove is really, really smart with superhigh energy," said Clay Johnson, a close friend. "Too much so. Nobody has that much energy. He doesn't drink coffee or alcohol. If he did, he would run through walls. He is going all the time. Sometimes you have to stop him and say, 'Stop. Sit down.' He is funny, a good friend, and real focused on George Bush."[64]

Bush gave almost everyone a nickname, and Rove's was either "Boy Genius" or "Turd Blossom." A mutual friend of theirs said the latter name was perfect because whenever the fifty-three-year-old Rove was around, "something was sure to pop up."

Rove recommended books to Bush to read, including Murray Myron's *The Dream and the Nightmare* and Marvin Olasky's *The Tragedy of American Compassion*. Both mirrored Bush's thoughts, arguing that the feel-good, permissive values of the 1960s undermined the strength of families and helped create dependency on government, ultimately harming the disadvantaged classes. As an antidote, Bush, in discussions with Myron, Olasky, and others, fashioned the concept of "compassionate conservatism."

It was not a catchy phrase, and conservatives didn't like it because it implied that there was something wrong with being a conservative—like calling someone a realistic liberal. But the phrase accurately described Bush's philosophy. His goal was to help people. He believed the best way to do that was to develop government programs and policies that allowed them to help themselves. He did not see government as an enemy, as traditional conservatives did. But he did not believe the solution to problems was necessarily to throw money around. Often, adjusting existing programs, discarding cumbersome procedures, energizing bureaucrats, or focusing the efforts of faith-based and other volunteer groups could achieve results while saving taxpayers money. Reducing taxes, in turn, was yet another way to help people.

"My philosophy trusts individuals to make the right decisions for their families and communities, and that is far more compassionate than a philosophy that seeks solutions from distant bureaucracies," Bush would say. "I am a conservative because I believe government should be limited and efficient, that it should do a few things and do them well."

Bush's optimistic philosophy and belief in limited government and personal responsibility went back to his roots in Midland. "The slogan when I was out there was, 'The sky's the limit.' That meant for everybody, not just a few," he said. During the 1960s, "The sharp contrast between right and wrong became blurred . . . We went from accepting responsibility to assigning blame. We became a nation of victims."

For years, Bush had been concerned about the decline in reading achievement in schools. Helping kids to read fit neatly within the mandate of a compassionate conservative. If kids were unable to read, they couldn't fathom a bus schedule or a soup label, let alone achieve success in life. Inability to read led to myriad social problems—unemployment, crime, drug use. Over the years, reading levels had been plunging, not just in Texas but throughout the country. Bush wanted to find out why, and what could be done about it.

Bush's mother had devoted herself to Neil Bush's reading problems, which resulted from dyslexia. She promoted literacy programs in the White House. Laura Bush had taught kids to read and was a voracious reader herself. The interests of the two most important women in his life focused Bush's attention even more on reading as an issue.

"I think it was a shared interest with Laura," Clay Johnson said. "They are very close to one another. She offers advice on things. He has an interest in reading, and she does too, so they are mutually supportive of that."

In the winter of 1992, Barnett Alexander "Sandy" Kress, a Democrat who was running for reelection to the Dallas school board, met with Bush at his Texas Rangers office to ask for his support. Kress, the president of the school board, had campaigned for Robert F. Kennedy, served in the Carter administration, and chaired the Dallas County Democratic Party. But he had heard through friends that Bush, while a Republican, reached out to both parties and was interested in how to improve the schools and reading scores in particular. At the time, Bush was thinking of running for governor. Among others, Alphonso Jackson, a leading black Republican leader whom Bush would later appoint secretary of Housing and Urban Development, was urging him to run.

Kress had been appointed by Bob Bullock, the conservative Democratic lieutenant governor, to serve on a task force that recommended that the state try to make schools more accountable, in part to improve reading scores. The concept of accountability was accepted in every other phase of life except in the schools. If schools could be rewarded or penalized based on how well students did, principals and teachers would put more effort into making sure kids read, or so the theory went.

Dallas had already tried a pilot program: During the 1980s, the school system gave extra money to schools that showed improvement in reading scores over time. The program seemed to work. By 1991, scores had jumped. Democratic governors James B. Hunt, Jr. in North Carolina and Richard W. Riley in South Carolina were also trying to raise school standards and, especially in Hunt's case, impose accountability.

Kress met with Bush for an hour and a half. Bush wanted to know about the accountability concept and what Kress was doing to try to improve reading scores. The next day, he agreed to support Kress for school board.

Six months later, Bush asked to meet with Kress again. This time, Bush wanted to probe deeper into reading and school accountability. Bush had dozens of questions: What did you learn? What are the best practices? What are other states doing? Taking notes on a legal pad, Bush wanted to know who had studied the issue. Kress mentioned six experts in the field.

"People think he shoots from the hip or that he's not smart," Kress said. "It baffles me. I had an intensive experience with him over that year. He was an incredible student of these issues. He had a voracious appetite for information. He looked into the problem and researched it. I had never had this experience with a politician before. Most politicians have a sound-bite view; some advisers come in with a little plan, and they speak it. His approach was exactly what a citizen would want. He followed through. I gave him six names. He called them all. They were as stunned as I was."[65]

The following year, based on the recommendations of the panel headed by Kress, the Texas legislature tied additional school funding for schools to improvements in test scores. When Bush became governor, he adopted the accountability concept and expanded on it.

"Three quarters of the politicians I know would pooh-pooh anything that had occurred before them," said Kress, who became the unpaid senior education advisor to Bush after his election as president. "He made it central to his own philosophy."

If Kress was amazed at how much effort Bush put into the problem, Dr. G. Reid Lyon, a reading expert at the National Institutes of

Health, was even more amazed when he answered his phone in Rockville, Maryland, in 1995 and was told the governor of Texas was calling.

A paratrooper during the Vietnam War, Lyon had taught reading to inner city third graders in Albuquerque, New Mexico. As he had been taught in his reading courses, he used what is known as the whole-language method. Developed by two professors, Dr. Kenneth S. Goodman of the University of Arizona and Frank Smith, formerly of the University of Victoria in Victoria, British Columbia, the whole-language method was a philosophy, rather than a teaching method. Introduced to American schools in the early 1970s, it held that teaching children the sounds of letters or combinations of letters—"b" or "th," for example—and having them sound out words by combining those sounds was a bore. Instead, under the whole-language method, children were given books to read. Because the books were interesting, the theory of the whole-language method went, the books will somehow by themselves motivate children to assume what the words mean from their context and accompanying illustrations.

The whole-language approach, in turn, was an offshoot of an earlier method called whole word, look and say, or look-say. That method, used in the "Dick and Jane" series of books which first came out in 1929, required kids to memorize words. After Rudolf Flesch's 1955 best-selling book *Why Johnny Can't Read* demonstrated why memorizing words did not help kids to read, the method began to go out of vogue.

Prior to the introduction of these so-called progressive methods promoted by education professors, schools going back to ancient Greece had taught kids to read by sounding out letters and combinations of letters, a method known as phonics. An "a," for example, has the sound or phoneme of "ay" as in "bay" or "ah" as in "cat." Any language with an alphabet is taught the same way.

The whole-language approach scrapped all that. It was predicated on a belief that reading came naturally and that kids would learn to read literally by osmosis. But reading, like devising algebraic equations, is anything but natural. It must be learned. Essentially, using the whole-language approach, learning to read became a guessing game. It was like expecting a child to learn to play the piano and read music without instruction. Whole-language proponents even said that when children guessed wrong, they should not be corrected.

"It is unpleasant to be corrected," Paul Jennings, an Australian whole-language enthusiast, said. "It has to be fun, fun, fun."

"Parents shouldn't be judgmental," another whole-language advocate said.

Lyon found that, especially with disadvantaged children whose parents had not helped them during their preschool years by reading to them and pointing out sounds, letters, and new words, the whole-language method was a fraud. Even middle- and upper-class kids who entered kindergarten and first grade with a vocabulary twice that of disadvantaged kids had trouble reading with the whole-language method.

"I was trained that reading developed in this holistic way," Lyon said. "I realized I didn't know what I was doing. The kids were not responding to the literature I was giving them. I was taught that when they struggled to pronounce a word, don't teach them to sound it out. Don't use phonics. Get them to use the surrounding context to predict the pronunciation of the word. That was the whole-language philosophy. It was goofy."[66]

Lyon later taught kids who were eleven and twelve. "By the time they came to me, they couldn't read, and their motivation was lousy," he said. "They were humiliated and discouraged by the fact that they couldn't read."

Lyon began asking how children learn to read. He took courses and became a psychologist specializing in reading development and reading disorders. He came to realize that the education establishment had adopted the whole-language method without any empirical evidence that it worked. And, in fact, since the whole word and whole-language approaches had been adopted, reading achievement in American schools had plummeted like a bad stock. Forty percent of fourth graders could not read a simple children's book. The California schools, which embraced whole language in 1987 and tossed out phonics workbooks, had had the highest level of reading achievement in the country. But by 1994, after seven years of whole language, the state was tied with Louisiana for last place in the country. Yet because California was one of the largest buyers of school textbooks, publishers had already switched to the whole-language approach.

As whole language became the predominant method, blacks and Hispanics suffered the most. Nationally, an unbelievable sixty-five percent of black fourth graders were below what is called the basic reading level, meaning they could not read a simple children's book. Only ten percent were deemed proficient in reading. Fifty-nine percent of Hispanics could not read a children's book. Only twelve percent were proficient. Each child who could not read faced a possible lifetime of failure.

When studies showed phonics to be superior to whole language, professors of education dismissed the results. Yet million-dollar studies were not needed: For a child who couldn't read, phonics was like pouring gasoline in a car that was out of gas. It usually worked immediately.* With phonics, even kids placed in special-education classes because of learning disabilities, mental retardation, and other impairments could be taught to read.

Many education professors convinced themselves, as the fifty-four-year-old Lyon put it, that "evidence is in the eye of the beholder." They considered written tests invalid and claimed that the success of the whole-language method should be evaluated by watching kids read—"kid watching" they called it. Of course, none of this had anything to do with whether they could read. Education colleges even dropped statistics courses that might help teachers evaluate which method worked best. They looked down their noses at testing kids' reading ability. It was as if IBM declared that earnings were no longer relevant to judging its own performance. A company that disregarded the need for profits would soon go bankrupt, and its employees would lose their jobs. But in the educational system, if kids could not read, no one suffered except the kids.

Whole language had one thing going for it: Instead of teaching the forty-four phonemes, or sounds, that the twenty-six letters of

---

* The author has personal experience with phonics. Having been taught by the whole-word method in the New York City schools, I could not read when I entered fourth grade in Cambridge, Massachusetts. I was placed in a remedial reading class using phonics and began learning to read immediately.

the English alphabet can make, with whole language, teachers could sit back and relax. They gave the kids books and passively watched as students struggled to make sense of the material placed in front of them. When their children failed to learn to read, they could blame it on their homes or on poor motivation. Yet even among white children with more advantages, twenty-eight percent of fourth graders could not read a simple children's book. Nationally, a heartbreaking forty-one percent of fourth graders could not read a simple children's book. In comparison, in the early 1900s, when phonics was the only form of instruction, illiteracy was almost unknown. In 1910, the U.S. Department of Education reported that 2.2 percent of children between the ages of ten and fourteen could not read.

Lyon began designing research that would rigorously compare whole language with different instructional methods, including phonics. In 1991, he joined NIH, becoming chief of the Child Development and Behavior Branch of the National Institute of Child Health and Human Development. In that capacity, he headed the institute's reading research program. Eventually, Lyon amassed data based on studies of 44,000 students. Now he and other reading experts could draw a firm conclusion: Whole language simply did not work. It was common sense that, rather than expecting kids to guess what was in books, learning the building blocks that make up language was the way to learn to read. The test scores proved it. When taught with phonics, only three to seven percent of blacks and Hispanics could not read, Lyon found. Except for children with dyslexia, nearly all the children in high-income areas learned to read when taught with phonics.

Lyon discovered that some teachers, recognizing that whole language didn't work, would secretly teach their classes phonics, even spending their own money to buy phonics materials. (Hooked on Phonics is one of many commercially available phonics teaching programs.) But most teachers came up with an endless stream of nonsequiturs to justify teaching whole language. They would claim that imposing phonics on them took away their "creativity" as teachers or that it was wrong to insist on using one method for everyone. They even said that giving tests—a mainstay of education—"reduces kids to numbers." Yet if children could not pass reading tests, they could not learn other subjects and would often drop out of school. Unlike employees of IBM, teachers did not lose their jobs if what they were doing didn't work. They were paid the same regardless of whether their students learned to read.

"Many professors of education and teachers simply don't want to change," Lyon said. "Careers and egos are built on whole language. The argument for whole language is driven by beliefs and by untested assumptions and philosophies. It's more like a religion. These arguments have gone on as reading failure rates have gotten worse. Most teachers want to do good, but they can only provide what they've been taught. The educational academic establishment has been enamored with these belief-system approaches to reading instruction rather than using evidence to determine what works. There has been intellectual laziness and scientific laziness involving something so important to a child's life as literacy. I see it in the eyes of youngsters who have failed to learn to read. It's educational malpractice."[67]

By the time Bush called Lyon, he knew about phonics. Sandy Kress, who became a lawyer with Akin Gump Strauss Hauer & Feld in Austin in 1995, had brought up the subject at their first meeting in 1992. Since then, Bush had learned that Lyon's federally funded research—some of it conducted in the Houston schools—had demonstrated the superiority of phonics. Rod Paige, the Houston school superintendent who would become Bush's secretary of education, was a proponent both of phonics and accountability. Once it became clear how the schools have let down kids by blindly adhering to the whole-language method, the need for holding teachers and principals accountable became far more apparent.

"Bush called and said, 'We have a problem,'" Lyon recalled. "He said he had thousands of kids who could not read, both English-speaking and Spanish-speaking. He is a businessman. He makes decisions based on facts, and he likes to see results. He said he understood there was empirical, scientific evidence that could help Texas make better decisions about how we teach kids to read."

By then, "science" had become a code word for phonics. When scientific comparisons were made, phonics always came out ahead. But the educational establishment was so fanatically wedded to the whole-language method that Lyon and other proponents of phonics tried to avoid the word. Instead, they referred to what the "science" had found about reading. The word "phonics" created an emotional reaction. Never mind that it saved kids from a lifetime of humiliation.

Similarly, Lyon and other proponents of phonics soft-pedaled it by saying they advocated a balanced or comprehensive approach, combining phonics with spelling, vocabulary, writing, work on comprehension, and actual reading. Of course, that was always part of teaching phonics. It was like learning to drive a car. No one would think of conducting driver education without actually driving. But the missing ingredient needed to teach kids to read was phonics.

Bush asked Lyon to meet with him at his office in Austin. Lyon spent hours with Bush on the intricacies of phonics. Lyon was skeptical of Bush, but Bush won him over. In Clinton's Department of Education, it was not politically correct to favor a particular reading instruction method. Clinton had proposed spending $2.75 billion over five years to pay tutors to read to young students. Lyon considered that a colossal waste of time and money.

"If kids learned to read by being read to, we wouldn't have problems," he told Bush.

Bush was impressed by the evidence that phonics works, and he was not afraid to take a stand if he thought it would bring results. Unlike most politicians, Bush did not operate in the gray areas. He saw the world in terms of black and white, right and wrong. If whole language was a sham, he would say so. If phonics worked, he was willing to launch a crusade to implement it, and damn the critics.

Bush was what Professor David Reisman of Harvard called an inner-directed personality. In his 1950 book *The Lonely Crowd*, Reisman described such people as self-reliant and purposeful. He contrasted them with other-directed personality types, who were passive and brought up to rely on the cues from others, particularly peer groups, coworkers, and mass media, in addition to parents, to find their way in the world.

Bush and Lyon discussed how to retrain Texas teachers who had learned to teach using the whole-language approach. But the biggest mystery was why the teaching establishment clung so tenaciously to something that didn't work.

"He thought it was outrageous," Lyon recalled. "I could tell he felt an urgency to turn around the reading failure."

With Sandy Kress, Bush's education aide Margaret Spellings, and others, Bush devised legislation that would tie Texas state funding to use of a reading method whose efficacy had been proven, meaning phonics. To create more accountability, schools that did not improve were penalized. Ultimately, the state could take them over.

Meanwhile, Bush asked Lyon if any research had been done on the best way to teach Spanish-speaking children to read in English. Looking into the matter, Lyon found few studies on the subject and none based on rigorous evaluation. Lyon began a massive program to get the answers.

As the Texas schools shifted back to teaching reading with phonics, scores started improving dramatically. Blacks and Hispanics who faced a life of illiteracy suddenly could read. Kids in wealthy neighborhoods were doing better as well.

"It is amazing to me that Bush is thought of as a right-winger who doesn't care about minorities," Lyon said. "He saved so many of their lives."

Yet nationally, the vast majority of public schools continued to teach the whole-language method. The media—unlike Bush—rarely dug into the subject.

"Nobody wants to write the real story of why kids can't read," Spellings said. "I don't know if it's too hard."[68]

Ironically, many of the reporters and editors who ignored what amounted to a scandal of monstrous proportions sent their kids to private schools that taught reading through phonics. While the New York City schools have turned out hundreds of thousands of kids who can't read because the public schools have long refused to teach phonics, the most competitive private schools in New York—the Collegiate, Brearley, St. David's, and Dalton Schools—all used phonics to teach reading.

"Of course we teach phonics," said Beth Tashlik, the head of the Collegiate School's lower school, which charges $22,500 in tuition a year. "You can't teach reading without it."

The major exception to the virtual media blackout was a series of articles that ran on the editorial pages of the *Los Angeles Times* in 1998. Called "Reading: The First Skill," the series examined why children were falling behind. It reported that a shocking sixty-two percent of California's third graders were reading below the national average. By the fourth grade, seventy-seven percent could not read.

The paper blamed the disastrous decline in reading skills on the state's "botched experiment" with whole language. As an example of what the California schools should be doing, the paper cited reforms in Texas and the resulting dramatic improvement in test scores there. After the series ran, California switched back to phonics.

"In Texas, when you realize there is a goal that needs to be accomplished, you get on your horse and go do it," said Beth Ann Bryan, a former elementary school teacher who was Bush's education policy director in Austin during his first year as governor. "You don't have a work session and study it endlessly. You just go do it."[69]

"In the presidential campaign, they used to say he wasn't adept at policy," Clay Johnson said. "The policy people in Austin would laugh at this because he was a greater policy person than they were. Not because he reveled in taking the documents and poring over every graph. But he has the ability to take most any subject you are discussing with him, and he can fast forward to the concluding paragraph and say, 'So you're saying that this is the point.' "[70]

Bush was reelected governor in 1998 by sixty-eight percent to thirty-one percent. By the time he left Austin to become president, only 36,000 third-grade kids out of 262,000 could not read, according to state tests.* By 2003, the number failing had been cut

* National tests do not necessarily show the same improvement recorded by Texas state tests. According to Reid Lyon, national tests may not show the same results as state tests for many reasons, including differences in the purposes of the tests, the specific knowledge being assessed by the tests, and those chosen to take them. When adjustments are made to account for differences in the makeup of student groups who take the tests, the national and state tests show more similar improvement in Texas, according to Darvin M. Winick, who helped develop the state testing system and is chairman of the governing board that oversees the national tests.

to 28,000. Instead of giving them "social promotions" and passing them along to the next grade level, the schools began putting them in special reading programs using phonics, a program Bush got the legislature to pass in 1999. The intensive work was done in the spring and summer at the end of third grade. After the additional work, which began in 2003, only 5,000—less than two percent—failed reading, according to Kress. That compared with 52,000 out of 230,000 third graders—an appalling twenty-three percent—who could not read in Texas when Reid Lyon picked up his phone and found George Bush on the other end of the line.

8

WE MADE IT

More than a month before the January 20, 2001, inauguration, the Secret Service and the General Services Administration began making preparations. The Secret Service checked the 1.9-mile parade route from Third Street to Seventeenth Street along Pennsylvania Avenue. Manhole covers were welded shut. Mailboxes were removed. Agents determined who the tenants were in each office and checked for criminal records or threats they might have made. They warned tenants not to open their windows or to go on the roof when the president's motorcade passed. Spotters with binoculars would scan the windows to make sure everyone complied. If they did not, the Secret Service had master keys to many offices or required superintendents with keys to be on duty.

"If someone opens a window, a team of agents responds," said a Secret Service agent. "We'll hold the motorcade until the danger has passed."

GSA had worked with the Bush transition team to make sure the new administration had parking spaces, computers, cell phones, and pencils. Detailed floor plans of the West Wing were drawn up so that offices could be assigned. Desks were emptied, stationery supplies distributed, walls touched up or repainted.

The Secret Service worked with White House aides to issue passes. Until the administration of Franklin Roosevelt, the White House grounds had been open. Anyone could walk through the front door of 1600 Pennsylvania Avenue NW and be greeted by the chief usher.

"That was changed when the king and queen of England came

over to visit the Roosevelts in 1939," William Hopkins, a former executive clerk who began working at the White House under Herbert Hoover, told me. "That was when they first issued White House passes. They also closed the gates."

When Lyndon Johnson's aide Walter Jenkins was caught making a pass at another man in the men's room of the Washington, D.C. YMCA, Johnson ordered the FBI to perform the first background checks on White House aides. Now everyone except the president, the vice president, and their families must undergo a security check and obtain a pass to enter the White House.

Visitors with appointments in the West Wing are asked beforehand for their Social Security number and date of birth. The Secret Service checks to see if the individual is on their threat list or has a criminal record or has warrants for their arrest outstanding. The threat list is divided into three categories: Category 3 lists about a hundred people who present the most serious threat. In all, the Secret Service lists about 50,000 people who are potential threats. Typically, the Secret Service receives 3,000 to 4,000 new threats against the president each year.

To enter the West Wing, visitors press a white button on an intercom mounted at the northwest gate and announce themselves. If they appear legitimate, a uniformed Secret Service officer electronically unlocks the gate, allowing them to enter. They pass their driver's license through a slot in a bullet-proof booth to one of four uniformed Secret Service officers. If the visitors are on the appointment list and have been cleared, they are given a pass and allowed into the booth. They swipe the pass and go through a metal detector before they're allowed to walk outside again toward the West Wing. They pass more than a dozen TV cameras on tripods that sprout along the driveway leading to the entrance to the West Wing lobby. The strip, where correspondents broadcast from the White House, was once known as Pebble Beach. Now, because flagstone has replaced the pebbles, wags in the press corps call it Stonehenge. A separate entrance to the left of the lobby entrance goes directly to the James S. Brady press briefing room.

At the very moment when Bush was being sworn in at the Capitol, GSA was removing the former president's flag in the Oval

Office and replacing it with a new one. Glossy color photographs of Clinton were being replaced by photos of Bush. Combinations to safes were being changed. New telephone lists were being distributed. The Cabinet chair with Clinton's name on it would be shipped to him, to be replaced by a new chair bearing Bush's name.

By himself, the president can do very little except—in the words of Bradley Patterson, a White House aide in three administrations— go to the bathroom. While the president sets policy, he needs a staff that will carry it out. As in any organization, that requires answering telephones, returning calls, opening and responding to mail, making decisions promptly, treating people with respect, and following the rules. GSA found that the Clinton people were either incapable of or unwilling to perform those simple tasks. In fact, as if at a giant fraternity party, they spent much of their time gabbing. Behind it all was an arrogance and lack of judgment that began with the president and radiated throughout his staff.

"The Clinton administration was not set up to do anything," Charles B. "Buddy" Respass, the GSA building manager in charge of the White House, said. "If they had any preplanning, no one was aware of it."

Once the Clinton people moved in, GSA manager Lucille Price found they were "just goofing off—a lot of walking around and drinking Cokes and hanging around." She compared the White House under the Clintons to a college campus.

"They didn't like to work. They didn't return calls. They were rude," Price said. "They were the most unprofessional people I'd seen since I'd been here, which was since Gerald Ford."

"When it came to the White House staff, it was almost like, 'My goodness! We're at inauguration day, we better bring in a lot of people who worked in the campaign,' " Leon E. Panetta, a former California congressman who was Clinton's second chief of staff, told the White House Interview Program, funded by Pew Charitable Trusts, in May 2000. "You cannot do that," Panetta said. "They've got to know how the White House operates. You have to have grown-ups."

In contrast, the Bush team was competent, organized, and professional. As executive director of the transition, Bush chose Clay

Johnson. Johnson recommended that Bush select his chief of staff as early as possible so that they could start putting together the White House staff, and a few weeks before the election, Bush asked Andy Card to take the job. Clinton, on the other hand, did not select a chief of staff until a week before inauguration day. Unlike Card, who had served in the White Houses of Presidents Reagan and the first President Bush, Thomas F. "Mack" McLarty, Clinton's first chief of staff, had no Washington job experience.

Johnson proposed clear goals, which Bush, Cheney, and Card approved: select the senior White House staff and develop the organizational structure by mid-December; select Cabinet secretaries by Christmas and have them briefed and ready for confirmation hearings by January 8.[71]

Back in August, Johnson commissioned development of a web site to receive the more than 60,000 resumés that would come in. Johnson asked Karl Rove if he would develop a preliminary schedule for the president covering initiatives and possible events for the first 180 days. At the same time, Cheney, Card, and Johnson reminded everyone that "this was not the time or place for hubris or triumphant partisanship," as Johnson put it. Cheney, who was chairman of the transition, was plugged in to Washington and knew the players.

Drawing on his experience at PepsiCo's Frito Lay division and at Citicorp, Johnson developed a protocol for interviewing candidates. The idea was to draw out and assess how they had performed in situations similar to those they would encounter in Washington.

"We wanted to know what kind of people they were," Johnson said. "How did they tend to make decisions? Why did they leave jobs? Why did they want to come here? Why did they choose to study law or math or whatever? How did they think?"

In addition, the administration asked why the candidates were applying. "Did they want to come here to serve, or was it to drive a narrow agenda or to be compensated for past political work?" Johnson said. "It's very hard to get things done here. We are told 'no' a lot by Congress and various entities. You can't go marching forward with whatever idea you have. So we wanted to find out if, in the past, they were involved in a situation where they were not able to get their way and how they handled it." Finally, Johnson said, the administration wanted to find out if candidates "have the ability to do the right thing when it may not be the popular thing. That has to happen a lot here. The popular thing is to reward the short term and the right thing oftentimes is to do what is best long term, but it may be a difficult pill to swallow in the short term."[72]

Rather than ask candidates to list their strengths and weaknesses, Johnson and others asked them what kind of colleague they would recommend to complement their own strengths. If an individual was a good organizer but not strong on creativity, he might respond by saying that the colleague should have a creative mind. Instead of asking how the individual handled a difficult issue, Johnson would ask how a colleague or fellow board member would describe how he handled it. Then Johnson might check with that other individual to see how his perception jibed with that of the candidate.

"One thing we pay attention to is candor," Johnson said. "How comfortable is he with self-deprecation? If somebody contends he has the answer to all questions, the answer probably is he is not comfortable with it."

Before nominating candidates and having them undergo FBI background checks, Johnson had Fred F. Fielding, who was White House counsel in the Reagan administration and deputy counsel in the Nixon administration, meet with them to try to elicit anything in their backgrounds that might be problematic.

Even with the shortened transition period, the Bush people made sure the White House staff was set to go when Bush took the oath of office as the forty-third president at a minute past noon on Saturday, January 20, 2001.

It was a raw, chilly day, and the TelePrompter at the Capitol had to be covered with a plastic sheet until Bush was ready to speak. After Chief Justice William H. Rehnquist administered the oath, the new president teared up. Bush, fifty-four, spoke of his love for his country and desire to "work to build a single nation of justice and opportunity." He pledged to conduct himself with "compassion and character." In retrospect, his references to reclaiming America's schools, cutting taxes, building up the country's military capability, and confronting weapons of mass destruction seem especially significant.

"We must show courage in a time of blessing," he said, "by confronting problems instead of passing them on to future generations."

At the conclusion of his speech, Bush hugged his father, tearing up again. Previously, only John Quincy Adams had followed his father into the presidency.

As in his run for governor, Bush had waged a highly disciplined campaign that focused on a few core issues. Over and over, he referred to his desire to restore dignity to the office, a thinly veiled reference to Clinton's escapades with Monica Lewinsky and to other ethical and moral lapses of the Clinton administration. As if to confirm Bush's point, the night before the inauguration, Clinton had stayed up almost all night issuing pardons to fugitive financier Marc Rich.

To Bush, disgracing the office of the presidency in this way was unthinkable, yet in his three debates with Al Gore, Bush had come across to many as unprepared for the job. In contrast to Gore, he did not display a command of issues, and he seemed to shrug at some of the points Gore made, as if they were not worth his time or energy. Occasionally, Bush made his trademark smirk or half smile, a gesture that many took as a sign of arrogance.

Clay Johnson thought the entire performance was a manifestation of Bush's intense distaste for acting and pretense. When responding to loaded questions from reporters or an unfair charge by Gore, Bush's honesty impelled him to signal, if ever so subtly, what he really thought. The smirk was not a sign of arrogance but rather an effort to convey his true feelings: that he was participating in a charade. When emerging from sessions with political types he was supposed to stroke and pacify, he would roll his eyes and grouse under his breath about the "B.S." meeting he had just had. In debates with Gore, he could not very well say, "That's B.S.," so he would smirk.

"He's a bad actor, a bad pretender," Johnson said. "He doesn't get up and say, 'One and one is two' unless he really knows it's two. What you see is what you get. So when you see him working that lip or showing discomfort, he can't act that away. It means he's bored or perturbed. A real actor would not show that."[73]

After the inauguration, the Texans and would-be Texans took over, staging eight inaugural balls, complete with live steers, 3,000 pounds of smoked ham, 3,500 pounds of barbecued beef brisket, 35,000 jumbo shrimp, eight hundred pounds of peach cobbler, and 12,000 cases of beer. The entertainers included Clint Black, the Beach Boys, Troy Aikman, George Strait, Tanya Tucker, and Lee Greenwood, who sang *I'm Proud to be an American.*

"This is our night to be outrageously Texan," said Senator Kay Bailey Hutchison, president of the Texas State Society. "We know that Texans brag, but I always tell people that our hearts are as big as our mouths."

Bush and Laura attended every ball. He joked about his rusty dance steps. Then it was to bed before midnight, a harbinger of things to come: The Bush administration would not spend their time going to parties. The place you'll find me at night, Bush would say, is at the White House in bed.

"I'm not somebody that says, 'Gosh, gosh, I can't wait to get to Washington so I can go to all the cocktail parties,'" he said. "That's not what I'm about."

"It was seven days a week and twelve to fourteen hour days in the first six months," Johnson said. "Andy Card and Condi Rice are on call 24/7. For others, after nine or ten months, it's five days a week with twelve- or sixteen-hour days. You just don't have energy to do social things."

The morning after the inauguration, the Bush staff moved into their offices. They found that they had been trashed. The "w" on dozens of computer keyboards had been removed, usually damaging them permanently. Obscene messages had been left on voice mail. The entire contents of desk drawers had been dumped on the floor. Stickers in the West Wing depicted Bush as a chimpanzee, and notes left in desks and filing cabinets said, "Hail to the Thief." In all, the General Accounting Office, the audit arm of Congress, reported, the Clinton staff had caused $15,000 in deliberate damage.

"Never having experienced a presidential transition, I was

surprised at what I saw," Alberto R. Gonzales, Bush's White House counsel, said. "It was a mess. There was trash all over, primarily in the Old Executive Office Building. There was graffiti. We learned later there were things taken."[74]

After press reports of the damage, the Democrats accused the Bush administration of purposely leaking the stories. They claimed such vandalism is routine when administrations change. In fact, GSA managers recalled only one previous episode: After Ronald Reagan was inaugurated, GSA found that the Carter staff had left rotting garbage in the White House and had trashed furniture in the Eisenhower Executive Office Building.

"It was enough to look like a cyclone had hit," Buddy Respass, the GSA manager, said. "They were mean-spirited people."

"They left chicken bones and White House mess dishes with food," another GSA manager said. "It smelled."

Bush said he wanted to move on and not dwell on the matter, but the vandalism by the Clinton people offended the sensibilities of the Bush team. They considered it an honor to serve in the White House. Next to the flag, it was the number-one symbol of the country.

Workers laid the cornerstone for the White House on October 13, 1792. The original building, based on a Georgian design by James Hoban, consisted of a sandstone box that measured 165 feet from east to west and 85 feet from north to south. Gray in color, the home was referred to as the President's House. That was the name preferred by George Washington, who never got to live there but who guided the project through Congress. When the building received a coat of whitewash in 1797, people began referring to it as the White House, the name Theodore Roosevelt officially gave it in 1902. Over the years, the White House has been sacked and burned, gutted, extended, modified, improved, renovated and redecorated. How could anyone dishonor the country's heritage by vandalizing the building that stood for America?

On Sunday after the inauguration, the Bush family attended an inaugural prayer service at Washington National Cathedral with their daughters and Vice President Dick Cheney and his wife Lynne. The Reverend Billy Graham, who had been instrumental in Bush's reaffirmation of his religion, asked God to "place his great hand of protection on each and every one, and specially on you, Mr. President, and your family."

After the service, Bush and Laura invited their family and close friends to a brunch at the White House. Since the U.S. Supreme Court gave Bush the election on December 12, 2000, and Al Gore conceded defeat, Clay Johnson had seen the president-elect just two or three times, when Bush came to Washington and held meetings with Cheney and Card at the Madison Hotel a few blocks from the White House, and then at Blair House, which was right across the street from the White House. At those meetings, they discussed nominees for Cabinet posts—Johnson and his team had developed a list of two hundred possible candidates—and other top positions. Bush wanted quality first, politics second.

"We asked, What is the job, what is the person statutorily allowed to do, what do we want the person to accomplish, and what kind of person is the best person to accomplish that?" Johnson said. "Then we looked at who else is on that team. Maybe others are already from Washington, and you want someone from a western state, or we already have a lawyer and we want a manager. Then and only then did we choose people to recommend. It's not a beauty contest. It's not what senator supports him. Yes, it's a political environment, but doing the right thing will stand us in good stead politically. Instead it's, What is the goal? What do we want the person to do?"

Johnson looked for people who emulated Bush's qualities: Civility, genuineness, friendliness, and an orientation toward getting results.

In selecting ambassadors in posts that are traditionally political, campaign contributions played a role. But Johnson said, "There are forty-five to fifty political ambassadors out of one hundred sixty-two. People can say that of the forty-five, thirty gave money to the presidential campaign. Okay, fine. I can show you a hundred others who gave a whole lot more money who wanted desperately to be ambassadors. They did not become ambassadors, not because we felt they were not as good as they needed to be, but because they were not as good as the others we made ambassadors."

Reid Lyon noticed the difference in the education field. Instead of selecting assistant secretaries of education based on political criteria, Bush chose people who were "first and foremost out-standing educational scientists, as well as excellent managers and people who could forge collaborations across programs and agencies," he said.[75]

When Clay Johnson went to the brunch on January 21, it was the first time he had seen Bush since he had become president. All day, Bush had been emotionally greeting his friends and supporters.[76]

"I came upstairs in the White House," Johnson said. "I turned left to the East Room. He was standing there. He looked at me. I looked at him."

Tears welled up in Bush's eyes as he hugged his friend from Andover.

"We made it," the president said.

9

POTOMAC FEVER

Back in the summer of 1997, Karen Hughes, Bush's communications director, walked into his office in Austin and said, "You're leading in the poll."

"What poll?" Bush asked.

"The poll that shows you are a front-runner for the Republican nomination," she said.

The thought of running crystallized when Bush attended a service at First United Methodist Church in Austin two hours before being sworn in as governor for the second time on January 19, 1999. In his sermon, the Reverend W. Mark Craig said America was starved for honest leaders with "ethical and moral courage." At the time, Bill Clinton had been impeached for allegedly committing perjury and obstructing justice in connection with investigations of his relationship with Monica Lewinsky. He was being tried by the Senate. The minister called for everyone to make the most of every moment and rise to the challenge.

After the church service, Barbara Bush turned to her son.

"He was talking to you," she said.

Just after Bush was sworn in as governor, Collister "Terry" Johnson, Jr., one of his Yale roommates, was jogging with him in downtown Austin. Bush confided that he was thinking of running for president. After their jog, Bush and his lawyer friend returned to the Governor's Mansion and chatted about running for president. Bush would declare his candidacy five months later.

"George, the only thing I hope is that if you become president, you adhere to the no asshole rule—all Dick Cheneys, no Al

Haigs," Johnson said. He was referring to Secretary of State Alexander Haig's "I'm in charge here" declaration, after John Hinckley had shot Ronald Reagan.

Bush gave Terry Johnson a quizzical look. Having known Bush for almost forty years, Johnson knew it meant: "Have you been reading my mind?"[77]

As it turned out, Bush not only placed Cheney, a former congressman, secretary of Defense, and White House chief of staff, in charge of recommending candidates to serve in his administration, he asked him to run as his vice president. Bush's other selections fit the same mold. They were team players, loyal to Bush, and highly experienced, either in government and the private sector, or both.

The media and liberal critics pounced on Bush's selections as evidence that he did not know what he was doing. Otherwise, why would he need such strong, seasoned people around to advise him? The truth was just the opposite. Because he had confidence in himself and his own abilities, Bush did not hesitate to select the most accomplished people. As the first president to hold an M.B.A., Bush knew that his administration would only be as good as those he chose to serve in it.

"Unless you're very confident as a leader, you don't surround yourself with people like Colin Powell, Condi Rice, Don Rumsfeld, or Dick Cheney," Karen P. Hughes told me. "They are smart, strong-willed people. Meetings with them are not for the fainthearted. But when you sit in meetings with them, it's very clear who the leader is."[78]

In most cases, Bush's team had done well financially. In fact, two thirds of Bush's Cabinet members were millionaires. A third had a net worth of ten million dollars or more. Cheney was worth between $22 million and $104 million, according to his financial disclosure statement. Donald H. Rumsfeld, Bush's secretary of Defense, was worth $62 million to $116 million. Colin L. Powell, Bush's secretary of State, was worth $15 million to $66 million. Bush himself was worth more than $20 million. He reported adjusted gross income for 2000 of $894,880, while Cheney reported income of $36 million.

The selections were notable in another respect. Never before had women and minorities been placed in such high government positions. Bush named retired Army general Powell secretary of State, former Stanford University provost Condoleezza Rice national security advisor, Texas Supreme Court justice Al Gonzales White House counsel, Karen Hughes communications director, and Margaret Spellings domestic policy advisor.

Besides Hughes and Spellings, Clay Johnson, Karl Rove, Al Gonzales, and Deputy Communications Director Dan Bartlett were Texans who had served with Bush in Austin. The Texans considered themselves the inner circle, the ones who understood Bush the best and were most comfortable around him. As Rove told a Texas paper, "Texas clout? Yeah, it starts at the top." When Bush's staff moved into the West Wing the day after the inauguration, the Texans would dominate the second floor.

For years, when most people thought of the White House, they thought of the main building at 1600 Pennsylvania Avenue NW, which serves as the president's home and once served as his office. Abraham Lincoln had his office in what is now known as the Lincoln bedroom on the second floor of the White House. Only with the recent TV series has the public come to understand that the West Wing now houses the presidential offices.

Only about fifty people work in the West Wing. In contrast to the TV show, they are not constantly rushing around, engaging in dramatic conversations. Their offices are well-lighted but in most cases are quite small. The staircase that leads from the first to the second floor of the West Wing is wide enough for only one person. The West Wing may be a "rabbit warren," as Carter's and Clinton's White House counsel Lloyd Cutler described it, but it is the most coveted office space in the country.

The West Wing was added to the White House in 1902. In 1909, the president's Oval Office was added in the center of the south side of the West Wing. In 1934, it was moved to its current location on the southeast corner, overlooking the Rose Garden. Finally, in 1942, the East Wing was built to house the offices of the first lady as well as the White House military office.

Other changes have reflected technological progress. When John Adams, the second president, and his wife Abigail moved into the White House on November 1, 1800, with their eight servants, they had an outdoor privy. In 1801, an iron cook stove replaced an open fireplace. In 1803 Thomas Jefferson replaced the privy with two custom-made water closets. Two wells were installed just outside the White House in 1814. Previously, servants had hauled water from half a mile away. A bathtub was installed, but water was poured in by hand. In 1834, indoor plumbing was installed. Gaslights were installed in 1848, and in 1845, the White House got its first refrigerator.

In 1879, a telephone was installed. Its number—1—was easy to remember, but it got little use because so few people had telephones. For three decades, it remained the only telephone in the White House. In 1880, the White House got its first typewriter. To cool the fever of James Garfield as he lay dying for almost three months from an assassin's bullet, a primitive air conditioning system was developed for the White House in 1881. Ten years later, the White House got electric lights and, in 1926, the first electric refrigerator. In 1929, the White House got its first electric washing machine.

Today the 132-room White House is a four-star hotel complete with priceless paintings. Motion detectors, infrared, audio, and pressure sensors detect any intrusion on the White House grounds. Video cameras on the roof and on the grounds record every movement. After 9/11, security was enhanced, with dozens of plainclothes and uniformed officers stationed around the White House and in buildings across the street.

Any time the president leaves or enters the White House, a SWAT team on the roof is ready with machine guns. A digitalized locator box tracks the location of each member of the first family from room to room within the White House and around the world, listing the president as POTUS, for President of The United States.

When J. Bonnie Newman first began working for the George H.W. Bush White House as assistant to the president for management and administration, her secretary gave her a schedule that said she was to attend a reception with POTUS.

"I said, 'I haven't heard of this group,'" Newman said. "My secretary hadn't either, but it turned out POTUS was president of the United States."

The twenty White House operators can, if necessary, obtain unlisted numbers. They even accommodated Caroline Kennedy when, at age five, she asked to speak with Santa Claus. They connected her with a gruff-voiced man in the White House Transportation Department, who is said to have taken her order for a helicopter for her brother John Kennedy, Jr.

The real cost of the White House is anybody's guess. Bush receives a salary of $400,000 a year plus an expense allowance of $50,000 and $100,000 for travel expenses. He also receives $202 million a year for what the U.S. Budget lists as the White House account, plus another $52 million for "unanticipated needs." These figures are but a token of what the White House costs. The real costs—totaling well over a billion dollars—are unknown even to Congress and the General Accounting Office, the audit arm of Congress, because dozens of other government agencies help support the White House.

"The total cost of the White House isn't in any records," said John Cronin Jr., who directed the GAO's audits of the White House for twelve years. "The Navy runs the mess and Camp David, the Army provides the cars and drivers, the Defense Department provides communications, the Air Force provides airplanes, the Marine Corps provides the helicopters. The State Department pays for state functions, the National Park Service maintains the grounds, the Secret Service provides protection, and the General Services Administration (GSA) maintains the East and West Wings and the old Executive Office Building and provides heat."

The Executive Office of the President employs nearly 1,700 people, but again, this is only the tip of the iceberg. The White House Communications Agency, a Defense Department entity that provides the president with instant worldwide communications, alone has more than a thousand employees. Hundreds of people from other agencies are detailed to work for the White House on specific projects, either full-time or part-time.

The cost of Secret Service protection—including for presidential candidates and former presidents—is classified, but it is more than three-quarters of the Secret Service's budget of more than a billion dollars a year.

The Secret Service refers to members of the first family, the vice president and his family, and other top government officials by code names. Bush is Trailblazer and Laura Bush is Tempo. There often seems to be a connection between the code names and the personalities of the people who have them. In fact, the code names are produced randomly by a Defense Department computer from a list of suitable everyday words. Words that are difficult to understand or are derogatory are not included in the list.

"There is no connection with the person," an agent said. "Sometimes it sounds like there is an association, but it is not there."

The code names for each family all begin with the same letter. Clinton is Eagle, while Hillary Clinton is Evergreen. Chelsea Clinton—who no longer receives Secret Service protection—was Energy. Bush's daughters, Barbara and Jenna, are Turquoise and Twinkle, respectively.

When Clinton was president, the press claimed that Roger Clinton, Clinton's brother, was code named Headache, presumably because he replaced Billy Carter as the black sheep of the first family. But because he was not protected by the Secret Service, Roger Clinton had no code name.

After his inauguration, as his father beamed in the Oval Office, Bush tried out the desk John F. Kennedy once used. Called the Resolute desk, it was made from timbers of the HMS. *Resolute*, a British ship that had been abandoned, only to be discovered by an American vessel and returned to the Queen of England as a token of friendship and goodwill. When the ship was retired, Queen Victoria commissioned the desk to be made in 1880 and presented to President Rutherford B. Hayes. To conceal the fact that he had braces on his legs from a bout with polio, President Franklin Roosevelt had the kneehole fitted with a panel carved with the presidential coat-of-arms. Ronald Reagan had the desk raised on a two-inch base to accommodate his six foot, two inch frame.

Bush had had the Oval Office redecorated in cream and peach tones. On one wall he placed an oil painting by W. H. D. Koerner. A gift from his Midland friends Joe and Jan O'Neill, it had hung in Bush's office in the Governor's Mansion. The painting was entitled

A Charge to Keep after a hymn written by Charles Wesley, a founder of the Methodist Church. It showed a man on horseback charging determinedly up a steep, rough trail. The message of the hymn, Bush would say, was, "We serve One greater than ourselves."

Busts of Harry S. Truman and Franklin D. Roosevelt were moved out, replaced by busts of Dwight D. Eisenhower and Winston Churchill, the leader Bush most admired. It was Churchill who said, "If you want peace, prepare for war."

On Thursdays, the White House mess in the basement of the West Wing began serving Tex-Mex food. The Texans groused that it didn't meet their standards. Nor did the Tex-Mex fare at Washington restaurants. Still, Bush and Laura made a foray to Arlington, Virginia, to have dinner at El Paso Café with Clay Johnson and his wife Anne and Michael M. Wood and his wife Judy. A friend from Andover and Yale, Mike Wood succeeded Bush as head cheerleader at Andover and as president of DKE at Yale. Bush and Laura also went to Cactus Cantina in Washington with Pam Nelson, a Kappa Alpha Theta sorority sister of Laura's, and Bush's Yale friends Rex W. Cowdry, M.D., and Robert McCallum and their wives, Donna and Mimi. Bush's father, on the other hand, liked Rio Grande in Bethesda, Maryland.

Bush would awake at 5:30 A.M., brew coffee for Laura, and feed the pets. He took multivitamins, an aspirin, and chondroitin with glucosamine for joints. By 6:45 A.M., he was in the Oval Office, checking in with Condoleezza Rice to get the latest developments overseas. Once or twice a week, he would drop in at the 7:30 A.M. meeting of his twenty senior staff members, presided over by Andy Card in the Roosevelt Room. By 8 A.M., he was being briefed by CIA analysts and George Tenet, the director of central intelligence. After the events of 9/11, Bush added a briefing at 8:30 A.M. by FBI Director Robert S. Mueller III. Dick Cheney, Andy Card, and Condoleezza Rice usually sat in on the briefings. By 6:30 P.M., Bush was back in the residence, where he usually read a two-inch stack of memos and papers after dinner. He was in bed by 9:30 P.M. and turned out the lights by 10:00 P.M.

Throughout the day, Logan Walters, Bush's personal assistant, stayed with him. While attending the University of Texas, Walters began working in 1995 as an intern in the governor's office. He became Bush's personal assistant—known in politics as a body man—in 1997. Walters traveled with Bush during the campaign and continued in the White House until February 2002.

On trips, Walters helped Bush adhere to his schedule. Walters kept key phone numbers in his PalmPilot, lugged around briefing books and speeches, collected small gifts people wanted to give the president, kept track of matters that Bush wanted pursued, ordered hamburgers, and provided him with fresh black Sharpie pens when his signature started to fade. Before events and meetings at the White House, Walters went over logistics with the president, like where he was to stand and what he was to do after his remarks.

Like many of Bush's aides, Walters became a personal friend. On Walters's twenty-sixth birthday, Bush was vacationing in Kennebunkport. Walters had planned to go fishing, but Karl Rove insisted that he attend a meeting of key aides. Walters was unhappy but agreed to go. It turned out to be a surprise birthday party and lobster dinner. From Austin, Bush flew in Walters's girlfriend, Kate Marinis, a niece of Don Evans's who was a campaign worker.

When Walters married Kate in April 2002, Bush and Laura attended their wedding in Houston. When Bush's cow Ofelia—named for Ofelia Vanden Bosch, his administrative assistant when he was governor—gave birth, Bush named the calf Logan. After Walters left to work for the Energy Department and then attend Rice University to work toward an M.B.A., Bush twice invited him and Kate to stay over at Camp David, a stamp of Bush's friendship. The first time, the couple was not married. Grinning impishly, Bush said they would have to stay in separate cabins.[79]

"We would have anyway," Walters told me.

Walters helped Bush get acclimated to the Oval Office, working with another aide to roll in multiple models of desk chairs from which the president could choose. Bush selected a simple chair to replace an elaborate one that Clinton used.

Bush's first act as president was to issue a broad set of ethical standards for all government employees.

"Everyone who enters into public service for the United States has a duty to the American people to maintain the highest standards of integrity in government," the memo said.

When Bush found that Linda Chavez had not been forthcoming about her employment of Marta Mercado, a Guatemalan housekeeper who was in the United States illegally, he withdrew her nomination for secretary of labor two days after ABC broke the story about her. In contrast, Clinton let Zoe Baird dangle for a month before she withdrew as his nominee for attorney general amid charges she had hired an illegal immigrant as a nanny and didn't pay her Social Security taxes.

Just as decisively, Bush moved to change the atmosphere of the White House, code-named Crown by the Secret Service. Under Clinton, the White House operated like an all-night pizza parlor. Aides attended meetings in jeans and T-shirts. As in a college debating society, business was conducted late into the night and all weekend. Clinton would throw out ideas and endlessly circle the subject rather than come to a conclusion. He would not hesitate to wake up aides at home with trivial questions. The lobby of the West Wing was like a subway station, packed with visitors coming and going. Carpets and upholstered furniture were fraying, and empty pizza cartons were everywhere. Because he was almost never on schedule, the Secret Service joked about CST—Clinton Standard Time.

"Under Clinton, staffers would bring in girls they had picked up in Georgetown to see the Oval Office at midnight," said a former Secret Service agent. "Bush changed that. If a staffer wanted to bring a guest in, he had to make an appointment in advance. There were no more late night visits to the Oval Office. Bush restored respect."

"Clinton would say, 'This is the People's House,'" another agent said. "He may have said that, but he didn't have any respect for it himself."[80]

Bush thought the White House should be run like any efficient business. Obvious as that might seem, previous administrations either did not see it that way or were not competent enough to operate efficiently. In the Bush White House, meetings would start precisely on time. Planning for State of the Union speeches would start as many as three months in advance. Men would wear jackets and ties in the Oval Office. Television sets would not be constantly turned on, distracting aides from their work. The lobby of the West Wing would be a place of dignity, with few visitors. Salaries and position titles would be downgraded. Bush would urge staffers to spend time with their families and get enough rest. He would only call them at home when it was urgent. But while Bush treated employees with respect, he also made it clear he would not tolerate any Al Haigs or John Sununus.

"There are two kinds of people who are attracted to working in the White House," said William P. Barr, who worked in the Reagan White House before becoming attorney general under Bush's father. "One is the person who is caught up in the superficial aspects of it—the pomp and circumstance and the perks. They tend to become absorbed over time with who is going to ride on *Air Force One*, who has mess privileges, and who is going to sit in which car in the motorcade. That, unfortunately, is usually a very large number of people at any White House. Even people going in initially who think they are going to change the world somehow get seduced by that atmosphere. Then there are people who really care about policy or people and who are interested in substance."[81]

To Bush, one case of "Whitehouse-itis"—a malady of arrogance that commonly afflicts presidents and White House aides— was one too many. After about a year, Clay Johnson began hearing of a few appointees insisting on large hotel suites when traveling or saying they were too busy to meet with their staff.

"My sense is when people come here and get in trouble, they come here with an attitude that they are very important people because of the position they have here, and if they just do things naturally they'll be okay," Johnson said. "They don't pay attention to the ethics rules, lose the common touch, and take themselves too seriously. We try to take people who will be good team members who will be comfortable being George Bush's assistant secretary rather than THE assistant secretary."[82]

On a Web site for administration appointees, Johnson added a section listing warning signs of Potomac Fever. According to the site—www.results.gov—individuals suffering the dread disease may have an inflated notion of self-worth. They may use phrases such as: "Let's get one of the cars and drivers here to take us to dinner," or "Hello, I'm THE assistant secretary of [blank]" as opposed to "President Bush's assistant secretary of [blank]."

Such individuals may get upset at industry gatherings when they're not instantly recognized. They have "more material and pictures of themselves on their 'I love me' wall than paper in their policy files." Their office hallway pictures and blow-ups are "two times life size." According to the Web site, such people may suffer bouts of memory loss, forgetting who appointed them to their position or that they serve at the pleasure of the president.

Under the heading "Prevention/Treatment," it is suggested that appointees visit "any small town outside the D.C. media market, go into a local store or restaurant to ask how many Cabinet officials and senior staff members the person waiting on you can name. Watch the local news in the same small town, notice how many seconds they devote to the most important issue you are currently working on. Ask your children or siblings if they know how important a person you are."

"We decided to have fun with this and also remind people that the work we do is important, but we are not," Johnson said. "Don't start to believe that you are critical to the Earth turning. These newfound friends are interested in the work you do, but you are not as cute as they would suggest. The invitations you get have a lot to do with the job you have—not the quality of your cocktail chatter."

10

WHY JOHNNY STILL CAN'T READ

During the campaign, Bush hammered at the need to improve public education, the first of his six campaign pledges. To many, it sounded like a sop to liberals. How could a conservative Republican be interested in the plight of lower-income families who send their kids to public schools? Once elected, most presidents quickly discard many of their campaign promises anyway—as Bush's father did after promising "no new taxes"—in favor of what they regard as more realistic goals.

But Bush devoted much of his first week as president to education reform, which would be his first legislative initiative. Going back to his roots in Midland, Bush thought of America as the land of opportunity, with limitless horizons. But if a child never learned to read, his horizons may extend no farther than a welfare program, a crack house, or a jail cell.

In fact, Margaret Spellings, Bush's domestic policy advisor, thought that, until the events of 9/11, reforming education was a principal reason Bush wanted to be president.

"If he wanted to do anything, I would say Bush wanted to change American education," Spellings told me in her office on the second floor of the West Wing. "That's why he's here. That's why he wanted to come here."

Spellings met Bush through her friend Karl Rove when Bush was thinking of running for Texas governor in 1990. A graduate of the University of Houston, she was then associate executive director of the Texas Association of School Boards, working with the Texas legislature on school accountability issues. Spellings became Bush's political director during his first campaign as governor and then became his education advisor in Austin.

The divorced mother of two, Spellings married Austin-based attorney Robert Spellings in August 2001. Bush's nickname for her—La Margarita—melded her first name of Margaret with her previous married name, La Montagne.

While she was never in the media, Spellings was just as sharp as Rove, with a computer-like brain that kept track of hundreds of things at once. Asked in her blue-carpeted office to name the members of the senior staff who meet every morning at 7:30, she identified each one in order of where they sat at the conference table. No matter how many threads she pursued after being asked something, she unerringly returned to the original question. With the practiced delivery of an auctioneer, she reeled off the names of dozens of agencies and programs that fall within her purview, from tort reform to going to Mars. Like the rest of Bush's inner circle, she referred to him in e-mail as "GWB."

Spellings's power office in a corner of the West Wing was L-shaped, one of the few with access to the outside through a balcony. It was two doors down from Rove's office. Like most West Wing offices, Spellings's had large photos of Bush and her framed commission signed by Bush on the walls.

One day when she was in Bush's office in the Governor's Mansion, Spellings noticed a strange-looking, two-inch-high jar on his desk. Inside, suspended in clear liquid, were what looked like a dozen tiny human buttocks.

"What the hell is this?" she asked Bush.

He picked up the jar and showed her the label: Pickled Fresh Big Spring Heinie Farms. Bush took out a black felt pen, signed the red metal cap, and handed her the jar.

"From one heinie to another. George Bush," the inscription said.

After Bush was elected president, startled state archivists discovered the jar in Spellings's office in Austin. Seeing that it had been signed by Bush, they wanted to know what it was and whether it should be sent to the archives and catalogued. Instead, Spellings had them forward the jar to her West Wing office. She kept it on a shelf, an example of Bush's "impish" sense of humor.

When it became clear that Bush would ask Spellings and Karen Hughes to go with him to Washington, Andy Card began preparing them for the punishing hours, warning they might rarely see their kids.

"I thought, 'I'm a single mother. I can't do this,' " Spellings said. "Then Karen called me in high anxiety."

"Are you believing this?" Hughes said. "We're never going to be able to see our kids. I don't think I can do it."

"I don't think I can do it either," Spellings replied.

Hughes told Bush she had concerns about the pace of life in Washington and the prospect of not seeing her kids.

"The next thing that happened was Bush called Andy Card and said, 'Are you running off the mothers?' " Spellings recalled.

Like the other seven senior aides he brought to the White House from the Lone Star State, Spellings was unabashedly Texan.

"We were proud of what we had done with reading in Texas," she said. "Texans are proud no matter what."

Describing working for Bush, she couldn't help but put in a plug for the Texans.

"He's a really good motivator and manager," Spellings said. "He's the kind of person you want to follow because you like him. He makes it fun to work here. People want to be working with someone who is fun and engaged and interested and appreciative and has a vision of what he wants to do. He's direct. There are no sideshows. That's more true with the people who have been around for a while and are from the Lone Star State."

As Bush's domestic policy advisor, Spellings was with him when he met in the Oval Office on Tuesday, January 23, with Senator Edward M. Kennedy to try to establish agreement on his No Child Left Behind Act and its Reading First Program. While Kennedy, the ranking minority member of the education committee, opposed Bush's idea of giving publicly funded vouchers to children so they could attend private schools, he understood the need to reform reading instruction by introducing phonics and accountability.

Rove had laid out the sequence of initiatives, beginning with education.

"Karl thinks education is obviously a huge issue," Spellings said. "He's quite the policy wonk. He was responsible for us leading out with this issue in the first days of the administration. It was so important to the president. It spotlights the fact that we were different kinds of Republicans, trying to change the tone in Washington. We were going to talk with Ted Kennedy about an issue that used to belong to the other side, where we had done our homework and knew a whole lot about it, but it was a subject where he was also an expert."[83]

Bush wanted to provide money to states that agreed to administer standardized reading and math tests annually in grades three through eight. Previously, schools gave tests in the third and eighth grades. When students did badly, teachers could blame the reading instruction the children received in the years in between.

Under Bush's proposal, schools would be required to make steady progress toward raising proficiency, with all students required to reach state-defined acceptable levels by 2014. Schools deemed failing for two consecutive years would have to begin to allow students to transfer to better schools. After a third year of failing, they could use public money to hire private firms to tutor students. If a school continued to fail, it had to replace its principal and teachers or reopen as a charter school. Bush wanted vouchers so parents could send their kids to such schools.

A charter school is a public school that has its own management and some private funding, allowing more flexibility and accountability. The best example was the KIPP (Knowledge is Power Program) chain of thirty-two charter schools in twenty-six cities. Started in Houston, the schools pay teachers more to teach from 8 A.M. to 5 P.M. on weekdays plus three Saturdays per month and three weeks in the summer. The schools issue cell phones to teachers so students can call them easily. In Washington, D.C., the average fifth grader enters KIPP DC: Key Academy, which is ninety-nine percent black, reading at the third grade level. Using phonics, the charter school in southeast Washington brings them up to grade level in less than a year. In two years, they are reading ahead of their grade.

Along with Spellings and Karl Rove, Sandy Kress, Bush's unpaid education advisor from Texas, attended the meeting between Bush and Ted Kennedy on Bush's reading initiative.

"As they got into it, it became clear to Kennedy, I think, that behind whatever pasteboard figure had been created about Bush, there was a thoughtful person, someone who had devoted a lot of energy to this," Kress said. "The president said we have a difference of opinion on vouchers, but I don't want that to get in the way of creating these reforms for children," Kress recalled. "I want to make this offer to you: that we work seriously and closely together to get to the result we both want."[84]

Kennedy, who later became chairman of the education committee, agreed.

"There are going to be reporters out there waiting for you when you leave the White House," Bush said. "They will try to separate us. Let's not let that happen."

Emerging from their first working meeting, Kennedy said he was encouraged by what he had heard. Later that day, in the East Room, Bush announced the broad outlines of his legislation.

What most troubled Bush was what he called the "soft bigotry of low expectations." In a satire, a Vermont school principal wrote to the *Burlington Free Press* about the "No Cow Left Behind Act." The principal wrote, "Now I'm sure farms have a mix of cows in the barn, but it is important to remember that every cow can meet the standard. There should be no exceptions and no excuses. I don't want to hear about the cows that just came to the barn from the farm down the road that didn't provide the proper nutrition or a proper living environment. All cows need to meet the standard."

In other words, children who grew up in poor neighborhoods or came from uneducated families were hopeless. In contrast to that attitude, the motto of the KIPP charter schools was "no shortcuts; no excuses."

In the East Room, Bush took aside Dr. Reid Lyon, his reading advisor from the National Institutes of Health. By now, Bush referred to him as a "good man," his highest accolade, picked up during his Skull and Bones days. Bush wanted to know from Lyon if any government agency had conducted research on how preschool children develop, not only educationally, but socially, emotionally, nutritionally, and physically. If more could be learned about these areas, the government could help prepare less privileged children for school.

"No, not in any formal or well-coordinated sense," Lyon said.[85]

Bush asked if different agencies were doing their own thing on these issues, not collaborating. When Lyon said that was correct, Bush said, "That's not acceptable."

Now, as president, Bush could issue instructions directly to Lyon rather than suggesting ideas for research programs, as he had when he was governor. Bush asked Lyon to develop a research program that integrated the work being done on children's total development within the NIH, the Education Department, and the Health and Human Services Department.

On Friday, January 26, Bush visited the Merritt Elementary School in northeast Washington, a nearly all-black school. With him were Laura Bush, Senator Ted Kennedy, Senator Jim Jeffords of Vermont, and Representatives John A. Boehner of Ohio and George Miller of California. Bush perched on a table in the teachers' lounge and asked the principal, Dr. Nancy R. Shannon, about her methods.

In theory, a school principal is like the CEO of a company, insisting on good results and taking action if employees are not doing a good job. In practice, most principals tend to the infrastructure—making sure the buses run on time and the safety patrol gets its badges—rather than concentrating on education.

For years, Dr. Shannon had been acting as a real CEO, making her teachers accountable. When children did well, she recognized the teachers with award nights and achievement certificates. When children did poorly, she downgraded teachers on evaluations, observed their teaching methods, and worked with them to improve. While the evaluations had no impact on their salaries, teachers singled out for having students with low reading scores recognized that they had to work harder. Within a few years, Shannon brought reading scores in her school up above the national average.

The No Child Left Behind Act was passed in the spring but,

because of the need to work out differences between the House and Senate versions, Bush did not sign it into law until the following January. Besides mandating more frequent reading tests and imposing accountability, the law provided $1.1 billion to schools that adopted reading instruction methods proven to be effective—meaning phonics. The money was allocated specifically to train teachers to teach phonics and provide new teaching materials. In all, Bush would eventually propose spending $22 billion a year on education, most of it for funding existing programs. Still, most school systems resisted. Even after the act became law, a stunning sixty percent of the country continued to teach reading by the whole-language method.

"They would submit plans, which would really be for a continuation of whole language," Lyon said. "We would reject them, then they would submit a new plan, which was still whole language," Lyon said. "Then we would go through the process all over again."

In particular, the New York City schools, which were most in need of a reading program that worked, stubbornly clung to their whole-language program. Called Month-by-Month Phonics, it was whole language disguised as phonics—a wolf in sheep's clothing, as Lyon put it. In rejecting a true phonics program, the city's schools stood to lose $44 million a year, the city's allocation from the No Child Left Behind Act.

Describing why the New York City schools rejected phonics, Lyon said that Joel I. Klein, the New York City schools chancellor appointed by Mayor Michael R. Bloomberg, would "look at the fact that a hundred professors from Columbia and Boston University say whole language is great. Only seven will say phonics is better. So he'll say it's a hundred against seven, not understanding that the quality of the research by the hundred professors does not meet research standards at NIH."[86]

Teachers' unions either rejected phonics or took a neutral approach.

"For some kids, Month-by-Month might work," Randi Weingarten, president of the New York City teachers union, said. "For others, another program might do better."

By this rendering, it was like choosing between a Mounds bar and an Almond Joy. It didn't make much difference which teaching method was used. But the truth was it did: Taught by the whole-language approach, sixty to seventy percent of New York City's schoolchildren were illiterate. In contrast, after Bush introduced phonics in Texas and required failing kids to take additional reading instruction, less than two percent could not read.

Because it was a third rail in the education establishment, the White House downplayed the need for phonics, the key ingredient in making a difference in teaching kids to read. Instead, Bush would emphasize the need for accountability, raised expectations, and teaching methods validated by research.

"The term 'phonics' is loaded," Margaret Spellings told me. "We talk about research-based or science-based instruction. If you're a twenty-year teacher and you've been doing it wrong all your career by using the whole-language approach, you don't want to be humiliated. Teachers are people of goodwill. Otherwise they wouldn't be teachers. You can't say they are evil and wrong. We have to make them want to buy into teaching phonics. The old-style Republican approach would have been to abolish the Department of Education, expose the educators, and voucherize, as opposed to trying to lead them out of the wilderness."

"The president tends to be positive," Karen Hughes said. "He doesn't like to point fingers or blame people."[87]

Aside from teachers' resistance to change and tackling more work, what fueled the movement to retain whole language and resist the No Child Left Behind Act were the arguments of the two professors whose ideas originally brought the concept to American schools: Dr. Kenneth Goodman of the University of Arizona and Dr. Frank Smith, formerly of the University of Victoria in British Columbia, Canada.

In an interview, Goodman told me that the Bush effort was part of a vast right-wing effort. It involved textbook publishers, the Heritage Foundation, and assorted other culprits who wanted to deprive teachers of the right to teach as they see fit, to impose federal control on education, and to cruelly force children to drill and take tests. The real goal, Goodman insisted, was an education system "like third world countries have, where people who can afford to send their kids to private school."

Why would all these people want to do that? I asked.

"The same reason the neoconservatives have pushed us into dangerous foreign policy, to centralize control and maximize profit." The Bush plan was an "inquisition" driving teachers from education, Goodman maintained.[88]

"Teachers don't like to be controlled, to be forced to teach in ways that damage the kids, to have the knowledge they've developed and the reason they went into education canceled out by federal mandate," Goodman said. Reading, Goodman said, should be taught by exposure to literature, allowing children to "experiment with reading and writing," a process he grandly called a "psycholinguistic guessing game."

Given Goodman's approach to letting children learn "naturally," should teachers correct spelling errors?

"What's an error?" Goodman said. "Language is a social invention, and it's also personal. My voice isn't yours, my dialect isn't yours . . . You learn to spell through misspellings. A skilled teacher can look at a child's writing and see that, though some of the spellings aren't conventional, they show the children's growing skills at the spelling system." He added, "What we're doing is turning our schools into drill camps for testing."

Even though it is a basic component of any kind of instruction, the education establishment quickly adopted Goodman's professed aversion to testing. No one objected to science and history tests, but educators contended reading tests were punitive or that teachers would "teach to the test." On reflection, that made perfect sense. Whole language is not an instructional method but rather a hope—a hope that if kids are given reading materials, they will miraculously learn to read if left to their own devices. Since that does not in fact occur in up to seventy percent of the student population, educators' natural reaction was to cover up kids' failure to read by rejecting testing that documents it. At the same time, they sneeringly portrayed Bush's desire to conduct exams as Gestapo-like.

"If you're teaching to the test, you're teaching what you want children to know, what's part of the curriculum," Laura Bush, a former teacher, noted. "I'm not worried about it. Accountability is absolutely fundamental to making sure that schools are doing well, and not as a punitive test but as a way to correct, to find out where the problems are."

"Don't read, don't tell," was how Robert W. Sweet, Jr., co-founder of the National Right to Read Foundation, aptly characterized the education establishment's campaign against testing.

Even though the California schools discarded whole-language instruction because they found kids were not learning to read, Goodman insisted that California test scores had not declined. Nor, he said, had the schools there had a problem with whole language, as their own administrators have said.

Why do test results show that phonics is superior to whole language?

"It's a misrepresentation," Goodman said.

Why is Bush pushing phonics if it isn't superior to whole language?

"I think he's pushing it because he's dedicated to promoting business interests," Goodman said. "It's the same reason he pushed it in Texas. Ken Lay [of Enron] was connected to the Texas Governor's Business Council," he added ominously.

But the business council was hardly fodder for a good conspiracy theory. Established by Democrat Ann Richards when she was Texas governor, the council promoted Texas economic development by providing the governor with research and advice, including on programs to improve literacy. Richards appointed then Enron chairman Kenneth Lay to head the council, and Bush reappointed Lay after he became governor.

If phonics is not superior to whole language, why do the toniest private schools in New York swear by it?

"There is tremendous pressure," Goodman said. "Through parents, through propaganda." In any case, Goodman said, "Only about five percent of kids go to private schools or parochial schools."

The plot thickened.

"The feds give money to PR firms to promote phonics," Goodman said.

Thus, private schools that teach phonics do so not because they have found it works, but because sinister forces have pressured them. The players in the campaign against whole language include "coopted scientists," the National Academy of Sciences, the religious right, Congress, governors, legislators, and, of course, George W. Bush, according to a diagram Goodman prepared for one of his academic papers.

In the end, Goodman's argument for teaching whole language turned not on whether it worked but on his contention that no one should be "forced" to change to phonics.

In an astounding statement, Goodman told me: "Even if tests show phonics works better, you shouldn't be telling teachers how to teach. They know better. Not only shouldn't you do it, but it doesn't work . . . You can't compel people to do what they don't believe in."

Comparing teaching to medicine, Goodman said, "If we decided that one treatment was better than certain other treatments, we wouldn't use the kind of strong-arm techniques that they [Bush administration officials and Congress] are using. We wouldn't go back through the research and expunge from it anything that differs with the Bush administration."

Wouldn't a doctor who did not use the technique proven to be best subject himself to medical malpractice suits and loss of his license and hospital privileges?

"No, he would not," Goodman said. "You can have conflicting research. There is no agreement in the field of education."

In the same vein, Professor Frank Smith, the other father of whole language, argued that testing somehow harms children, taking away teachers' freedom, controlling children, and creating a "heartless" environment. Like Goodman, Smith portrayed phonics as a way of imposing on children "linguistic purity that would limit children to arbitrary 'proper' language." Reading is, in fact, overvalued, according to Smith.

"Literacy doesn't make anyone a better person," Smith observed.

Thus, on the word of Goodman, who says whole language should be taught even if it is inferior to phonics, and Smith, who says reading is overrated, the nation's public schools have been teaching whole language since the 1970s, turning out millions of kids who cannot read.

Nutty as their arguments were, Spellings never failed to become angry when she heard them. Shaking her head, she said, "I don't know why Ken Goodman is on this planet, but I don't think it's to teach kids to read."

When told that Goodman, comparing them with doctors, said teachers should not be forced to teach a method even if it is proven best, Spellings said, "That's bull. We don't practice medicine like that, obviously. There are standard practices and best practices." Referring to the followers of whole language, she said, "It's crazy. It's a religion."

Goodman was right about one thing: For reasons that are unclear, the reading wars have transmuted into a struggle between the right and the left. Liberals saw the laissez-faire approach of whole language as being liberating, joyful, and creative. In her book *It Takes a Village*, Hillary Rodham Clinton endorsed Reading Recovery, a whole-language approach to remedial reading that produces shockingly poor results. New Zealand researchers reported that children who took Reading Recovery in that country showed no signs of accelerated reading performance. In Fort Wayne, Indiana, almost a quarter of the students who took Reading Recovery still could not read. That compared with less than two percent in the Texas schools after Bush introduced phonics.

Conservatives, on the other hand, saw nothing wrong with practice, drill, and testing, the methods schools have used for centuries. There is nothing joyful or liberating about being illiterate— unable to read phone books, ballots, manuals, or the directions for taking a medicine.

"People say, 'Don't drill,'" Karl Rove said. "What they're saying is you don't need to sound out a word or know its meaning. I say, How can that make sense to anybody?"[89]

"How do you get to Carnegie Hall or play tennis?" Spellings said. "You practice. Not only is that not punitive, it's a good thing. Many of these same proponents of whole language say some of these kids can't be taught to read anyway. That's what Bush calls soft bigotry."

Since the failure to teach reading with phonics has the greatest impact on blacks, whole language, in effect, has made blacks "subservient" to the rest of the population, Robert Sweet, now an aide to Representative Boehner, noted.

The greatest irony was that children of New York liberals, who were the first to ridicule Bush for everything he did and said, were illiterate because of the teaching method he was trying so hard to banish.

How could education colleges and teachers be taken in by such transparently absurd theories? Aside from pure negligence, one reason was that the media covered the subject like a political campaign, reporting on charges and countercharges but rarely delving into how whole language has rendered large segments of the population illiterate.

Spellings shook her blond head again.

"People don't understand how profoundly our country is being harmed by this," she said. "Our poverty, our crime stem basically from these kids' inability to access society. It's crazy."[90]

11

A Trip on *Air Force One*

On Friday, February 16, 2001, Bush took his first international trip as president on *Air Force One*, paying a visit, with Laura, to Vicente Fox of Mexico. Like his predecessors, Bush on the plane was like a boy in a candy store, wearing his blue *Air Force One* windbreaker, trying out the communications, and marveling at being able to fly anywhere in the world on a moment's notice.

Air Force One got its name when Dwight D. Eisenhower was president. Prior to his presidency, the aircraft used by Franklin D. Roosevelt and Harry S. Truman had been known by their actual Air Force designations. Because a flight controller had mistaken it for a commercial plane, the pilot suggested calling any plane the president happened to be using *Air Force One*. The Secret Service codenamed it Angel.

Beginning with Eisenhower, presidents used Boeing 707s. The 707 carried just fifty passengers, including staff members, guests, Secret Service agents, and fourteen reporters, photographers, and TV camera crew members called the press pool, which distributes reports to others covering the White House. After George H.W. Bush became president, the present 231-foot-long Boeing 747-200B bubble top jumbo jet was used.

The current *Air Force One* has a range of 9,600 miles and a maximum cruising altitude of 45,100 feet. It cruises at 600 miles per hour but can achieve speeds of 701 miles per hour. In addition to two pilots, a navigator, and a flight engineer, the plane carries *Air Force One* stewards and seventy-six passengers. The plane has eighty-seven telephones.

While the average 747 has 485,000 feet of electrical wire, the presidential plane has 1.2 million feet, all shielded from the electromagnetic pulses which would be emitted during a nuclear blast. Near the front of the plane, the president has an executive suite with a stateroom, dressing room, and bathroom with a shower. The president also has a private office near the stateroom and a combination dining room and conference room. Toward the rear are areas for the staff, Secret Service, guests, and the press.

The crew that flies *Air Force One* is part of the Air Force's Eighty-Ninth Airlift Wing under the Air Mobility Command. The unit provides transportation for government officials, including members of Congress. Based at Andrews Air Force Base east of Washington, *Air Force One* costs $34,400 per hour of flight time for fuel and supplies alone. *Marine One*, the helicopter that flies the president to Andrews Air Force Base at the start and end of each plane trip and back and forth to Camp David, costs $5,597 per hour.

Under Federal Aviation Administration regulations, *Air Force One* takes precedence over other aircraft. When approaching an airport, it bumps other planes that have arrived first. Before it lands, Secret Service agents on the ground check the runway for explosives or objects such as tires. Generally, other aircraft may not land on the same runway for fifteen or twenty minutes before *Air Force One* lands.

By its very nature, *Air Force One* brings out the true character of presidents and first families. In command of their own flying carpet and confined to a small space over many hours, presidents who are arrogant and haughty tend to exhibit those traits more. Bill Clinton's escapades on *Air Force One* were prime examples.

In May 1993, Clinton ordered *Air Force One* to wait on the tarmac at Los Angeles International Airport while he got a haircut from Christophe Schatteman, a Beverly Hills hairdresser whose clients have included Nicole Kidman, Goldie Hawn, and Steven Spielberg.

"We flew out of San Diego to L.A. to pick him up," recalled James Saddler, a steward on the fateful trip. "Some guy came out and said he was supposed to cut the president's hair. Christophe cut his hair, and we took off. We were on the ground for an hour. They closed the runways."

While Clinton got his haircut, two LAX runways were closed. Because that meant all incoming and outgoing flights had to be halted, Clinton's thoughtlessness inconvenienced passengers throughout the country.

The press reported that the haircut cost $200, Christophe's fee at the time for a haircut in his salon at 348 North Beverly Drive. But Howard Franklin, the chief *Air Force One* steward, said Schatteman told him on the plane that his charge for the cut was $500. Staffers informed Franklin that someone at a Democratic fund-raiser paid for the haircut.[91]

In typical Clinton fashion, when he learned of the flight delays, Clinton blamed his staff for arranging the haircut. But it was his hair that was being cut, and he gave the orders to delay takeoff. As president, he was aware that if *Air Force One* sat on a runway, traffic would be stopped.

Masters of spin, Clinton White House staffers ardently tried to turn the fiasco into a plus. "Is he still the president of the common man?" White House Communications Director George Stephanopoulos was asked at his daily White House briefing. "Absolutely," he responded. "I mean, the president has to get his hair cut. Everybody has to get their hair cut . . . I think he does have the right to choose who he wants to cut his hair."

After Clinton's inauguration, Franklin told Clinton's advance people that "the key to being effective was planning." That novel idea brought a vigorous retort. "They said, 'We got here by being spontaneous, and we're not going to change,'" Franklin recalled. Besides an aversion to planning, Clinton and his people brought with them the attitude that "the military were people who couldn't get jobs," Franklin said.

Like an adolescent, Clinton would exchange with male crew members observations about the anatomy of any women who happened to be on the plane. To female crew members, he would make off-color remarks.

Caught up in the latest scandal involving the firing of the White House Travel Office employees, Clinton wandered into the press compartment at the back of the plane on Friday night, September 2, 1995. He spoke about how America was in a "funk" because the world was changing so fast.

"What makes people insecure is when they feel they're lost in the fun house," he announced to puzzled journalists. "They're in a room where something can hit them from any direction at any time. They always feel living life is like walking across a running river on slippery rocks, and you can lose your footing at any time."

It was a telling description of the way Clinton felt about himself. With his strongest conviction the desire to be elected, he had little moral compass. Clinton's refusal to keep a schedule was a way of asserting control, just as Lyndon Johnson had done.

Johnson "would be an hour late and would expect the crew to make it up so he would be on time," said Robert MacMillan, an *Air Force One* steward who flew with him. "We hedged our bets and would add forty-five minutes to an hour for every stop. He finally figured that out. He said, 'How come it takes the [commercial] airplanes an hour, and we take two hours?' We said, 'Mr. President, that's because you are often an hour late.' He would say, 'That's my business.'"

Gerald F. Pisha, another *Air Force One* steward, said that on one occasion when Johnson thought a steward had mixed a Cutty Sark and soda that was too weak, the president threw the drink on the floor.

"Get somebody who knows how to make a drink for me," Johnson said.

"He had episodes of getting drunk," George E. Reedy, his press secretary, said. "There were times where he would drink day after day. You would think this guy is an alcoholic. Then all of a sudden, it would stop. We could always see the signs when he called for a Scotch and a soda, and he would belt it down and call for another one, instead of sipping it."

Dr. Bertram Brown, the psychiatrist who has seen many White House aides, said Johnson's humiliation of his employees was an exercise of his power. He would, for example, issue instructions to his staff while sitting on the toilet.

"Johnson was a megalomaniac," Brown said. "He was a man of such narcissism that he thought he could do anything." In the same vein, Clinton was "intoxicated and overwhelmed, as any-body might be, by the thrills of the presidency—the fame, the ex-citement, the importance." But, he said, Clinton did not do the hard work of being a CEO, of thinking, planning, and strategiz-ing. "He is a mediocre guy getting his kicks out of being the top politician in the land," Brown said.

While Carter cultivated the image of a simple peanut farmer who was a man of the people, he couldn't be troubled to greet the crew.

"Carter came into the cockpit once in the two years I was on with him," said James A. Buzzelli, an *Air Force One* flight engi-neer. "But Reagan never got on or off without sticking his head in the cockpit and saying, 'Thanks, fellas,' or 'Have a nice day.' He [Reagan] was just as personable in person as he came across to the public."

Carter's effort to show he was a man of the people extended to carrying his own luggage when traveling. But that was for "photo ops," said Charles Palmer, the chief *Air Force One* steward. When the press was not around, Palmer said, he "stopped doing it."

Even Carter's claim that the White House would be "dry" was a sham. Each time a state dinner was held, the White House made it a point to tell reporters that no liquor—only wine—would be served.

"The Carters were the biggest liars in the world," said Bill Gul-ley, who was in charge of the White House military office. "The word was passed to get rid of all the booze. There can't be any on *Air Force One*, in Camp David, or in the White House. This was coming from close associates of the Carter family. I said to our White House military people, 'Hide the booze, and let's find out what happens.' The first Sunday they are in the White House, I get a call from the mess saying, 'They want bloody marys before going to church. What should I do?' I said, 'Find some booze and take it up to them.' "

"We never cut out liquor under Carter," said Palmer, the chief of the *Air Force One* stewards. "Occasionally, Carter had a mar-tini," Palmer said. He also would have a Michelob Lite. "Rosa-lynn may have had a drink . . . She had a screwdriver."

After he was voted out of office, Carter occasionally stayed in the townhouse which GSA maintains for former presidents at 1716 Jackson Place. Like other presidents, Carter stayed there on the evening of his successor's inauguration.

On the walls of the townhouse are photos of former presidents. Because GSA managers had to check on the premises while Carter was there, they found that Carter would temporarily remove the photos of Republican presidents Ford and Nixon and decorate the townhouse with another half-dozen photos of himself.

Each time, Charles Respass, then the GSA manager over the White House, became irate because GSA had to find the old photos and hang them again. Lucille Price, another GSA manager who reported to Respass, said Carter "didn't like them [Ford and Nixon] looking down at him. We would find out he would put photos of himself up . . . Then he would take the photos of himself back with him."

While he was in the White House, Carter did not want the Secret Service uniformed division to greet him. For the president who claimed to be a populist, saying hello to the hired help was beneath him.

"We never spoke unless spoken to," said Fred Walzel, who was chief of the White House branch of the Secret Service uniformed division. "Carter complained that he didn't want them [the officers] to say hello."

"The Carters were the world's worst," said a longtime White House residence staffer. "They would walk over you like you were dirt under their feet. Carter wouldn't even say 'good morning' to you."

In contrast, George W. Bush remembered the names of every member of the White House residence staff and the crew of *Air Force One*. Rather than snubbing them, he would play baseball with Secret Service agents.

Bush's father and mother were the same way. When Bush's father was president, Bonnie Newman, assistant to the president for management and administration, recalled that George Prescott Bush, his twelve-year-old grandson, was hitting tennis balls off the back of the White House tennis court when she and Joseph W.

Hagin, deputy assistant to the president for scheduling, approached the court to play. The two White House aides had reserved the court, but seeing the president's grandson, they turned away and began walking back toward the White House. Just then, Barbara Bush came along and told George, son of Jeb Bush, to get off the court.

"Mrs. Bush saw it and just plucked him off," Newman said. "She really sent the message not only to staff, but to family as well, that you remember your manners."

"With the Carters, you had to get off the elevator in the residence when they got on," a member of the residence staff said. "With George H.W. and Barbara Bush, they wouldn't let you off."

Of all the recent presidents, George Bush had the simplest tastes. While his father relished barbecued beef brisket and would snack on pork rinds dipped in hot sauce, Bush preferred peanut-butter-and-jelly sandwiches and would snack on Fritos. Logan Walters, Bush's personal assistant, said that during the campaign, the word got around that those were his two favorite foods.

"Everywhere he went, there were peanut-butter-and-jelly sandwiches and Fritos," Walters said. "At one hotel, there was a towering stack of peanut-butter-and-jelly sandwiches—enough for a dozen people—and a gigantic bowl of Fritos. He called for me and said, 'Logan, enough with the peanut-butter-and-jelly sandwiches. I don't want to see any more of them.' "[92]

But Bush soon returned to his two weaknesses. He liked creamy peanut butter—usually Jif or Peter Pan—with raspberry jam. While he preferred them on white, whole wheat was acceptable, as was grape jelly. Occasionally, he might have an egg salad sandwich. When visiting friends, he would often go into the kitchen and prepare it himself. Bush drank Diet Coke and unchilled bottled water. He liked his coffee black with an artificial sweetener like Equal.

"Bush is not demanding," Howard Franklin, the *Air Force One* steward, said. "He is the best passenger on the plane."[93]

In contrast, "Clinton and Hillary wanted everything low fat," said Franklin. "Low-fat Reubens made with low-fat turkey, low-fat Monterey Jack cheese, and low-fat dressing. They would say they only wanted a half a sandwich, but then they would wind up having three halves." All the while, they snacked on Heath bars and Reese's peanut butter cups, which they had *Air Force One* stock.

Bush banished chocolate bars from the plane. He brought his workout clothes wherever he went. After flying to Europe and China, he did ninety-minute runs. In the White House, he tried to block off an hour and a half beginning at 11:30 A.M. for exercise and lunch. He used free weights and an elliptical trainer, then took a quick shower. Three times a week, he jogged up to three miles. He averaged seven-minute, fifteen-second miles. The jog, on a White House track Clinton had installed, helped Bush sleep better, reduced his stress, and kept him disciplined, he would say. Because of knee pain, he had to give up running temporarily in late 2003. He weighed 194 pounds and was five feet, eleven and a half inches tall.

At his Crawford ranch, Bush established the "100 Degree Club" for Secret Service agents who could keep up with him in the West Texas heat. He presented them with commemorative T-shirts and certificates.

"Bush runs agents into the ground," a Secret Service agent said. "Only Ed Marinzel, the special agent in charge of the White House detail, and a handful of other agents are fast enough to run with him. Clinton would run and work out at 2 A.M. Then he would go for months without any exercise and gain weight."

Clinton traveled with an entourage of literally hundreds of people and liked to linger on foreign trips, taking in the sights. On a trip to Africa, Clinton spent $42.8 million. That included the cost of operating two 747s—one as a backup—and more than sixty other aircraft to haul personnel and equipment. A trip to Asia cost $63.5 million. Nor did that include the cost of Secret Service protection.

"Clinton drained the Secret Service," said a former agent. "Each event requires fifty to a hundred agents. The number of foreign trips eclipsed both George H.W. Bush and Ronald Reagan's trips. They [the Clintons] just wanted to see the world. They gave no thought to cost."[94]

Bush slimmed down the entourage, although his presidential motorcade could include up to fifty to sixty vehicles, including security cars, VIP vehicles, press cars and vans, and an ambulance and local police escorts. Bush could be in any one of the cars or vans. The president's vehicle is code-named Stagecoach.

After his first official flight on *Air Force One*, Bush discussed trade and immigration issues with Vicente Fox at his San Cristobal farm. The farm primarily grows broccoli. Bush confided to Fox's mother that, like his own father, he hates broccoli.

That same day, Bush called "routine" a series of air strikes on Iraq air defense positions.

"Saddam Hussein has got to understand we expect him to conform to the agreement that he signed after Desert Storm," Bush said.

After eight years of hearing Clinton threaten Hussein and seeing him fail to follow through, no one took Bush's words seriously.

After spending eight and a half hours in Mexico, Bush flew to Waco for a weekend visit to his ranch in Crawford, which is eighteen miles west of Waco.

"I like my own bedroom," Bush said.

During the campaign, two king-size, nonallergenic pillows traveled with him so he would not have to acclimate himself to a strange pillow in a hotel. He continued the practice after he became president.

Reporters who regularly cover the White House take turns writing the press pool report for other reporters. The one covering the trip to Mexico noted that the "lure at the end of this long day was that of a first class meal and drinks on the charter flight to Waco, Texas, where nobody wanted to go. The media's inclination was to stay in Mexico, have a look around, and get some sleep. But the president was determined to sleep at his ranch . . ."

According to the pool report, after announcing the safety instructions, the chief steward of the plane chartered for the press noted some grumbling and made the mistake of adding, "Now, the FAA wouldn't make these rules unless they knew what they were doing."

"This confidence in the infallibility of the FAA was greeted with jeers and catcalls," the pool report observed. "The crew also had not been told the media has [sic] a low opinion of rules in general and government agencies in particular. Attempts by the cabin crew to get the media to watch the safety demonstration brought forth more catcalls and derisory clapping."

The visit to Crawford was Bush's first since his inauguration. Located on a stretch of the Santa Fe railroad line that runs north along the Blackland Prairie, Crawford had one traffic light and four churches for seven hundred residents. A handful of stores lined one side of the two-block span of Main Street, which ran parallel to the railroad tracks and grain silos. The two-man police force was based in a one-room police station.

"Welcome to the Texas White House," said a sign at the Coffee Station, a restaurant beside the solitary stoplight. Soon, Colin Powell, Condoleezza Rice, and Bush himself would be ordering hamburgers there.

On his Prairie Chapel Ranch, Bush loved to clear brush, which one wag suggested was trucked in every night by the Republican National Party. On Saturday morning, February 17, Bush managed a three-mile run, breakfast, a workout on weights in his own gym, and some serious fishing time on his eleven-acre man-made lake stocked with black bass, bluegill, and perch.

That night, the locals threw a belated inaugural ball for Bush at the Crawford Community Center. A longhorn steer named Frito, surrounded by Christmas lights, was tethered to a nearby tree. Many of the men were dressed in what is called "Texas tuxedo"—formal jackets, shirts, and bow ties with blue jeans and boots. A fiddler scratched out a version of "Hail to the Chief."

Wearing a suit, Bush told guests at the shindig that beyond his own delight in returning to his ranch, it was a way to "stay in touch with real Americans." But journalists covering the president were dismayed at the thought of spending August in Crawford, where Bush would be vacationing in heat of more than a hundred degrees. They stayed in a roach-infested Motel 6, which, according to the pool report, did not supply the complimentary shampoo normally offered at fine hotels.

The pool report quoted an unnamed journalist who asked, "Why can't he just visit his parents in Kennebunkport?"

12

SPITE

I f anyone was responsible for the nasty tone of politics in Washington, it was Newt Gingrich. When he was in the minority in Congress, he called former Speakers Jim Wright, Tom Foley, and Tip O'Neill a "trio of muggers." House Democratic leaders were "sick."

Gingrich orchestrated the Republican takeover of the House on the premise that he and his supporters were paragons of virtue who would restore family values to America. Yet while married to his high-school math teacher, Jackie, Gingrich had engaged in extramarital affairs. When Jackie lay in a hospital recovering from a third cancer operation, Gingrich appeared at her bedside with a yellow legal pad to discuss the terms of a divorce.

If Gingrich was a hypocrite, he was also ruthless. After he became House speaker in 1994, quoting Mao Tse-tung, Gingrich said, "Politics is war without blood."

"It was confrontational politics," said David K. Rehr, a former aide to one of Gingrich's lieutenants who sat in on many of Gingrich's strategy sessions. "He ended comity," Rehr said. "He felt the only way to save the House was to destroy it."

During the campaign, Bush pledged to change the tone in Washington and encourage civil discourse. Two days after his inauguration, Bush invited a group of respected Democratic elders to the White House, including former Carter press secretary Jody Powell and former senator John Glenn of Ohio. In his first week, he met with ninety members of Congress in the White House. A third of them were Democrats. Bush attended an orientation of congressional Democrats, the first time any president had done so. He invited all thirty-eight members of the Congressional Black Caucus to the White House for coffee, telling them he would work to insure that voting machines function as they should. By October 2002, Bush had signed a bill to improve the way elections are held.

"Do you believe that pardons were for sale in the Clinton White House?" a reporter asked at a press conference on February 22, 2001. "And what specifically do you think should be done to look into, to investigate the circumstances of the president's brother-in-law accepting money to lobby him on pardons?"

"As far as this White House is concerned, it's time to go forward," Bush said. "I have too much to do to get a budget passed, to get reforms passed for education, to get a tax cut passed, to strengthen the military, than to be worrying about decisions that my predecessor made."

After Bush took office, the White House made a particular deal with the Democrats. If the White House appointed a few specific candidates to a board, they would support some Bush appointees whose confirmations were being held up. Bush made good on his promise, but the Democrats reneged. At a meeting with Bush, Clay Johnson, as his personnel director, brought it up and said some form of retaliation was needed.

"We need to show we're in charge," Johnson said. "They can't push us around, and they can't take us lightly."[95]

"What?" Bush said. "Go over this again."

"We have to set a tone and let them know with whom they're dealing," Johnson said. "They have to honor their deals."

"If I understand you correctly, this is all about spite, isn't it?" the president asked his friend from high school and college.

After Johnson paused for a moment to think about it, he responded, "Yes, sir. But it feels so good. Please join us in this spiteful act."

"No, I'm not going to do the spite thing," Bush said.

"I sort of meekly left the Oval Office like a lower form of humanity," Johnson said. "That was one of the most telling encounters I've had with him. He doesn't do things to get back at people. He thinks that's what fifteen-year-olds do. It's not about him advancing himself."

With that approach, Bush made steady progress in advancing his agenda. At the same time, Bush's tendency to speak his mind and his refusal to waffle on delicate issues contributed to the image of him as an arrogant cowboy. Bush would tell it like it was, and people could either accept it or not. With Bush, there would be no pretense about not drinking in the White House or about the president carrying his own luggage.

For presidents like Carter and Clinton, the White House was a stage where they would create a story line. As in the movie *Dave*, Bill and Hillary Clinton would emerge from the marine helicopter holding hands. But once they got inside the White House, they would start screaming at each other, and Bill would slink off to have phone sex with Monica Lewinsky.

Until the *Miami Herald* revealed Gary Hart's fling with Donna Rice in May 1987, the media had not exposed extramarital affairs of presidents and presidential candidates. Yet the hypocrisy and lack of judgment exhibited by a politician engaging in extramarital relations were clues to character that the electorate needed to consider.

Ironically, the tip that led the Miami paper to the Donna Rice story began with a column by political editor Tom Fiedler defending Hart, the Democratic Party's leading contender, against unsubstantiated rumors of being a womanizer. A woman who refused to identify herself called Fiedler and said she disagreed with his column. In fact, she said a friend of hers who was a part-time Miami model was flying to Washington that Friday evening to spend the weekend with Hart. The caller described the woman as being attractive and blond.

Fiedler, reporter Jim McGee, and investigations editor Jim Savage looked at airline schedules and picked the most likely nonstop flight to Washington that Friday evening, May 1. McGee took the flight and spotted several women who matched the description. One was carrying a distinctive shiny purse. When they touched down in Washington, she disappeared into the crowd.

Taking a cab to Hart's town house, McGee saw the same young

woman with the shiny purse. She was walking arm in arm with Hart out the front door. Joined by Savage and Fiedler on Saturday, McGee watched their comings and goings at the town house for the next twenty-four hours. When Hart came outside and seemed to have spotted them, they confronted him and asked about the beautiful young woman sitting inside his home.[96]

"No one was staying in my apartment," Hart told the newspaper. "I have no personal relationship with the individual you are following." Hart described the woman as "a friend of a friend of mine" who had come to Washington to visit friends of hers.

That night, after the story had been filed with Rice still unidentified, Savage, Fiedler, and McGee met with a Washington friend of Hart's who had introduced him to Rice. Savage pointed out that the effort to identify the woman would create a media feeding frenzy, and it would be in Hart's interests to name her. The story ran in the *Miami Herald* on Sunday, May 3. That morning, a spokesman for Hart told the Associated Press that the unidentified woman was Rice.

On the same Sunday, the *New York Times* ran a story quoting Hart as denying the allegations of affairs. He challenged the press to "follow me around . . . it will be boring." Hart continued to deny he had been having an affair with Rice, but CBS ran an amateur video of them together aboard the luxury yacht *Monkey Business* in Bimini. CBS noted that Rice, who was not identified, later left the yacht to compete in a "hot bod" contest at a local bar. The *National Enquirer* followed with a photo of Rice sitting on Hart's knee on the boat. Hart was forced to withdraw as a presidential contender, a victim of his own arrogance and deceit.

In fact, there was more to the story. According to a former Secret Service agent who was present, well before his encounter with Rice, Hart routinely cavorted with stunning models and actresses in Los Angeles courtesy of Warren Beatty, one of his political advisors.

"Warren Beatty gave him a key to his house on Mulholland Drive," the agent said. "It was near Jack Nicholson's house." Beatty would arrange to have twenty-year-old women—"tens" as the agent described them—meet him at Beatty's house.

"Hart would say, 'We're expecting a guest,'" the former agent said. "When it was warm, they would wear bikinis and jump in the hot tub in the back. Once in the tub, their tops would often come off. Then they would go into the house. The 'guests' stayed well into the night and often left just before sunrise. Beatty was a bachelor, but Hart was a senator running for president and was married."[97]

Sometimes, the agent said, "There were two or three girls with him at a time. We would say, 'There goes a ten. There's a nine. Did you see that? Can you believe that?' Hart did not care. He was like a kid in a candy store."

Asked for comment, Gayle Samek, his spokesperson, said, "Senator Hart tends to focus on the present rather than the past, so there's no comment."

In contrast to Hart and Clinton, Bush had a committed relationship with his wife, and their love was genuine. Bush would not make a cheesy spectacle of their love by parading in front of the media perpetually holding hands with Laura.

Bush's fixation on truth even extended to verifying with his partner his golf score (ranging from seventy-seven to ninety-five) before announcing it to the press.

"He plays the game by the rules, plays the ball where it lies, and counts every stroke," said David Sibley, a lawyer and former Texas state senator who is a golfing partner. "You can tell a lot about a person by the way he plays golf."[98]

Clinton, on the other hand, would try to inflate his scores by taking mulligans, do-over golf shots. Admitting to the practice, Clinton told an interviewer, "You'd be surprised at how many times you don't get a bit of good out of it."

Bush's golf game also reflected his decisiveness.

"He plays very fast," said Michael M. Wood, his friend from Andover and Yale who runs Hanley-Wood, a housing and construction media company. "Usually, it takes four hours to play a game, but it usually takes him three. If you ask him how he did, instead of giving you his score, he'll say, 'Three hours and ten minutes.' He doesn't agonize over shots, waiting until the wind is blowing the right way or until a particular blade of grass is standing up straight."[99]

To determine the wind velocity and direction before hitting a golf shot, serious players will pinch some grass out of the ground and throw it into the air.

"He considers tossing grass and multiple practice swings a waste of time, and he doesn't tolerate such behavior by his playing partners," Wood said. "He'll yell, 'Hit it, Woody!' "

When it came to policy initiatives, Bush's honest approach gave critics more ammunition. Like Harry Truman, Bush saw no need to sugarcoat the issues. He was interested in action, not words. The fact that many Bush initiatives were complicated made it that much harder to explain them to the public. Their complexity also made it easier for critics to pick away at one facet to the exclusion of all others.

The Kyoto Protocol was an example. On its face, the treaty sounded as desirable as apple pie. How could anyone be against measures to curb global warming? But the 1977 treaty, negotiated in Kyoto, Japan with 167 nations, would have required the United States to reduce emissions by seven percent below 1990 levels. Because of the extraordinary economic growth since then, that would have meant a cutback in emissions of thirty percent. The impact on the economy, already in recession, would have been devastating. While the United States was supposed to cut back drastically, developing countries with fast-growing economies like India, Mexico, and China were exempted.

In fact, the Kyoto treaty was nothing but a PR gambit, an effort by leaders of countries around the world to convince their citizens that they were doing something to stop global warming by imposing limits on carbon dioxide emissions and other heat-trapping gasses. In fact, only Romania had adopted it. The Senate had refused ninety-five to nothing to ratify its key points. While Clinton gave lip service to the treaty and had signed it, he didn't dare submit it to the Senate for ratification. He knew it would never pass.

Bush would have none of that. If there was anything he hated, it was charades. He forthrightly announced that he would not support the treaty and would instead devote funds to study how to reduce global warming through less drastic measures, including building more environmentally friendly vehicles. Those studies were continuing.

"The emperor Kyoto was running around for a long time, and he was naked," Andy Card said. "It took President Bush to say, 'The guy doesn't have any clothes on.' "

That unleashed a backlash that intensified when Bush rolled back a Clinton regulation to reduce the amount of arsenic allowed in drinking water below what occurs naturally in many parts of the country. The cost of the regulation would have been in the billions. Convinced that the economic impact would be severe, Bush simply wanted to maintain the status quo. But the episode conveyed the impression that because of Bush, arsenic levels in drinking water would be going up.

"There are always a handful of things you wish had been done differently," Card said. "When he took office, he realized that Kyoto would cause great damage to our economy and was not realistic. It would have hurt the United States and made it more difficult to achieve economic growth. He pushed us hard to come up with an alternative. It would not be a command and control stifling regulation on our economy. It would produce cleaner air, fewer carbon dioxide emissions, and produce better technology that could be shared around the world. More and more countries recognize, even if they don't have the courage to say it, that the expectations under Kyoto were false expectations."[100]

On the arsenic issue, Bush wanted to "look at the science," Card said. "It wasn't that the president wanted to put more arsenic in the water." Yet on both issues, "From a communications point of view, they were not handled as well as they could have been. We probably should have done a better job of explaining what the regulations were."

Bush's later proposal to ease industrial pollution rules was a more calculated decision. The rules would make it easier for thousands of older power plants, refineries, factories, chemical plants, and paper mills to make major upgrades without installing costly new antipollution controls. The old rules created "too many hurdles, and that hurts the working people," Bush said. Encouraging power companies to install new equipment would help the country's power infrastructure, he maintained. At the same time, Bush would cut power plant emissions over fifteen years by seventy percent, reducing the largest pollutant, sulphur dioxide, from eleven million tons a year to 4.5 million tons in 2010 and three million tons in 2018.

What was not noticed at the time was the legislation would also regulate emissions of mercury, which is found in the coal burned by power plants. These plants emit an estimated forty-eight tons of mercury in vapor form each year. No administration had ever proposed a cap on mercury admissions. Chiefly for that reason, the utility industry did not like the bill, and that was a major reason the legislation became stalled in Congress.

"He looks at cost and the benefit," Clay Johnson said. "We want clear air. We like forests. But yet you can't legislate your way to any extreme. He tries to find a balance."

But to many, Bush's decision to reject the Kyoto treaty and scrap the arsenic regulation looked as if he had arbitrarily decided to do away with well-considered environmental measures. It fed the growing perception that the president was a cowboy out of the Wild West. European nations, in particular, were incensed that Bush had rejected the Kyoto treaty. The French environment minister called it a "scandal." Yet none of those countries had agreed to honor the treaty.

"The impression that he's arrogant probably comes from knowing what he wants to do and doing it," said Bush's friend and former Yale roommate Terry Johnson. "He is a very unpretentious, self-deprecating person. But when he makes up his mind to do something, he considers the pros and cons and advice, and once he decides, he does it. It took fewer than two months to decide he wanted to marry Laura. So when he goes ahead and does it, and people say, 'Wait a minute! You have to think about that,' that's perceived as arrogance. But he's already listened to those arguments."[101]

"There is a confidence there," Clay Johnson said. "There is a swagger to him. But he's not overly overconfident. He's not someone who has let the office go to his head or believes the laws of physics don't apply to him."[102]

The fact that Bush and many of those around him talked of their religious faith made some fear that he was a "far-right nut," as Barbara Bush put it. While Bush did not regularly attend church, he made no secret of the fact that he started every day on his knees in prayer and sometimes prayed several more times during the day. He read the Bible every day. Like Bush and Laura, Andy Card was a Methodist, and his wife Kathleene was a Methodist minister in McLean, Virginia.

Typically, twenty-five to fifty of the nearly 1,700 employees who work in the White House complex attended weekly hour-long prayer and Bible study sessions in the Eisenhower Executive Office Building. Neither Bush nor Card attended. Federal workplace guidelines permit such activities as long as employees do not feel coerced to attend. Clinton also had prayer meetings, and Nixon, a Quaker, invited evangelists to speak to staffers at the White House.

Like every president, Bush invoked God and asked for his blessing. He often thanked his audiences for praying for him and argued that there was a role for religious faith in government.

"Our government must not fear faith," he would say. "We must welcome faith in our society."

After 9/11, Bush added a Hanukkah party with a kosher buffet and an iftar dinner celebrating the end of the Muslim holy month to the traditional Christmas celebrations at the White House.

As one of his key initiatives, Bush pushed to allow religious groups to compete for federal money to operate programs for the needy. At first blush, mixing religion with government appeared to be a violation of the principle of separating church and state.

"This is one more example of a president who seems to think he's the pastor of the country," said Barry Lynn, who heads Americans United for the Separation of Church and State, after Bush announced his faith-based initiative.

But as in the case of many of Bush's ideas, further examination revealed that it made perfect sense. If organizations were already in place to help the needy, why not give them more funds to do their jobs? Those funds were available for organizations that had no religious affiliation. The fact that an organization that was affiliated with the Catholic, Jewish, Protestant, or Muslim faiths received federal money did not mean the money would be used to fund religion. It meant the money would be channeled to help those who are hungry, addicted to drugs, or illiterate in the most efficient way possible because the overhead for attacking those problems and the volunteers to work on them already existed. Thus, taxpayers would not have to pay for new layers of bureaucracy to distribute the aid. In effect, it was a way to leverage the government's money. The faith-based initiative was another example of Bush's compassionate conservative approach—a practical way to attack social problems without massive federal spending.

To head the program, Bush chose Jim Towey, a Democrat who had been Florida's secretary of health and social services under Governor Lawton Chiles. For twelve years, he was legal counsel to Mother Teresa. In 1990, he lived as a volunteer in a home she ran in Washington, D.C., for people addicted to drugs or alcohol, many of whom had AIDS. In 1996, Towey founded Aging with Dignity, a Tallahassee organization that promotes better healthcare for people with terminal illness.

When he became director of the Office of Faith-Based and Community Initiatives, Towey replaced John J. DiIulio, Jr., who, after he left the White House, told Ron Suskind for a piece in *Esquire* that Bush's policy staff was weak on substance. He said they "consistently talked and acted as if the height of political sophistication consisted in reducing every issue to its simplest black-and-white terms for public consumption, then steering legislative initiatives or policy proposals as far right as possible."

After presidential spokesman Ari Fleischer called the DiIulio comments "baseless and groundless," DiIulio, a Democrat, agreed. He said he would never again comment publicly on "any aspect of my limited and . . . unrepresentative White House experience or any matters or persons related thereto."

Towey, who took over the job in February 2002, told me that, in most cases, government regulations already allowed religiously affiliated groups to receive federal money, but either the organizations themselves or the bureaucrats who approved federal grants did not realize it.

"There were perceptions of barriers and governmental hostility," said Towey, a friend of Governor Jeb Bush's. "A lot of my work has been a communication effort to say, 'It's okay, government grant makers. You're not violating separation of church and state if you give money to a church organization that does job training, as long as the money goes for job training.' "[103]

While organizations with political clout received money before Bush became president, those without leverage were "harassed locally by some grant official who said, 'Wait a minute. Either you take that scripture verse off the wall or we'll pull your grant,'" Towey said. "The groups with political muscle received money, but the small groups were intimidated. In many neighborhoods, they're the only groups there."

In other cases, organizations were prohibited from applying "simply because they had a religious name or identity, even though their programs may be turning lives around," Towey said. For example, even though a church controlled its board, a group that changed its name from St. John's Shelter to John's Shelter would more likely be successful in obtaining federal money.

Before Bush became president, well-known groups like the Salvation Army, Catholic Charities, and local Jewish federations received federal money. After his faith-based initiative, local organizations like Exodus Transitional Community in New York; the Jewish Renaissance Medical Center in Perth Amboy, New Jersey; Notre Dame School in Warren, Ohio; and Inner-City Muslim Action Network in Chicago received it. The Muslim group offers high school equivalency courses and computer training to low-income and minority families in the community. The Jewish medical center provides free healthcare to those who have no insurance and cannot pay. The Protestant-affiliated Exodus group helps prisoners return to society.

Traveling with Bush to visit the programs, Towey got a better understanding of how both faith and Bush's own experience with alcohol addiction play a role in his life.

"You have these perceptions that he is a heartless Republican," Towey said. "I've traveled with Mother Teresa. He's not a saint, of course, but he's a very caring guy. In his private life, he prays. He doesn't hold himself out as some great Christian. He doesn't see himself that way. For him, religion isn't a show. It's intensely personal. You see this when he is talking with addicts. He knows how his recovery was fueled by a faith experience."

The fact that devout Christians were Bush's strongest backers led to charges that the faith-based initiative was a sop to them.

But Jewish and Muslim groups were just as happy to receive the money.

"The faith-based initiative got off to a shaky start from a perception standpoint," Towey said. "There was a feeling this would be payback to the religious right. The reality is they have not been that interested. The new applicants have been mostly inner-city groups."

"Bush recognizes that there are more people saved by individuals than by government," Andy Card said. "He celebrates that and recognizes that faith-based initiatives are often fostered by a community of faith where one individual touches another." In the past, "Government would sometimes get in the way. He said the government should get out of the way. So we looked at all our regulations to make sure they are not in the way. That's a hard thing to ask a bureaucrat to do, to remove regulations."

The fact that Bush rolled out his faith-based initiative in the second week of his presidency suggested how deeply he cared about it.

"Education and faith-based initiatives are the two domestic-policy subjects that the president just riffs in speeches," Spellings said. "On those two subjects, he seldom sticks to the text of his speeches. He just gets up and emotes. He speaks from the heart. He knows the subject and has his own construct of how it all fits together."[104]

Like Bush's reading initiative, the faith-based initiative was both populist and iconoclastic: Both efforts helped the needy and minorities the most. By holding schools to account and by permitting interaction between government and religion, both initiatives challenged politically sensitive dogma.

Liberals refused to see it that way. They could not accept the fact that a conservative Republican who wore cowboy boots was a champion of the underdog. Rigidly, they saw monumental federal spending as the only way to solve problems. But Bush, whom they derided as brainless, had used his head to devise ways to help people without the need for massive spending.

At the heart of Bush's approach was his trust in people. He believed that if schools were held to account, children could be taught to read. If existing programs for the needy were allowed to compete for federal funds, they would help those who needed it the most. It was like the difference between communism and capitalism, with communism imposing government solutions and capitalism allowing people to achieve success by making their own decisions.

While the media were fascinated by Bush's prayer habits, he only talked about his religion when asked. But if he did not proselytize, his tendency to mangle his speech provided plenty of fuel for critics. Even though he knew how the word nuclear was normally pronounced, he insisted on pronouncing it NOO-kyoo-ler, a southern rendering which happened to be similar to Jimmy Carter's NOOK-ee-yuh.

"He loves to say NOO-kyoo-ler," Clay Johnson said. "I think he likes the way it sounds, or maybe he's trying to affirm his southern roots. We were going to have a meeting about nuclear energy one time. Before the meeting, I kidded him and said, "Just remember, it's NOO-klee-er. During the meeting, he said NOO-kyoo-ler. Andy Card looked at me and shrugged, meaning: 'What can you do?' "

In fact, the *Merriam-Webster Dictionary* lists the way Bush pronounced nuclear as an alternate, even including that version in an audio clip on its web site.

"Though disapproved of by many," the dictionary notes, such pronunciations "have been found in widespread use among educated speakers, including scientists, lawyers, professors, congressmen, U.S. cabinet members, and at least one U.S. president and one vice president. While most common in the U.S., these pronunciations have also been heard from British and Canadian speakers."

"He is widely misunderestimated," Card said jokingly. As for what have come to be known as Bushisms, "His mind is faster than his mouth sometimes," Card said. "He presumes you know the topic, so he rushes ahead."

"I think he starts talking without having a clear idea of what he wants to say," said Michael Alexander, M.D., associate clinical professor of neurology at Harvard Medical School. "Then he gets tangled up trying to finish the thought."[105]

Ironically, the liberals who made fun of Bush's speech patterns and called it dyslexia would be the first to pounce if Bush ridiculed the way others spoke. But Bush, possessed of a self-deprecating sense of humor, thought his gaffes were hilarious. Clay Johnson was in the Oval Office a few days before Bush was to speak at the Radio and Television Correspondents dinner.

"I'm going to give the funniest speech you've ever heard," Bush told "Big Man," as he called Johnson. "They have this tape of ridiculous phrases I used in the campaign. I can't believe that a candidate for president said those things."[106]

Bush recited some of the examples:

"Africa is a nation that . . ."

"Dick Cheney and I do not want this nation to be in a recession. We want anybody who can find work to be able to find work."

"Families is where our nation finds hope, where wings take dream."

"The woman who knew that I had dyslexia—I never interviewed her."

"I've never seen him laugh that hard," Johnson said.

At the Radio and Television Correspondents dinner, Bush said, "This is my most famous statement: 'Rarely is the question asked, is our children learning.' Let us analyze that sentence for a moment," he said. "If you're a stickler, you probably think the singular verb 'is' should have been 'are.' But if you read it closely, you'll see I'm using the intransitive plural subjunctive tense. So," Bush said to laughter, "the word 'is' is correct."

A month later, at the White House Correspondents Dinner, Bush put on a slide show about growing up in Texas. One slide was of one of his elementary school report cards. Miraculously, he had received As in writing, reading, spelling, arithmetic, music, and art.

"So my advice to you is, don't peak too early," Bush said.

During the campaign, Clay Johnson and Donald Evans talked about whether Bush really had the burning desire to be president. His body language in some of the debates seemed to indicate to them that he really did not have his heart in it. But within a week or two of becoming president, Johnson changed his mind.

"He was so into the job and on point," Johnson recalled.

"Here you had Colin Powell and Cheney and Rumsfeld who had all this previous experience in Washington. But he was clearly in charge. He was providing the leadership for these people, most of whom were more senior and more experienced."

After their second Cabinet meeting, Johnson went up to Evans.

"Remember that conversation we had about whether he really wanted the challenge?" Johnson said. "I don't have that feeling now."

"I don't either," Evans said.

"He's really being president now," Johnson said.

13

EAT, SLEEP, AND BE MERRY

In speeches, Andy Card would ask audiences how many would like to see the president for just five minutes and give him some advice. Predictably, every person would raise his or her hand.

"There are any number of ideas that the president would love to hear," Card would say, "and an infinite number of people who would love to bring those great ideas to him."

Card saw his job as making sure Bush saw everyone he should, while ensuring that the president was not overwhelmed by demands.

"The president is a man of great discipline," Card said. "His discipline extends to every aspect of his life. His faith, his love for his family, doing his homework, making decisions, his health, what he eats, exercise, and getting sleep. He knows he needs to relax, so he will find time to relax. My job is to make sure that every twenty-four-hour day includes time to eat, sleep, and be merry so he can do his job as president," Card said.[107]

Card imposed a test: "If you *need* to see the president as a White House staffer, you will see the president. If you *want* to see the president, you won't," he said. "Many people show up and say they need to see the president, and I'll scratch away at the veneer and find out it's a good old-fashioned want. The same goes for the pieces of paper that float around the building. Memos are written by the thousands. They are written for the president. Most of the people who wrote them really want him to see them. My job is to make sure he sees the ones he needs to see. There are a finite number of minutes in a day. So I have to be a conscience for the schedulers. I have to make sure he has time to go to the bathroom, to eat, to talk to Laura, call the twins, read a book, exercise, eat, and relax. And to meet with his senior staff, make a decision, talk to the press, and meet with members of Congress. Those jobs are easy. The eat, sleep, and be merry challenge takes more of my attention than the rest of the world believes."

When Bush entered the White House, the media portrayed him as a puppet. Either Dick Cheney, the competent grown-up, or Karl Rove, the powerful Svengali, was pulling the strings. Calling Cheney "a man in charge," *Time* said that according to a joke making the rounds in Republican circles, "We have to keep Dick Cheney healthy. Otherwise, it will be the first time in history that the Number One will have to take over."

Referring to an incident just after Bush became president, Jay Leno said on NBC's *The Tonight Show* that "when that crazy gunman started firing shots at the White House, the press spokesman said that Bush was working out in the gym while Vice President Dick Cheney was hard at work at his desk. See, now that the election's over, they're not even trying to hide who's really running the country anymore."

The big secret was that Bush was not only making all the decisions, he was making them decisively. In Bush's view, "Making a decision in time is probably even more important than making the decision," Card said. "We've all known leaders who made decisions too late or have allowed time to make the decisions for them. This president will make a decision in time for it to be implemented well. That requires courage. The easy decisions don't make it to the Oval Office. They can be made in the name of the president. The ones that do make it to the Oval Office are tough ones. If it's a tough decision that is fifty-fifty, you can make it in time, you can implement it well, and you can turn it pretty quickly into a fifty-one to forty-nine decision."

Rather than being uninformed, "He takes these big briefing books back to the residence at night," Card said. "There isn't a morning I can think of when he hasn't challenged me on something that needs more work. He'll go from a heated foreign-policy discussion about Israel and the Palestinian situation to Iraq and Afghanistan, Kashmir and India, Nepal, China and Taiwan, South Korea, and North Korea and Japan," Card said. "And then he deals with Medicare and Medicaid and an education bill. He is amazingly conversant on almost every issue that is presented to him."

Bush became impatient when others did not carry out assignments as quickly as he thought they should or gave vague, rambling answers to his questions.

"He is real big on follow-through and doing things quickly," Johnson said. "He's a high-energy guy. He doesn't believe in ambling along. When he feels that something's not happening as quickly as he understood it would, he'll get agitated and say, 'What's the deal on this? When are we going to see tangible results? We have to get going.' When somebody gives him a smoke-and-mirrors answer, he'll say, 'What does that really mean?' He is interested in results, in tackling big issues, and in changing and elevating the way this place works."

Bush's White House functioned like a seasoned football team, with each member keeping a low profile and contributing to the final result. Their loyalty was first to him and to each other: Aside from calls from their families, Bush insisted that they return calls from each other before returning calls of others. It was entirely different from the way the White House operated under previous administrations, with individuals or factions leaking to the press to enhance their own status and policy positions, conducting war against each other.

"He's a real team person," Clay Johnson said. "If somebody stumbles or trips or misspeaks, his inclination is to give them every benefit of the doubt. But if they are on a different team— and he'll have to be convinced it's true—then he's not above saying, 'Let's find a replacement.' But he's not a quick-trigger guy. He's very loyal to people."[108]

"He trusts the people he has worked with for a long time," said Margaret Spellings, the domestic policy advisor. "He has seen me execute judgment on his behalf for a long time. I have a track record. That means a lot to him."[109]

In one case, Bush had a problem with a speechwriter who could not seem to comprehend the points he wanted to make.

"He would say, 'Here's the policy we want to communicate,' " a staffer said. "The draft would come back, and it wouldn't make that point. He went back and forth over this." Finally, Mike Gerson, the chief speechwriter, eased the person out.

"Does he get mad and frustrated? Yes," Spellings said. "He's more apt to have an edge and say, 'Dammit.' But he won't say, 'I'm discouraged.' That's not like him. He is feistier than that. He's a very happy, high-energy, very optimistic person."

Like Ronald Reagan, Bush never failed to ask about a staffer's sick parent or write a handwritten note when a family member had passed away.

"Around Labor Day before 9/11, I moved my kids up to Washington from Texas," Spellings said. "After a Cabinet meeting dealing with the tragedy on September 14, he asked me how school was and how my kids were doing."

"The way presidents treat people reflects the way their administration treats people," former Secret Service agent Charles Taylor said. "As an agent, you see whether they are genuinely concerned about people and try to learn from them."[110]

Like any CEO, a president is only as good as the advice he gets. Presidents such as Johnson and Nixon ignored or ostracized those who presented them with opposing opinions. In his book *A Look Over My Shoulder*, Richard Helms, Lyndon Johnson's director of Central Intelligence, recounted Johnson's instruction to him in the summer of 1967 that he obtain proof that the direction and funding of the antiwar movement in the United States came from abroad.

"I explained that such an investigation might risk involving the agency in a violation of the CIA charter limiting our activity to operations abroad and forbidding anything resembling domestic police or security activity," Helms wrote. "LBJ listened for some fifteen seconds before saying, 'I'm quite aware of that. What I want is for you to pursue this matter and to do what is necessary to track down the foreign communists who are behind this intolerable interference in our domestic affairs.' "

Helms and his predecessor John McCone repeatedly warned Johnson that the war was not winnable, largely because the entire rationale for the war was based on a misconception: that the struggle between the North Vietnamese and the South Vietnamese was a critical battle in the cold war rather than a civil war that had nothing to do with U.S. interests. In a June 11, 1964, memo to McGeorge Bundy, Johnson's national-security advisor, McCone debunked the "Domino Theory," Johnson's rationale for prosecuting the war.

"We do not believe that the loss of South Vietnam and Laos would be followed by the rapid, successive communization of the other states of the Far East," McCone wrote. In April 1965, McCone hand-carried a memo to Johnson. "I think we are . . . starting on a track which involves ground force operations [that will mean] an ever-increasing commitment of U.S. personnel without materially improving the chances of victory," McCone wrote. "In effect, we will find ourselves mired in combat in the jungle in a military effort that we cannot win, and from which we will have difficulty extracting ourselves."

When Leonard Marks, Johnson's lawyer for twenty-five years who headed the United States Information Agency, suggested as Johnson was getting dressed that he declare victory in Vietnam and get out, Johnson thundered, "Get out! Get out!"

Marks gathered his papers and left. After that, he heard nothing from the White House. Even invitations to NSC meetings stopped coming. Finally, Marks told his wife he had decided to resign. His wife suggested that he be patient. A few days later, Lady Bird Johnson called with an invitation to attend a surprise birthday party for the president. Eventually, Marks asked Johnson why he had been so tough on him.

"He shook his head and said, 'You know, I secretly agreed with you and [Senator George] Aiken, but I knew I could not go that route without being torn apart by the Kennedys.'"

As he sent more troops into battle to get killed, Johnson would brood over whether he had made the right decision. As if that validated the wisdom of his decision, Johnson made sure the press portrayed his hand-wringing, complete with photos showing him looking solemnly out of an Oval Office window.

"One of the real problems of the presidency is he gets no resistance to his personality," George Reedy said. "That is very unhealthy. Most of us go through life meeting all sorts of resistance: the hotel clerk who gives us a fishy look when we try to cash a check; the old-maid aunt who flushes bright red when you happen to say damn or when you light a cigar; the people who stand up and say, 'Oh, no you don't.' There's a healthiness to that. But suppose you're a person whom everybody says 'yes' to. You want a Coke, and all of a sudden there it is in your hand. You want a cheeseburger, and all of a sudden, it's there in front of you. You want to go to Texas at 4 P.M., and you just have to say it out loud and by 4:30 P.M., there's a helicopter on the lawn ready to take you to *Air Force One* to take you to Texas. Think of what that would do to you every day for four years."

As Gerald Ford's chief of staff, Donald Rumsfeld warned of this corrosive influence. To guard against it, he listed proscriptions for White House aides to follow. Rumsfeld's first rule was: "Don't accept the post or keep it unless you have an understanding with the president that you're free to tell him what you think with the 'bark off' and unless you have the courage and ability to carry that out." His last rule was: "Assume that everything you say or do will be on the front page of the *Washington Post* tomorrow. It may."

While Clinton solicited opinions, he had trouble deciding what to do with them.

"The Clinton people couldn't seem to decide what to do," said James Simon, who had extensive dealings with both administrations as assistant director of Central Intelligence for administration. "They had fifth or sixth thoughts about almost everything." In contrast, "The Bush people listen. If you said something in the Clinton White House, you would have a breach if you disagreed with their policy position. Bush made it clear it was our job to tell him, and it was his job to decide," Simon said.

Once Bush decided, he never looked back. At that point, he expected his White House staff to support him, but he allowed his Cabinet officers wider latitude.

"People say that Rumsfeld and Powell are at war with each other," Clay Johnson said. "No kidding. They're supposed to be. The State Department's answer to most anything is diplomacy. The Defense Department's answer to almost anything is weapons and warfare. The question is what is the right mix of those for each situation. You want those differences of opinion to exist in any organization.

"In manufacturing, you have operations people who want to make stuff really fast," Johnson said. "The quality control people want you to make stuff really slowly so it is perfect. If you go to either one of these extremes, your company goes out of business. So the question is where on the spectrum are you, and you have this ongoing dialogue. The glue that holds it together, according to the management consultants, is mutual respect. If you respect one another, you'll find the right balance. So do Powell and Rumsfeld respect each other? I believe they do. Are their disagreements excessive? Are they dysfunctional? I've never seen that."

The differences played out in the press, with Powell announcing early on, for example, that the United States would continue Clinton's efforts to work with North Korea, while Bush was saying otherwise. Press reports constantly attributed to Powell more conciliatory views than the White House position. It was a price Bush was willing to pay to keep Powell on his team.

By July 2001, Bush had succeeded in reducing income taxes by $1.35 trillion over ten years, and he raised military pay by $1 billion a year. While his education initiative had been passed by the House and Senate, it was stalled in conference because Democrats wanted a bigger increase in education spending. While Bush's faith-based initiatives also ran into trouble, he imposed many of them by executive order. His public speaking was gradually improving, with fewer verbal gaffes.

"People said he seemed to grow in his job," Clay Johnson said. "But the presidency is not a lateral move for anybody. For anyone, it's a huge step up. The president either gets better or gets decimated by the job. So he has to get better because he's never done something like that before."

But while Bush's job approval rating after 180 days in office stood at fifty-seven percent—well ahead of Clinton's forty-five percent at the same point—most people had only a vague idea of what Bush stood for.

That would soon change.

14

SARASOTA

Sandy Kress, Bush's unpaid education advisor, was puzzled. Bush was always on time. But on the morning of Tuesday, September 11, he seemed to want to linger, talking about politics and mutual friends in Texas.

They were in Bush's penthouse hotel suite at the Colony Beach and Tennis Resort on Longboat Key, an eleven-mile-long barrier island between the Gulf of Mexico and Sarasota Bay off the coast of Florida. It was a gorgeous day, the sky crystal clear. After waking up at 6:30 A.M., Bush had gone for a seventeen-minute run on the golf course with his Secret Service contingent. He returned to his suite and had orange juice and toast. He showered and dressed in a dark blue suit, a pale blue shirt, and an iridescent orange tie.

Just after 8:00 A.M., Bush's CIA briefer Mike* gave him the President's Daily Brief with the agency's hottest intelligence. They discussed developments in the Middle East, particularly with the Palestinians. Bush placed a call to Condoleezza Rice and asked her to follow up on a few points.

At 8:15 A.M., Kress began to brief Bush on their planned nine o'clock visit to the Emma E. Booker Elementary School in nearby Sarasota. With them were Andy Card, Secretary of Education Rod Paige, and Karl Rove. In an effort to spotlight the need for final passage of the languishing No Child Left Behind Act, the White House had scheduled two such reading events, one in Sarasota and

---

* Because he is now undercover, Mike's last name is not used here.

one in Jacksonville the day before. It was a positive way to demonstrate Bush's interest in improving kids' reading ability.

Kress went over some key points for a talk the president would be giving to the press after he read to second-grade students at the elementary school.

"We talked about accountability and the need to get it right," Kress said. "Increasing amounts of money had been spent, but the reading scores had not improved."

To get to the elementary school in Sarasota by 8:55 A.M., the president was supposed to leave by 8:30 A.M.*

"I've never known him to be late," Kress said. "But I remember we finished the briefing on that fateful day, and we continued to talk for another ten minutes about people and politics in Texas. The time to leave came and passed."[111]

Looking back, Kress would think those were the last moments Bush had without the burden of protecting the country from another 9/11 attack.

Kress was a Jew whose paternal grandfather's family had been largely wiped out by the Holocaust. After he visited the Holocaust Museum in Washington, Kress shared with Bush the pain he had felt, and the president seemed to understand. Sometimes with Laura, Bush would ask Kress about Judaism, and they had discussed the Jewish concept of *mitzvot*. The Hebrew term for commandment, the word is commonly used to refer to good deeds. Kress understood the word to have a broader meaning—directions to live well and do right.

"He had always been interested in my views on Judaism," Kress said. "He was just curious about it."

In his book *The Right Man*, former White House speechwriter David Frum, who came up with Bush's "axis of evil" declaration, weighed in on the president's faults as he perceived them: "He is impatient and quick to anger; sometimes glib, even dogmatic; often uncurious and as a result ill-informed; more conventional in his thinking than a leader probably should be."[112]

The analysis provoked tittering in the White House. Frum had

---

* Many 9/11 timelines use scheduled times rather than actual times. Those used here come from participants.

gotten it right that Bush was impatient when things did not move as fast as he wanted. But Frum had gotten it wrong on every other count. The reason Bush came under so much criticism was that his thinking was *unconventional*. His preemptive strike on Iraq was a prime example. Bush was a remarkably sanguine man who expressed frustration but rarely anger. When he did become angry, it was usually over substantive matters, such as administration leaks or kids' poor reading scores. While he was perceived as dogmatic, Bush not only listened to other views but aggressively solicited them. Rather than being uncurious and ill-informed, he constantly asked others about everything from religion to law. Thus Bush's discussions with Kress about Judaism. Bush's interest in people and issues was one reason everyone who met him found him so engaging.

The fact that Frum, like many in the media, had so many misimpressions of Bush was not surprising. As a low-level speechwriter, Frum had actually met with the president in the Oval Office only a few times, according to Karen Hughes and chief speechwriter Mike Gerson. Frum hardly knew Bush.[113]

"Who the hell is David Frum to even say this?" Spellings said. "The only reason Bush recognized him was he saw his picture blasted on TV ten thousand times. The president didn't know who David Frum was."[114]

On September 11, as the presidential motorcade finally made its way to the school where Bush was to read to the children, Ari Fleischer received a call. It was just before 9:00 A.M.

"Do you know anything about a plane hitting the World Trade Center?" Fleischer asked the CIA briefer after getting off the phone. He didn't.

Thinking of his own experience flying a fighter jet, Bush guessed that the pilot might have had a heart attack.

They arrived at the school at 9:02 A.M. A few minutes after Bush began to read to the children, Andy Card whispered to him that a second plane had hit the South Tower.

"America is under attack," Card said.

After thinking about what his response would be, Bush cut short his presentation, apologizing to the principal, Gwendolyn Tosé-Rigell. From a secure phone in an adjoining room, he called

Dick Cheney and FBI Director Robert S. Mueller III. Bush watched videos of the attacks on a television that had been wheeled in on a cart. Flame and smoke engulfed both towers, and people were jumping from windows.

"We're at war," Bush announced to his aides—Card, Fleischer, Rove, and White House Communications Director Dan Bartlett.

At 9:22 A.M., Bush appeared in the school's media center to make a brief statement on TV.

"Today, we've had a national tragedy," Bush said. "Two airplanes have crashed into the World Trade Center in an apparent terrorist attack on our country." Borrowing a phrase his father had used more than a decade earlier about Saddam Hussein's invasion of Kuwait, the president said, "Terrorism against our nation will not stand."

The limos carrying Bush and his entourage raced to the airport at speeds up to eighty miles an hour. At the end of the ride, Bush learned that a third jetliner had slammed into the Pentagon. Over a secure phone, he consulted with Cheney, who was in an emergency bunker beneath the White House grounds. The vice president urged him to authorize military planes to shoot down any commercial airliners that might be controlled by the hijackers. Bush called Rumsfeld, who had elected to stay in the burning Pentagon, and conveyed the order.

"We're going to find out who did this, and we're going to kick their ass," Bush told Cheney.

As a rule, presidential candidates choose running mates to balance the ticket rather than because they are competent. They feel threatened by accomplished people and look for vice presidential candidates who are nonentities and can be counted on to remain in the shadows. But Bush had had no second thoughts about asking Cheney, a man of far greater experience, to run with him.

Like Bush, Cheney felt no affinity for the academic world. Born on January 30, 1941, in Lincoln, Nebraska, he grew up in Casper, Wyoming. He attended Yale for two years but had to drop out because his grades were poor. Cheney got a union job laying power lines in Rock Springs, Wyoming. He kept in touch with Lynne Ann Vincent, his high-school sweetheart, who was going to college in Colorado. She "was firm that she did not want to spend the rest of her life married to a lineman," according to Tom Stroock, an oilman who helped Cheney get into Yale.

In high school, Lynne was a straight-A student who was elected Mustang Queen, the equivalent of most popular girl, and became a state baton-twirling champion. She persuaded Cheney to return to college. He started at Casper College, then transferred to the University of Wyoming at Laramie, where he majored in political science. He finally earned a B.A. degree there. They married in 1964.

Cheney went to Washington in 1968 as a congressional fellow, and Rumsfeld hired him as a White House aide under Richard Nixon. He returned to the White House to be deputy assistant to Gerald Ford and then his chief of staff.

In November 1978, Cheney was elected to the House as a Republican from Wyoming. He was reelected five times and served on the House Intelligence Committee, becoming the House Minority Whip. In 1989, Cheney became George H. W. Bush's secretary of defense. While in that position, he recommended that the president select Colin Powell to be chairman of the Joint Chiefs of Staff. Cheney directed the 1991 U.S. invasion of Iraq. In 1995, he became chairman and CEO of Haliburton Co., an energy equipment and construction firm based in Dallas, where he earned $2 million a year.

Bush and Cheney didn't know each other well before the election, but Bush's father suggested that his son ask Cheney to run the search for his running mate. During the summer of 2000, the two were sitting on the back porch of Bush's ranch in Crawford discussing candidates to be vice president. Bush turned to Cheney and asked if he would run with him. Later, Cheney told friends that the Texas heat was so stifling that he consented in hopes of getting off the porch and back into the air-conditioned house.

Bush said he chose Cheney as the person who could do the most to help him govern, not to help him win the election. With experience on the Hill, in the White House, in the Defense Department, and in private industry, Cheney would be invaluable to the president. But as Cheney later pointed out, "Those three electoral votes in Wyoming turned out to be pretty important."

Like Bush, Cheney was aggressive and willing to take risks.

While Winston Churchill was Bush's most admired leader, Cheney described Churchill as the first author to have had a profound impact on him. Churchill's six-volume history of World War II impressed upon Cheney the point that leadership in world affairs is about recognizing dangers and confronting them rather than wishing them away.

While the elite in England favored appeasing Hitler, Churchill early on recognized the Nazi threat. In the November 1935 issue of *Strand*, Churchill warned of the German menace, noting that German soil was "pock marked" with concentration camps. Here, masses of Germans, from "world famous scientists" to "wretched little Jewish children," were being persecuted. Churchill adopted the position that the truth would always be the opposite of what Hitler said. He cited Hitler's statement in *Mein Kampf*: "The great masses of the people . . . will more easily fall victim to a great lie than a small one."

Upon becoming prime minister in May 1940, Churchill told the House of Commons the objective was quite simple: "Victory: Victory at all costs. Victory in spite of all terror. Victory however long and hard the road may be: for without victory there is no survival."

"The reason that the twentieth century ended with the forces of communism and fascism defeated and with capitalism and democracy increasing as the political and economic models people aspire to," Cheney would say, "is due in no small part to U.S. leadership backed by military force."

In every previous administration, the vice president collected his salary and did little except wait to see if the president would die in office. Cheney, who made $181,400 as vice president, functioned like any other staffer. While most people had the impression that Bush relied on Cheney's advice only in the security area, Bush had him sit in on most policy meetings, on subjects from education and the economy to stem cell research. In making personnel selections, Clay Johnson consulted him as well.

"The vice president is not looking to be president," Andy Card told an interviewer. "Do you know how unusual that is? He is here to be an adviser and counselor to the president."

Even in that role, Cheney was self-effacing. Early in the administration, Clay Johnson was driving to work in his Volvo and

heard sirens. Cheney's motorcade, preceded by Metropolitan Police on motorcycles blocking traffic, was arriving from the vice
president's residence. A white house built in 1893 for the superintendent of the U.S. Naval Observatory, it overlooks Massachusetts Avenue at Thirty-Fourth Street. Police blocked Johnson's
way to the coveted parking area for top White House employees
at the southwest gate.

"The world stopped turning so he could get to work," Johnson
said. "A couple of hours later, I was in the basement of the West
Wing getting a cup of coffee at the takeout counter. The fourth
person waiting in line was the vice president."[115]

While Bush and Cheney were not social friends, they had a
comfortable, joking relationship. Bush called the slightly stooped
Cheney "Big Time" or "Vice." When Bush felt sick one day, he
called Dr. Richard Tubb, the White House physician. Tubb, an Air
Force doctor, said the president had an intestinal flu. As a cure,
the good doctor gave him a remote-controlled, battery-operated
fart machine. The next time the vice president walked into the
Oval Office, Bush turned on the machine.

The fact that Cheney recommended shooting down any commercial planes that might have been hijacked validated Bush's
decision to place him on the ticket. Only someone with his experience in the Defense Department could have conceived on the spot
of such a drastic but necessary measure.

At 9:57 A.M. on September 11, *Air Force One* took off from
Sarasota's Bradenton International Airport and climbed fast to
45,000 feet, with F-16s and AWAC radar planes as escorts. There
were reports of attacks on the State Department and fires in the
Eisenhower Executive Office Building.

"We didn't know if we were going to be attacked," Andy
Card said. "We didn't know if the White House was going to be
attacked."

At 10:00 A.M., the South Tower of the World Trade Center collapsed. The Secret Service ordered everyone to leave the White
House, telling women to take off their high heels and run. The
second tower collapsed at 10:29 A.M. Bush watched TV images
picked up from local stations. Clouds of smoke and ash obscured
the tallest buildings.

Card assured Bush that Laura, who had been on the Hill, was safe and had been taken to a secure location, the basement of Secret Service headquarters. The Secret Service would soon relocate Barbara Bush, a freshman at Yale, and Jenna, a freshman at the University of Texas, as well. Even Barney the dog was fine, the Secret Service told Card, who informed Bush.

Air Force One flew to Barksdale Air Force Base in northwest Louisiana, where camouflaged soldiers brandishing M-16s surrounded the plane. As extra food and water were brought on board, Bush consulted Cheney by phone and made another televised statement. The president looked dejected and deflated.

After they took off again, Bush, his jacket off, called Mike, the CIA briefer, into his cabin near the front of the plane. The president asked Mike who he thought had done it.

"I would bet everything on bin Laden," Mike said.

From its first briefing of Bush back in Crawford in December after he became president-elect, the CIA had been warning about Osama bin Laden and al Qaeda. In April and May, Mike began conveying reports of chatter indicating that terrorists could be planning a major attack. During the summer, Bush asked several times whether the CIA had any information indicating an attack might occur within the United States. The answer was that while bin Laden wished to launch a direct attack and had made such plans in the past, including a thwarted plot to bomb Los Angeles International Airport, no intercepted communications suggested it was about to happen. On August 6, the CIA gave Bush a background paper on bin Laden's interest in attacking the United States. Full of vague, uncorroborated information, it showed just how little the FBI and CIA knew about al Qaeda's plans and its presence in the United States.

As it turned out, the CIA had failed to put on a watch list Nawaf al-Hazmi, and Khalid al-Midhar, two of the terrorists. While the agency had agents in al Qaeda at low levels, it had not succeeded in penetrating bin Laden's inner sanctum. Back in 1998, the National Security Agency had succeeded in intercepting bin Laden's satellite phone calls. But on August 17, 1998, the *Washington Post* ran a story citing a claim by Vincent Cannistraro, a former CIA counterterrorism official, that bin Laden's calls were being intercepted. The story ran ten days after al Qaeda bombed American embassies in Kenya and Tanzania. Within a day or two of the article, bin Laden stopped using the phone. NSA Director Michael V. Hayden described the compromise of the intercepts as a "setback of inestimable consequences." The CIA believed the article was responsible.

George S. Tenet, the director of Central Intelligence, had warned as early as 1997 and 1998 that al Qaeda was the greatest threat to the United States. No one listened. Clinton had no use for intelligence. While he read the President's Daily Brief, Clinton stopped the CIA's morning briefings six months after he became president.

After the attack on American embassies in Africa, Clinton ordered a Cruise missile attack on an al Qaeda paramilitary training camp in Khost, Afghanistan and on the El Shifa pharmaceutical plant in Khartoum, Sudan's capital. The attack in Afghanistan killed twenty-one al Qaeda trainees from Pakistan but missed bin Laden.

"Today, we have struck back," Clinton said after the missile attacks.

If the statement was laughable, it diverted public attention from Clinton's televised admission three days earlier that he had misled the American people about his relationship with White House intern Monica Lewinsky. Even if bin Laden had been killed, such an attack could never inflict real damage on al Qaeda.

Bush thought the Clinton's administration's response to bin Laden only confirmed that the United States would do little to go after him. In effect, tossing Cruise missiles into tents was like waving a red handkerchief in front of a bull, goading him to attack again. Condoleezza Rice called it a "feckless" policy. It was the same short-sighted approach taken by Senator John F. Kerry, who voted to support the invasion of Iraq but then voted against reconstruction funds intended to keep it secure.

John M. Deutch, Clinton's appointee as director of Central Intelligence, had imposed a rule that CIA officers must obtain high-level clearance before recruiting an agent with so-called human rights violations. Yet agents who had murdered or tortured people were the ones who would know what the bad guys were up to. Deutch's rule sent a message to CIA officers throughout the agency that it was better to sit in their offices and collect paychecks than to take risks. It was as if the FBI had said it was no longer interested in obtaining help from people like Sammy Gravano, whose testimony was critical in convicting Mafia boss John Gotti, because Gravano had murdered nineteen people.

Deutch, a former MIT chemistry professor who was appointed by Clinton to be deputy secretary of Defense, had further shattered morale at the agency by saying publicly that CIA officers were not as competent as military people. He would tell guests at Washington dinner parties that the military was far superior to the CIA. At a meeting with the *New York Times* editorial board, Deutch bluntly made the same point. A watered-down version of his comments made its way into a piece about him in the *New York Times Magazine*. According to the December 10, 1995, article, he said, "Compared to uniformed officers, they [CIA officers] certainly are not as competent, or as understanding of what their relative role is and what their responsibilities are."

Deutch also made no secret of the fact that he had never wanted the CIA job anyway. In a characteristic parting shot after he resigned, Deutch told the *Washington Post*, "Everybody says it's a job I've been pushed out of, but I would recall it's a job I was pushed into."*

"The human-rights-violation rule had a chilling effect on recruitment [of spies]," said William Lofgren, who was chief of the CIA's Eurasian Division, which included Russia. "If faced with two possible recruitments, are you going to go after the one with a human-rights violation or the other one with no human-rights violation?" The result was that "people retired in place or left," Lofgren said. "Our spirit was broken. At the CIA, you have to be able to inspire people to take outrageous risks. Deutch didn't care about us at all."

To succeed Deutch, Clinton appointed Tenet, a former staff director of the Senate Select Committee on Intelligence who had been the CIA's deputy director and then acting director. Bush liked him immediately and asked him to stay on as director. Both had the same approach to life: Both were very focused, both prized action over words, both were highly patriotic. Accepting the Ellis

* See the author's *The CIA at War: Inside the Secret Campaign Against Terror.*

Island Medal of Honor on November 6, 1997, Tenet described how his Greek mother had fled southern Albania on a British submarine to escape Communism, never to see her family again.

Tenet's Greek immigrant father "taught me to value hard work, to honor this great country, and to take nothing for granted," Tenet said. "Nowhere in the world could the son of an immigrant stand before you as the director of Central Intelligence. This is simply the greatest country on the face of the Earth."

Like Tenet, Bush was an emotional man, tearing up when speaking of the sacrifices of American troops fighting to defend freedom. Bush might have been a product of Andover, Yale, and Harvard, but, like Harry Truman, who never graduated from college, Bush thought of himself as a simple man from Crawford, Texas. Similarly, Tenet considered himself a man with blue-collar roots. He once worked as a busboy in his father's diner and was not impressed by fancy academic credentials. In 1999, when speaking at his high-school alma mater, Benjamin N. Cardozo in Queens, Tenet told the students: "Many of you will go on to college, and you will run into people who went to fancy prep schools and who appear to have a higher quality education than you do. They don't."

Like Bush, Tenet could be blunt. Neither man was given to pretense or "hand-wringing," the phrase Bush applied contemptuously to those who endlessly worried about taking decisive action. With Tenet, there was no meandering academic analysis, just straight talk.

"He wasn't puffed up or pompous," Cheney said of Tenet. "The president clearly likes that."

Bush and Tenet had one more trait in common: They were both baseball fans. When Tenet was in New York seeing his mother in Queens or attending to CIA business, he took in a Yankees game whenever he could.

Although Tenet occasionally slept over at Camp David when attending meetings there, he and Bush were not personal friends. "He can like you, but that's not what he judges you on," Tenet told me. "Instead, it's, 'Are you doing your job? Are you delivering what you're supposed to be delivering?'" With Bush, "What

The West Wing, in the foreground, is the most coveted office space in the world. Correspondents broadcast on the flagstone strip along the driveway with the White House in the background.

After his election, President George W. Bush spent hours talking with Andrew H. "Andy" Card, Jr., his chief of staff, about the kind of White House he wanted.

Karl Rove, President Bush's senior advisor, described the president as using "conservative means to achieve liberal ends."

Margaret Spellings, President Bush's domestic policy advisor, led the battle to restore phonics to reading instruction under the No Child Left Behind Act so that schools would stop turning out millions of illiterate kids. At right are Secretary of Education Rod Paige and Tommy Thompson, secretary of Health and Human Services.

Clay Johnson III, left, President Bush's friend from Andover and Yale, was his chief of staff in Texas and became chief of presidential personnel in the White House. In that role, he helped Bush select the major players in the administration. At right is Andy Card, chief of staff.

Dan Bartlett, President Bush's communications director, said that Bush is "like a CEO—somebody who sets goals and builds a team. He views communication the same way."

National Security Advisor Condoleezza Rice and Stephen J. Hadley, her deputy, found President Bush would come up with innovative foreign policy approaches that had not occurred to them.

President Bush was proud of the fact that Alberto R. Gonzales, a Harvard Law School graduate who was his White House counsel, grew up in a two-bedroom house with seven other siblings and no hot running water.

At the Emma E. Booker Elementary School in Sarasota, Florida, on September 11, 2001, President Bush gathered information about the terrorist attacks. Dan Bartlett, director of communications, pointed to news footage of the World Trade Center towers burning. At right is senior advisor Karl Rove.

When President Bush addressed the nation from the Oval Office on the evening of September 11, 2001, he said, "We will make no distinction between those who planned these acts and those who harbor them."

After speaking at the service for America's National Day of Prayer and Remembrance at the National Cathedral, President Bush grasped the hand of his father, former President George H.W. Bush.

Three days after the worst terrorist attack on American soil, President Bush, standing upon the ashes, pledged that "the people who knocked these buildings down will hear all of us soon."

President Bush had Vice President Dick Cheney, shown after a meeting in the Oval Office on January 24, 2002, sit in on most policy meetings, on subjects from education to the economy.

The Secret Service code name for the White House is Crown.

President Bush met on the evening of March 19, 2003, with his national security and communications advisors after authorizing military operations against Iraq. From left are Stephen J. Hadley, deputy national security advisor; Karen Hughes, then special advisor to the president; Richard B. Myers, chairman of the Joint Chiefs of Staff; Dan Bartlett, communications director; Vice President Dick Cheney, Secretary of Defense Donald Rumsfeld (with his back to the camera); National Security Advisor Condoleezza Rice (partially hidden); and Secretary of State Colin Powell.

Following the swearing-in ceremony for Colin Powell as secretary of State, President Bush and Vice President Dick Cheney checked their watches in the Oval Office.

National security advisor Condoleezza Rice sees President Bush constantly throughout the day and often spends weekends with him and Laura at Camp David or at the Crawford ranch.

President Bush walked on stage before addressing military personnel and their families at Fort Stewart, Georgia, on September 12, 2003.

President Bush paid a surprise visit to troops having Thanksgiving dinner at Baghdad International Airport on November 27, 2003.

"We did not charge hundreds of miles into the heart of Iraq and pay a bitter cost of casualties, and liberate twenty-five million people, only to retreat before a band of thugs and assassins," President Bush said at Whitehall Palace in London on November 19, 2003.

Domestic Policy Advisor Margaret Spellings, seated, and Deputy Chief of Staff Harriet Miers, center, were two of President Bush's most powerful aides but almost never appeared in the media.

President Bush looked over one of countless drafts of his State of the Union address with then Senior Counselor Karen Hughes and chief speechwriter Mike Gerson in the Oval Office on January 24, 2002.

While they often had divergent views, President Bush valued the advice of Secretary of State Colin Powell and Defense Secretary Donald Rumsfeld, shown on the floor of the House prior to Bush's January 28, 2003 State of the Union address.
(AP/Wide World)

When President Bush said Osama bin Laden was wanted dead or alive, Laura Bush, shown with her husband at a state dinner for Kenya's President Mwai Kibaki on October 6, 2003, said, "Whoa Bushie!" (AP/Wide World)

A former teacher and librarian, Laura Bush helped push her husband's reading initiative and was an avid reader of novels. Her favorite was Fyodor Dostoevski's *The Brothers Karamazov*.

On long trips, President Bush takes along a treadmill on *Air Force One*, shown here arriving in Moscow on May 23, 2002 with him and Laura Bush on board.

President Bush, shown working at his desk on *Air Force One*, had the simplest tastes of any modern president. For lunch, he loved peanut butter— smooth, not chunky—with rasp-berry jam on white bread.

In contrast to the caricatures, President Bush aggressively solicited dif-fering views, then made the final decisions. With him on *Air Force One* on June 4, 2003, are, from left, Elliot Abrams, special assistant to the president on the National Security Council staff; Secretary of State Colin Powell; Dr. Condoleezza Rice, national security advisor; and Assistant Secretary of State William Burns.

President Bush's Crawford ranch was at the heart of his centered approach to life.

The Prairie Chapel Ranch provided President Bush with a creek, canyon, waterfalls, and meadows, along with plenty of brush to clear.

Even though Prime Minister Junichiro Koizumi of Japan does not speak English, he and President Bush hit it off, and Bush invited him to his Crawford ranch.

President Bush walked into the Eisenhower Executive Office Building on June 26, 2003, with Dina Habib Powell, chief of presidential personnel. An Arabic speaker, she came to the U.S. from Egypt with her family at the age of four.

Unlike Bill and Hillary Clinton, President Bush and Laura—shown here at the north entrance of the White House—treated military aides, Secret Service agents, and maids and butlers with respect.

you see is what you get," Tenet said. "He's not prepackaged. He tells you what he thinks. He's direct, and he's blunt."

When Mike first briefed the newly inaugurated President Bush the day before the president was to go to Mexico, a White House steward entered the Oval Office with coffee. Bush motioned to his guest to stop talking while the steward was in the room. Mike was impressed. Bush cared about security.

At the end of the briefing, Bush brought up the trip to see Vicente Fox.

"Are you coming with me?" the president asked.

From that point on, Mike or alternate CIA briefers traveled with Bush on every trip. They saw him six and often seven days a week, whether at Bush's ranch in Crawford, his parents' home in Kennebunkport, at Camp David, or in the White House. Since the founding of the agency in 1947, no other president had wanted to be briefed by the CIA when he was out of town.

As Mike briefed Bush after taking off from Sarasota, he went over some of bin Laden's previous attacks—the ones on two American embassies in East Africa and the one on the USS *Cole*. Bush asked how long it would take to know if bin Laden was responsible. Based on previous attacks, Mike said, it would probably be a matter of days.

Air Force One landed at Offutt Air Force Base in Nebraska, where Bush held a teleconference with members of the National Security Council (NSC) and with Cheney, Rumsfeld, Mueller, and Tenet. Again accompanied by fighter jets, *Air Force One* roared back into the sky at 4:36 P.M. for a return to Washington. Bush had overruled the Secret Service, which wanted him to delay his return.

"We need to get back to Washington," Bush told the Secret Service. "We don't need some tinhorn terrorist to scare us off. The American people want to know where their president is."

That evening at 8:30, Bush spoke to the nation. In a speech Bush gave in 1999 at The Citadel military academy, he had said that those who sponsored terrorism or attacks on the United States could expect a "devastating" response. Mike Gerson, Bush's chief speechwriter, returned to that text and crafted a sentence to say that the United States will "make no distinction between those who planned these acts and those who permitted or tolerated or encouraged them."

Saying that was "way too vague," Bush said he wanted instead to use the word "harbor." The final sentence read: "We will make no distinction between those who planned these acts and those who harbor them."

By using the broader term "harbor," Bush had not only expanded the definition of the enemy, he shifted the burden of proof the United States would use in going after those who support terrorism. Instead of having to show that another country was aware of and permitted terrorists to operate within its borders, the United States would now use military force or apply diplomatic pressure on countries simply because terrorists lived there.

The declaration became known as the Bush Doctrine. It was a sea change in foreign policy, one that would make all the difference in the war on terror.

15

"I HEAR YOU!"

On the morning of Friday, September 14, Andy Card arrived at his office at 5:45 A.M. As he usually did, he skimmed the newspapers, read over intelligence reports, and reviewed Bush's schedule. From the Secret Service locator box, he could see that POTUS was on the south grounds of the White House. At 6:45 A.M., Bush walked into the Oval Office.

Card started to go over the day's schedule, but Bush stopped him. The previous evening, the president had developed plans for reshaping the government's response to terrorism. Instead of passively waiting for the next attack, the United States would become the aggressor, taking on terrorists wherever they were. Instead of focusing on catching and prosecuting terrorists after they had done their damage, the government would switch its priorities to preventing attacks. Instead of relying on laws that created impediments to tracking down terrorists, the government would enact new laws so the FBI and other government agencies would not be handcuffed.

Bush told Card he wanted to rearrange the day's schedule so he could implement those plans. After the usual CIA briefing at 8 A.M., Mueller and Attorney General John Ashcroft began to brief Bush.

"They talked about how the terrorists got plane tickets, got on planes, moved from one airport to another, and then attacked our citizens," Card recalled. "And the president, while he was very interested in that report, said, 'Mr. Director, that's building a case for prosecution. I want to know what you have to say about the

terrorist threats that haven't materialized yet and how we can prevent them.'"

While the FBI in the previous six years had stopped forty terrorist plots before they happened, the bureau tended to look no
further than the latest case when going after terrorism. In the previous bombing of the World Trade Center in 1993, the FBI had
been content to catch those responsible without determining if it
was part of a larger plot. Years later, the FBI discovered that bin
Laden had connections through Al Kifah Refugee Center in
Brooklyn to some of those convicted in the 1993 attack and that
he was behind the bombing.

Bush and his aides were dismayed at the way the FBI almost
disintegrated under Louis Freeh. Appointed by Clinton in 1993,
Freeh had seemed the perfect candidate for FBI director. He was a
U.S. District Court judge who was a former FBI agent and former
federal prosecutor. But Freeh had no management experience and
had the habit of punishing anyone who disagreed with him or
brought him bad news.

"Freeh said he wants everything straight. The first person who
told it to him straight, he cut his head off," said Weldon Kennedy,
whom Freeh promoted to deputy director.

In one way or another, Freeh contributed to the problems at
the FBI laboratory, the flawed indictment of Wen Ho Lee, the fiasco involving innocent bystander Richard Jewell in the Olympics
bombing in Atlanta, the security breaches that allowed Robert
Hanssen to spy, the failure to turn over documents relating to
Timothy McVeigh, and the FBI's counterterrorism failure before
the attacks of 9/11 by al Qaeda.*

When Freeh took office in 1993, he had the computer in his office removed. He did not use e-mail. Over the eight years of
Freeh's tenure, that lack of appreciation for technology would
translate into disastrous consequences for the bureau. By September 2001, 13,000 of the FBI's personal computers were 386- and
486-chip pre-Pentium machines, incapable of using the current
software, handling graphics, downloading from a CD, or even
working with a mouse. Agents had to double up to use computers,

---

* See the author's *The Bureau: The Secret History of the FBI.*

and the FBI's internal e-mail was so slow that agents used their personal e-mail addresses instead. The FBI system did not allow e-mail outside the agency. Often, with funds from the Justice Department, local police were far more technologically advanced than the FBI. Because few of the FBI's computers could handle graphics, agents had to have photos of suspects e-mailed from local police departments to their home computers.

The result was that the FBI had mountains of information it didn't know what to do with. While the agents were smart and dedicated, they had few analysts who could sift the data and connect the dots to try to zero in on potential investigative targets. Thus, while none of the information the FBI had before 9/11 would have uncovered the plots, if the information and leads had been brought together and analyzed, they might have led to further investigations that could have uncovered the plan.

Despite the fact that the FBI was crumbling around him, Freeh survived because he was a wizard at manipulating Congress and the press. When the Democrats controlled Congress, he emphasized liberal issues, like minority hiring. When the Republicans took over, he railed about the FBI's previous fiascoes at Ruby Ridge and Waco, appealing to the right wing. Robert B. Bucknam, his chief of staff, leaked a memo Freeh wrote to Janet Reno, Clinton's attorney general, taking issue with her opposition to appointment of an independent counsel to investigate Clinton and allegations of illicit fund-raising in the 1996 presidential campaign. After that, in Republican eyes, Freeh could do no wrong.

In May 2001, Freeh resigned of his own volition to take a high-paying job at MBNA, a credit card company. But as he was leaving, he put out the word that the Bush administration had asked him to stay on until a successor was found. In fact, the White House did not ask Freeh to remain in his job. So skillful was Freeh at manipulating public opinion that he had an "associate" tell the *Washington Post* that when his sixth son was born in 1998, Freeh responded to rumors that he might resign by saying he had a mission to make the bureau "more efficient, more professional, more tech-savvy and, along the way, to rebuild confidence in the nation's largest law enforcement organization." To the unwary, it sounded as if the FBI was in trouble before Freeh took over eight years earlier, rather than the other way around. The comment was in line with Freeh's and Bucknam's strategy of having the FBI director distance himself from the bureau's problems—even if he had caused them—so that he could pose as a reformer.

Bush considered the FBI director one of his most important appointments. Above all, he wanted someone who knew how to manage a large organization. Clay Johnson's presidential personnel operation and Alberto R. Gonzales, Bush's White House counsel, had primary responsibility for finding the right candidate.

Born in San Antonio, Gonzales was a graduate of Rice University and Harvard Law School who attended the U.S. Air Force Academy and was a veteran of the U.S. Air Force. Gonzales's father was a construction worker who laid down concrete for freeways in Houston. Later, he got a job as a maintenance worker in a rice mill. Gonzales's father, mother, and seven other siblings lived in a two-bedroom house in North Houston. In Gonzales's last semester at Harvard, his father died in an accident at the rice mill.

"We didn't have a telephone until I was a junior in high school," Gonzales told me. "We never had hot running water when I lived there. We had cold water. To take baths, we would boil water on a stove and bring the water to the bathtub."[116]

Thanks to the G.I. bill, scholarships, loans, and part-time jobs, Gonzales managed to pay for his education.

Gonzales first came to Bush's attention when he turned down Bush's father's offer of a job in his White House. Bush's father was trying to recruit "up-and-coming minority stars," Gonzales, an Hispanic, said. He spurned the offer so he could focus on making partner in his law firm, Vinson & Elkins in Houston. After Bush became governor, he asked Gonzales to be his general counsel.

"You first got on my radar screen back . . . when you turned down my old man for the job," Bush told him after Gonzales accepted his offer.

After Gonzales spent three years in that job and became secretary of state, Bush appointed him to the Texas Supreme Court. When Bush came to Washington, he asked the forty-five-year-old lawyer to be his White House counsel.

Gonzales met Bush's "good man" test. There would be a catch

in his voice as he recounted how Gonzales had succeeded despite his humble background.

Like many of Washington's top lawyers going back to Edward Bennett Williams, Gonzales was brilliant but, at the same time, modest and empathetic. He could summarize complex legal issues in a few plain sentences but also rattle off citations and precedents as in a LEXIS search.

Gonzales admired Bush's balanced perspective on his job. Unlike presidents Johnson, Nixon, and Clinton, Bush had never been consumed by a burning desire to be in the White House. He had a life apart from the presidency. In his set of priorities, his family and faith came first, then his country.

"He understands the majestic power of the presidency to do big things, great things," Gonzales told me in his beige-carpeted, paneled office in the West Wing. "But he knows there are limits to what even a president can do. I think he's quite comfortable knowing there are limits. That comfort comes from his very real faith. He does the best he can. That's all he can do. At the end of the day, it will be over. He will have done his best as president. And he will just move on; it will be somebody else's turn."

Gonzales's appointment to the White House job touched off speculation that he would be a candidate for the U.S. Supreme Court. But like the rest of Bush's aides from Texas, Gonzales maintained he wanted to return to the Lone Star State.

"This job has a lot of trappings; there is a lot of power in this job," he said. "But I love my family and Texas more. I would not be here after two and a half long years but for this president. I believe in him. He wants me to be here. So I will be here because I want to help him. But I also look forward to the day I can return to Texas."

Like Bush, Gonzales thought the role of judges should be limited. While race could play a role in hiring decisions, it should never supplant competence.

"I should not be hurt because of my race," Gonzales would say. "Likewise, I don't think I should be helped solely because of my race."

While the names of several possible candidates for FBI director appeared in the press, Robert Mueller was the leading candidate from the beginning, Gonzales said. When Ashcroft became attorney general, Mueller, a Republican, was acting deputy attorney general. Ashcroft was a fan. But others recommended him as well.

"The fact that the decision to choose him was not made immediately is not a reflection that there was lack of confidence in Bob," Gonzales said. "We wanted to make sure we had looked at the entire universe. We concluded Bob was the right man for the job. Clay Johnson was involved in that process. I was involved."

"Let's go with him," Bush said to Johnson and Gonzales in the Oval Office, referring to Mueller. On July 3, 2003, Bush and Gonzales were playing golf at Andrews Air Force Base, Bush's first golf outing as president. He directed Gonzales to make arrangements for the president to call Mueller about the appointment, Gonzales recalled.

"We generally look for people who can do the job at hand—in the case of the FBI, manage—are good team players, want to be here for the right reason, and can do the right thing when it may not be the popular thing," Johnson said. "Bob was all these things."[117]

Mueller (pronounced MULL-er) was a no-nonsense former Marine with a long record as a seasoned prosecutor and manager. He received a B.S. degree from Princeton University and an M.A. in international studies from New York University. A first lieutenant in the Marines, Mueller served in the Vietnam War and was awarded the Bronze Star and the Purple Heart. Thinking he would become an FBI agent, Mueller obtained a J.D. degree from the University of Virginia Law School in 1973.

After serving as U.S. Attorney in Boston and San Francisco and becoming assistant attorney general in charge of the Justice Department's Criminal Division, Mueller returned to private practice. But in May 1995, he joined the government again to prosecute homicide cases for the U.S. Attorney's office in Washington, where he began working on knifings, batterings, and shootings. He answered the phone, "Mueller, Homicide."

When Bush interviewed him for the job, Mueller's cell phone rang. Mueller knew Bush did not like cell phones going off.

"I'm dead," Mueller said, and the president chuckled. The fact that Mueller was direct only endeared him to Bush.

The president announced Mueller's nomination in a Rose Garden press conference on July 5, 2001. Mueller, fifty-six, with a craggy face, slightly graying black hair, and ramrod-straight posture, spoke for forty-eight seconds, thanking Bush several times.

In contrast to Freeh, who claimed he would take a polygraph test but never actually did, Mueller, when asked during his confirmation hearing if he would take one, said, "This may be my training from the Marine Corps, but you don't ask people to do that which you're unwilling to do yourself. I have already taken the polygraph."

"How did you do?" Senator Orrin Hatch asked.

"I'm sitting here. That's all I've got to say," Mueller answered, and the senators laughed.

Mueller took office on September 4, a week before 9/11. Unlike Freeh, Mueller used e-mail and was a proponent of technology. Several weeks before taking over, Mueller met with Bob Dies, the FBI's computer guru. Mueller listed standard software, such as Microsoft Office, that he wanted on his computer. Dies told him he could have it installed, but none of it would be compatible with anything else in the bureau. Mueller was flabbergasted.

Mueller found that the bureau's mainframe computer system was so flawed that memos sent to agents never arrived. There was no way for the sender to know if a memo had been received. To store a single document on the FBI's Automated Case Support system required twelve separate computer commands. On these green-screen terminals, the FBI could search for the word "flight" or the word "schools"—retrieving millions of documents each time—but not for "flight schools."

In the days before 9/11, Mueller issued instructions that led to ordering thousands of new Dell computers to replace the bureau's existing PCs, which were so antiquated that no church would likely take them as donations. Rather than snubbing those who brought him bad news or disagreed with him, as Freeh had done, Mueller removed people when he found out they had *kept* bad news from him. Just before 9/11, Mueller visited the FBI academy at Quantico, Virginia. He said there that he wanted to institute training programs for analysts. Prior to that, the FBI had promoted secretaries to be analysts and had given them no training.

Now, because of Bush's instruction on October 14, Mueller had a new mission: To change the approach and culture of the FBI to emphasize prevention over prosecution. Rather than waiting years to obtain every last bit of videotaped evidence to convict terrorists, the FBI would roll them up quickly on any violation—from cigarette smuggling and credit card fraud to lying to an FBI agent.

Every morning when Bush met with Mueller and Tenet, he went over the latest threats, following up on previous ones and demanding to know what the CIA and FBI were doing to make the country safer. As Mueller would say, nothing concentrates the mind so much as having to report every morning to the president of the United States Bush was nothing if not focused, and he never forgot that his first priority was the security of the country.

"His concern is not the number of indictments and arrests," Mueller told me. "It's what we have done to assure that there will not be another September 11. That covers disrupting terrorist cells but also anticipating the attacks, looking at the threats, and making sure we track down every piece of information related to threats, whether it's here or overseas. He gets a report on that integrated investigation daily."[118]

Card pointed out that Bush's directive to the FBI to emphasize prevention was historic. But on the morning of September 14, Bush's day was just beginning. After the FBI and CIA briefings, Bush convened a Cabinet meeting in the Cabinet Room. As the president walked in, everyone stood and applauded. Bush choked up. Thinking of the speech Bush would be giving later at the National Cathedral, Colin Powell, who sat next to the president, penned a note:

"Dear Mr. President, What I do when I have to give a speech like this, I avoid those words I know will cause me to well up, such as 'mom' and 'pop.'"

Powell slid the note along the table. Bush read it and smiled.

"Let me tell you what the Secretary of State told me," Bush said, waving the note in the air. "Dear Mr. President, don't break down!"

The room erupted in laughter.

Bush told the hushed group that he was going to convene a war council to address the new threat. He issued instructions to each Cabinet officer whose agency would be involved. But he said he did not want the war to detract from domestic priorities. Addressing Rod Paige, the secretary of education, he said efforts must continue to make sure every child learns to read and has the opportunity to succeed.

At Bush's direction, Paige was working with Clay Johnson's presidential personnel group and with Margaret Spellings to select candidates to serve on a Presidential Commission on Excellence in Special Education. The commission, the first of its kind, would be charged with developing better ways to assess and educate the six million children placed in special-education classes because of learning disabilities and other problems, such as mental retardation and speech or hearing impairments. From Reid Lyon, Bush had learned that, too often, children who could not read because they had been taught with the whole-language nonmethod were "shunted aside," as Lyon put it, into special-education classes. Bush wanted to put a stop to it.

"Once you get in, you're not getting out of special-education classes," Spellings said. "We have a lot of misdiagnosed kids. That happens particularly with minority kids and particularly African-American kids. We don't teach them how to read. We put them in special ed. That's the end of the story."[119]

Bush was sensitive to the fact that while the United States was now on a war footing, Americans needed to conduct business as usual.

"We have to prepare the public without alarming the public," he said.

Bush dispatched Karl Rove to urge resumption of major-league baseball and professional football games. Bush was also concerned about hate crimes directed against Muslims. Rather than being an intolerant right-winger, Bush had always felt comfortable with people from every religion. One of his friends from Yale, Muhammed Ahmed Saleh, was a Muslim from Jordan.

"The only bias I can detect is, he doesn't like people who are hypocritical or who put on airs," said Robert Dieter, Bush's lawyer friend from Yale. "Other than that, he accepts people for who they are."[120]

A week after 9/11, Bush visited the Islamic Center of Washington, where he made the point that the acts of violence against innocents at the World Trade Center violate the tenets of the Islamic faith. Quoting from the Koran, a largely benign document, he said: "In the long run, evil in the extreme will be the end of those who do evil."

A week later, Bush went to the El Paso Café in Arlington, Virginia with his friends Clay Johnson and Mike Wood and their wives. The next day, Ari Fleischer told the press about the outing to make the point that Americans were returning to their normal lives.

On September 14, following the Cabinet meeting, Bush met in the White House Situation Room with the National Security Council, George Tenet and Cofer Black, who headed the Counterterrorism Center at the CIA. As they had discussed earlier, Tenet presented the president with a plan to track down bin Laden, topple the Taliban in Afghanistan, and confront global terrorism. The plan called for CIA paramilitary teams and U.S. Special Forces to hunt down the terrorists and kill them if necessary. The CIA would support and pay off the Northern Alliance to fight the Taliban, who harbored bin Laden and al Qaeda. And the agency would use its full complement of techniques—from human spying and interception of communications to satellite and reconnaissance plane surveillance—to find terrorists all over the world.

Black warned that Americans would die.

"That's war," Bush responded. "That's what we're here to win."

At noon, Bush went to the National Cathedral. He joined most of his living predecessors, hundreds of members of Congress, the justices of the Supreme Court, commanders of the armed forces, the Cabinet, the heads of the CIA and the FBI, former secretaries of State and of the Treasury, former attorneys general, and his opponent Al Gore, along with ordinary citizens, firefighters, and policemen, in remembering the victims.

The service, planned by Laura Bush and then White House Communications Director Karen Hughes, began with guitar music and children singing a folk rendition of the Twenty-Third Psalm. It included a Protestant minister, a rabbi, a Catholic cardinal, and a Muslim cleric. Looking frail, the Reverend Billy Graham spoke.

Bush told the mourners, "God's signs are not always the ones we look for. We learn in tragedy that his purposes are not always our own. Yet the prayers of private suffering, whether in our homes or in this great cathedral, are known and heard, and understood."

Bush cited some of the heroic acts that had taken place on 9/11 as examples of the national character. "Inside the World Trade Center, one man who could have saved himself stayed until the end at the side of his quadriplegic friend," he said. "A beloved priest died giving the last rites to a firefighter. Two office workers, finding a disabled stranger, carried her down sixty-eight floors to safety. A group of men drove through the night from Dallas to Washington to bring skin grafts for burn victims."

He closed his folder and walked deliberately back to his seat among his family. Reaching across Laura, his father squeezed his son's hand.

The service ended with the fiery resolve of *The Battle Hymn of the Republic*. The congregation sang, "Glory! Glory! Hallelujah!"

From Andrews Air Force Base, Bush flew to New Jersey on *Air Force One*, escorted by fighter jets. He helicoptered to Manhattan and hovered over Ground Zero, where smoke still rose from the ground. Thousands of workers were combing over the wreckage. After landing at 4:40 P.M. near Wall Street, Bush took a limousine to the site where the 110-story twin towers had stood three days before. Against Secret Service advice, he left the limo and began shaking hands, patting the backs of firefighters and volunteers, saying "Thank you." None of the New Yorkers lining the street had gone through magnetometers, the usual practice before the president waded into crowds.

Andy Card noticed a group of workers standing on scaffolding. They were chanting, "USA, USA," but they were waving a Japanese flag.

"They were volunteers from Japan who had come to help us," Card said.

Another group of rescue workers had Canadian flags sewn on their sleeves. Soon everyone was chanting, "USA."

A Bush aide asked sixty-nine-year-old Bob Beckwith, a retired firefighter from Queens who had joined the effort, if the president could use a crushed fire truck as a platform. Beckwith, gas mask dangling from his neck, bounced up and down on it a few times to make sure it was stable. Wearing a beige windbreaker, Bush grabbed a bullhorn and jumped up on the truck. Beckwith tried to leave, but Bush wrapped his arm around his shoulders.

"Thank you all," Bush began. "I want you all to know—"

"Can't hear you," a rescue worker shouted.

"I can hear you!" Bush shouted through a bullhorn. "The rest of the world hears you. And the people who knocked these buildings down will hear all of us soon."

The workers broke into spontaneous chants of "USA, USA." Bush took a small American flag and waved it.

Watching on TV, Dr. Rex W. Cowdry, one of Bush's friends from Yale, thought that for the first time he was seeing in public the George Bush he knew in personal settings. Cowdry, a psychiatrist who is a former acting director of the National Institute of Mental Health, said, "It seemed to be a turning point. The person I know came out. He was natural, unscripted. He stepped out from his handlers."[121]

The next morning at Camp David, Tenet gave a more detailed presentation of the covert action plan the CIA had developed. He distributed a packet labeled "Going to War." The cover featured a photo of bin Laden inside a red circle with a slash over his face. The CIA plan called for an attack on the network's financial support and a ferocious effort to track down bin Laden's supporters. In that effort, the CIA would enlist the help of eighty countries and would use friendly Arab intelligence services—those of Jordan, Egypt, and Morocco, in particular. The CIA would subsidize them with funds for training and equipment.

Tenet wanted broad authority to conduct the CIA's war, one that would allow use of deadly force as part of the U.S. effort at self-defense and thus would not require him to seek approval for each action. He presented it as a modification of Ronald Reagan's January 1986 intelligence finding—an authorization to conduct covert action—to allow the CIA to identify terrorists who had committed crimes against Americans abroad and to help bring them to justice.

Bush thanked Tenet for his presentation. He said he would consider his proposals and those of his other advisors and get back to them with decisions by Monday. By September 17, Bush decided to grant all of Tenet's requests, including an extra $1 billion. Bush wanted the CIA to be first on the ground, preparing the way for the military with both intelligence officers and paramilitary officers.

The events of 9/11 "fundamentally changed the way the president looked at the world," John E. McLaughlin, the deputy director of Central Intelligence who periodically briefed Bush and attended most of the meetings with the president to plan a counterattack, told me. "I'm convinced he wakes up every morning thinking about how to prevent anything like that from happening again."[122]

By the end of September, the United States had amassed 28,000 sailors and troops and more than 300 warplanes and two dozen warships in the Indian Ocean and Red Sea for an attack on the Taliban. On October 7, the bombing, aided by the British, began on Kabul, the capital and largest city in Afghanistan. Bombers, fighter planes, and Tomahawk cruise missiles pounded airfields and other strongholds.

In prosecuting the war, the Predator, a CIA unmanned aircraft, was critical. It allowed the troops and U.S. Special Forces on the ground to view targets remotely in real time.

By early December, it was almost all over. The Taliban had abandoned Kandahar, their last stronghold. In mid-December, U.S. and Afghan troops surrounded a giant cave complex in the eastern Afghan region of Tora Bora, where a radio transmission was believed to have come from bin Laden. U.S. warplanes blanketed the area with bombs, but the United States relied largely on local Afghan forces on the ground. Hundreds of al Qaeda suspects escaped across the border to Pakistan. Bin Laden was believed to be among them.

On December 13, the Bush administration released a videotape of bin Laden chatting with followers. Recovered in Afghanistan, the videotape showed he had had prior knowledge of the attacks. Bin Laden gloated over the roughly 3,000 deaths.

"We calculated in advance the number of casualties" that would result when two airliners crashed into the World Trade Center, he said. "I was the most optimistic of all" in predicting how many would be killed, he said. On the morning of the attacks, bin Laden turned on a short-wave radio to hear the news. His followers, he said, were "overjoyed when the first plane hit the World Trade Center, so I said to them, 'Be patient.'" Chuckling, he said that most of the hijackers recruited for the "martyrdom operation" had not been aware until the last minute that they were going to their deaths.

Illustrating the difference between Bush's approach to security and Clinton's, Clinton saw parallels between the 9/11 attacks, on the one hand, and acts of oppression or hatred perpetrated by white men. While he didn't say that the victims brought it on themselves, when he spoke on November 7, 2001, at Georgetown University, Clinton said that that "those of us who come from various European lineages are not blameless." He described America's record of slavery, oppression of Native Americans, and individual hate crimes as part of terrorism's "long history."

Putting aside the fact that these acts arguably do not fall within the definition of terrorism, Clinton seemed to be saying that bin Laden had a point because Americans over the years had engaged in wrongful acts. By that logic, when meting out justice to rapists and serial killers, the fact that Americans oppressed Native Americans and owned slaves should also be considered.

Bush was nothing if not a moral absolutist. In his system of values, there was such a thing as right and wrong, good and evil. Anyone who cried while watching terror-stricken Americans of all religions and ethnic backgrounds flee the World Trade Center knew that as well. For Bush, only one reaction was appropriate: "We will rid the world of the evildoers."

16

SNEAK AND PEEK

Within an hour of the attacks, commentators began referring to an "intelligence failure." Democrats began pointing fingers in every direction. But Bush recognized that the failure to catch the hijackers had been a systemic one. The truth was the government had never taken the al Qaeda threat seriously enough and dealt with it in a coherent, aggressive fashion. Instead of assigning blame, Bush began taking steps to correct the problems, making it clear that lack of cooperation between the FBI and CIA would not be tolerated and asking Congress for billions in additional funds for the CIA.

Bush understood that to protect America, the help of FBI agents and CIA officers would be critical. They—like Bush's White House aides—risked their lives by simply going to work. Along with the Capitol, the White House and the headquarters of the CIA and FBI were the most likely terrorist targets. After 9/11, the FBI and CIA came under constant criticism. Nothing they did was portrayed by the press in a positive light. If the morale of the men and women of those agencies was shattered and they became afraid to take risks, America's first line of defense against terrorists would fall.

Bush knew that he could not run the show alone. Leadership was all about making people want to follow you into battle. Rather than castigate the two agencies, as Democrats and a few Republicans were doing, Bush visited the FBI and the CIA to tell employees how crucial they were to winning the war on terror.

"One week after 9/11, Bush came to the CIA," George Tenet

recalled. "He said, 'I trust you, and I need you.' It doesn't often happen that way in Washington, D.C. The president could have easily cut us off at the knees. Instead, he came to us and said, 'I have enormous confidence in the men and women of this organization. I know what your work has been like.' If you don't think that made a difference in everything that has happened since," Tenet said, "you don't understand the relationship between the CIA and the president. It gave us peace of mind so we could do our jobs. Our boss was at our back. There isn't enough money in the world to tell you what that meant."[123]

Karen Hughes saw a parallel with Bush's reaction after he lost the New Hampshire primary in 2000.

"Most politicians look for a scapegoat," Hughes said. "That's the Washington blame game. Both John Kerry and John Dean fired campaign staff when things didn't look good [in 2004]. Not George W. Bush. After he lost in New Hampshire, he called us into the room and said, 'I don't want you to blame each other. We're going to hold our heads up high. We've got this far together, and we're going to win.'"[124]

After 9/11, besides hunting down terrorists all over the world, Bush wanted to give the FBI the tools to uncover plots within the United States before they unfolded. Critics seemed to think that the FBI could do this by moving a cursor around on a computer screen and "connecting the dots," the phrase that came into vogue to describe what the FBI and CIA failed to do before 9/11. But moving a cursor around a PC screen will not uncover the kind of carefully compartmented scheme hatched by bin Laden and a few of the top people in his organization. Many of the hijackers themselves did not know the dimensions of the plot and were unaware they were flying to their deaths. The problem before 9/11 was that the information that would uncover the plots simply was not there. Thus, there were no dots to connect.

Besides developing informants, the chief way to obtain the needed information was to seize records and conduct electronic surveillance. To make sure the FBI got such leads, within a few days of the attacks, Bush asked his counsel Al Gonzales to begin working with the Justice Department to craft what would become known as the USA Patriot Act. Congress passed the new law in record time, and Bush signed it in the East Room forty-five days after the attacks.

To liberal critics, the Patriot Act was an assault on civil liberties, if not the end of American freedom.

"This law is based on the faulty assumption that safety must come at the expense of civil liberties. The USA Patriot Act gives law enforcement agencies nationwide extraordinary new powers unchecked by meaningful judicial review," said Laura Murphy of the American Civil Liberties Union.

In fact, the legislation was nothing more than an effort to update existing law to keep up with technology and give the FBI the same powers in terrorism cases that it already had in cases targeting drug traffickers, spies, and Mafia figures.

Under the new law, the FBI could obtain authorization to wiretap a terrorist in a national-security investigation no matter what phone he used. Previously, the FBI would have to obtain new authorization each time a terrorist in such an investigation used a new or previously unknown pay phone, disposable cell phone, or fax machine. By the time the FBI obtained nearly a dozen signatures on a wiretap application and the approval of a judge, the terrorist had gone on to use a different phone. The FBI could never keep up with him. Since under the new law each roving wiretap, as they were called, had to be approved by a judge, there was no question about infringing on civil liberties any more than when a judge approved a search of the house of a suspected child molester. It was a question of making it at least as easy for the FBI to do its job as it was for a terrorist to do his. Yet the critics portrayed the change as a monstrous attack on civil liberties.

"We have begun to tamper with some of the basic laws—laws that strike at the heart of what this democracy is about," Anthony Romero, executive director of the ACLU, said after the law was passed.

Since the days when J. Edgar Hoover ordered illegal wiretaps and improper surveillance, the FBI as an organization had not engaged in illegal conduct. If the FBI could not be trusted to wiretap within the framework of the law, why trust agents to make arrests or carry weapons? What was the point of having an FBI if it was so hobbled that it could not perform its mission? Whose rights were being violated more, those whose phones were tapped by court order or those who died in the September 11th attacks?

If the FBI ever did abuse its authority, the appropriate response would be to prosecute those responsible and institute more oversight—not to make it more difficult to wiretap so that criminals could avoid detection and terrorists could attack again.

Prior to 9/11, because of relentless media criticism and a lack of clear authority under Justice Department guidelines, the FBI had become so gun-shy and politically correct that even though terrorists were known to hatch their plots in mosques, the FBI was averse to following suspects into them. Because he was a cleric, FBI and Justice Department lawyers debated for months whether to open an investigation of Sheik Omar Abdel Rahman, who was later convicted in the first World Trade Center bombing. Under the existing guidelines, FBI agents could not even look at online chat rooms to develop leads on people who might be recruiting terrorists or distributing information on making explosives. The FBI had to have determined that there was a sound investigative basis before it could sign on to chat rooms that any twelve-year-old could enter. In other words, "A crime practically had to be committed before you could investigate," Weldon Kennedy, the former FBI deputy director, said. "If you didn't have that, you couldn't open an investigation."

"I remember discussions when we said, unfortunately, it will take a tragedy before the issue of the tools we need is recognized for what it is," said Larry Collins, the former FBI special agent in charge in Chicago. "Maybe a congressman's daughter has to be kidnapped, and we can't track her. Congress tied our hands."

The other major problem before 9/11 was that the FBI, because of complex provisions of existing law, perceived that it could not share information developed in foreign intelligence–related investigations with agents investigating criminal matters.

"We had to report violations when criminal and intelligence agents talked to each other," Barry Mawn, who was assistant FBI director in charge of the New York field office, said. "The assistant special agent in charge over both sides had to try to keep it all separate in his head. My guys were always coming to me and complaining that they weren't allowed to share information between intelligence and the criminal side. We bitched about it at an SAC conference."

The Patriot Act made it clear that such information could be shared. The need for such a measure could not have been more obvious. Yet the American Civil Liberties Union mounted a massive effort against Bush and the Patriot Act. The organization claimed that the FBI now could use "sneak and peek" tactics in libraries to probe the reading habits of sinless grandmothers without informing the targets until after a search. But the FBI always had authority, with a judge's approval, to conduct a search without telling the suspect until a later point in the investigation. If the FBI were trying to stop a terrorist bombing and needed to search the computer of a suspect to round up the plotters without tipping them off, would anyone want the FBI to inform the suspect that his computer was about to be searched?

Nor did the FBI have any interest in anyone's reading habits. Its interest was in finding the bad guys before they killed again. Since some of the 9/11 hijackers used internet connections at libraries to communicate, the FBI might ask a judge for authority to search a particular library's computers to find such communications.

The ACLU whipped librarians into hysteria, and they began destroying charge-out records of patrons so the bureau would not get them. In Seattle, the public library printed 3,000 bookmarks to warn patrons that the FBI could obtain permission to look at their reading or computer records.

"The FBI . . . is all over the library threat, seizing library records at will under the Patriot Act," Naomi Klein wrote in *The Nation*.

Two years after enactment of the Patriot Act, Attorney General Ashcroft authorized the FBI to reveal just how many searches the FBI had conducted at libraries under the business records provision of the new act. The number was zero. Undaunted, some members of Congress—including Republican Representative C. L. "Butch" Otter of Idaho—insisted that perhaps agents were clandestinely conducting searches of library records on their own. Otter added that "some of these provisions place more power in the hands of law enforcement than our Founding Fathers could have dreamt and severely compromises [sic] the civil liberties of law-abiding Americans."

Since no libraries had been searched, the critics said the provision in the act should be repealed because there was no need for it.

"If they haven't used it, they shouldn't have any problems with our efforts to get it repealed," Representative Dennis J. Kucinich, one of ten Democratic presidential candidates, said.

That was like saying that because a policeman had never used his gun, it should be taken away. If the provision were needed to stop a dirty radiological bomb attack that might kill hundreds of thousands of people, would the Democrats oppose the law? Bush wanted to have the provision in place before it was needed, not when it was too late.

The ACLU said Bush was exploiting the 9/11 tragedy to gain wider powers. That was like saying that President Franklin Roosevelt exploited the Japanese attack on Pearl Harbor to get the United States into World War II. Finally, the ACLU warned ominously that the number of wiretaps was increasing. That was like complaining that arrests were increasing. The reason the number of wiretaps was increasing was that the FBI was doing a better job of tracking down terrorists and other criminals. When Democratic Senator Dianne Feinstein of California asked the ACLU if it knew of any actual abuses by the FBI under the Patriot Act, the organization admitted that it knew of none.

If there were any doubt about how Al Gore would have responded to the 9/11 attacks, it was dispelled when he joined the critics.

"I want to challenge the Bush administration's implicit assumption that we have to give up many of our traditional freedoms in order to be safe from terrorists," he said in a speech. He called the Patriot Act a "broad and extreme invasion of our privacy rights in the name of terrorism."

If so, Congress was complicit. The Senate had passed the Patriot Act by a vote of 98 to 1. The House passed it 357 to 66. Unlike Al Gore, Congress understood that without security, there is no freedom. Whether in the United States or in Saudi Arabia, al Qaeda's aim was to destroy civilization.

"The attacks of September 11 were a classic attack on our Constitution," Andy Card said. "Other attacks on the U.S. have been by other nations trying to impose a different form of government or ideology. But the attacks of 9/11 were an invitation to anarchy. They wanted anarchy to spread."[125]

Ironically, the same liberals and pundits like Senator John F. Kerry and Maureen Dowd of the *New York Times* who assailed Bush for not stopping the attacks of 9/11 were the ones who railed against him for proposing the Patriot Act in an effort to prevent the next attack. *New York Times* columnist Paul Krugman attacked Bush for not putting more federal money into homeland security measures. In doing so, he failed to recognize that with no additional expenditure, the Patriot Act could do more to stop the next attack than billions of dollars spent on defensive security. Those who claimed, as Senator Edward M. Kennedy did, that Bush was leading the nation to a "perilous place" forgot that the country was in a perilous place when the attacks of 9/11 occurred.

Invariably, the media reported on the new powers contained in the Patriot Act without saying that the FBI already had such authority in pursuing lesser threats. But Bush did not take his cues from the media. Beyond sports and an A&E special or two, he rarely watched television. In the morning, he glanced at the news stories in the major papers—the *Washington Post, New York Times, Los Angeles Times, Wall Street Journal,* and *USA Today.* In addition, he relied on Andy Card to brief him each morning on what the press was saying. But through his FBI and CIA briefings, Bush had an inside view of world events.

The big secret was that Bush did read the *Dallas Morning News.* It was delivered to the White House each day around noon. When controversy erupted over Bush's reference in his State of the Union speech to Saddam Hussein trying to obtain uranium in Niger, the Dallas paper ran ten stories mentioning it, compared with eighty-four in the *Washington Post.* But even when reading the Dallas paper, Bush focused mainly on state politics and the sports pages.

"I don't think he really pays that much attention to media criticism," Margaret Spellings said. "He doesn't know, and he doesn't care. That helps him keep his glass-is-half-full mentality. If you sweated out every bad thing that was said about you, you'd never get out of bed."

"Dad, don't do that to yourself," Bush would say to his father, who consumed all the news of his son, good and bad.

"This president is very good about making decisions," Gonzales said. "He likes to hear from all sides, make a decision, and move on. To reconsider means you may have made a wrong decision. Obviously, new facts may come to light, and you may have to reconsider. But he's very comfortable in terms of where we are with the Patriot Act. This is all about preventing the next attack and protecting America, all within the limits of the Constitution. He believes the American people understand that and support him."[126]

To Rex Cowdry, Bush's psychiatrist friend from Yale, Bush's transformation of the government to prevent further attacks was merely an extension of his Yale activities. "He had leadership and found the right venue," Cowdry said.[127]

17

AN AGENT FOR CHANGE

In his inauguration speech, Bush said, "We will confront weapons of mass destruction, so that a new century is spared new horrors." No one paid much attention. After all, back in February 1998, Bill Clinton had said, "Iraq still has stockpiles of chemical and biological munitions, a small force of Scud-type missiles, and the capacity to restart quickly its production program and build many, many more weapons." Clinton insisted then that the world had to address the "kind of threat Iraq poses . . . a rogue state with weapons of mass destruction, ready to use them or provide them to terrorists . . . who travel the world among us unnoticed."

But Clinton's idea of addressing the problem was to support more United Nations resolutions, which Saddam Hussein ignored. When Saddam made it impossible for weapons inspectors to continue their work in 1998, Clinton sent in bombers and missiles for a three-day shoot-'em-up. The Clinton team called this a "proportional response." The same defeatist approach led to the United States being trounced in the Vietnam War.

If there was anything Bush hated, it was pretense. Making a show of force and giving lip service to toothless resolutions was worse than taking no action at all. Saddam Hussein had used chemical weapons on his own people and invaded Kuwait. Bush was not willing to wait to find out if he would use them on the United States or would share them with terrorists.

After 9/11, Bush's thinking crystallized. During the cold war, the policy of containment worked because the Soviet Union was

171

governed by rational leaders who did not want to see themselves annihilated in a retaliatory strike. Now the enemy were terrorists who did not care if they were killed and had no national assets to protect. The terrorists were working on acquiring weapons of mass destruction that could kill hundreds of thousands of Americans.

To most Americans, Bush's grasp of foreign affairs was symbolized by his inability in a TV interview during the campaign to name the leaders of Taiwan, Pakistan, India, and Chechnya. In August 2000, *Time* magazine said that Bush "stands a chance of becoming the president with one of the thinnest resumés in a century."

But Jack Welch did not need to know how to design jet engines to run General Electric. As Bush's aides saw it, foreign affairs was all about leadership and interpersonal skills. That had always been Bush's strength, along with surrounding himself with smart, capable people. Bush's foreign-policy team, headed by forty-nine-year-old Condoleezza Rice, was a prime example.

Rice grew up in segregated Birmingham, Alabama, where blacks had to eat separately from whites and use different bathrooms and water fountains. When Rice was nine, Denise McNair, one of her friends, was killed in the 1963 bombing of the Sixteenth Street Baptist Church. But Rice's parents gave her a strong sense of self-worth. In their neighborhood of Titusville, an enclave of rising black middle-class families, the motto was "twice as good," meaning that kids had to be twice as good as white children to pull even. No one was going to push her around.

Rice vividly remembered going into a store when she was seven with her mother Angelina. Rice spotted a dress she liked, and her mother asked the saleswoman if her daughter could try it on. The woman took the dress from Rice and motioned to a storage room.

"She'll have to try it on there," the woman said.

But Angelina Rice addressed the clerk as the hired help she was.

"My daughter will try on this dress in a dressing room or I'm not spending my money here," she said.

Hoping to make a commission, the sales clerk furtively showed them the way to a dressing room.

An only child, Rice started taking piano lessons at age three. At age four, she began accompanying the choir at the church of her father, the Reverend John W. Rice, Jr. By age five, Rice could read. When the Negro schools, as they were called, would not let her start school because she was too young, her mother took a year off from teaching school herself and taught Condoleezza at home.

"My parents," Rice said, "were very strategic. I was going to be so well prepared, and I was going to do all of these things that were revered in white society so well, so that I would be armored somehow from racism. I would be able to confront white society on its own terms." Rice lived in a place where restaurants wouldn't serve her a hamburger, she once said, "But my parents were telling me I could be president."

When Rice was eleven, her father became dean of Stillman College in Tuscaloosa, and Rice and the family left Birmingham. Two years later, her father became an administrator at the University of Denver, and Condi Rice entered her first integrated school, a private Catholic academy. She became a competitive ice skater as well as an accomplished pianist.

As a freshman at the University of Colorado, Rice was one of two or three blacks in a lecture hall of 250 students when a professor began to embrace William Shockley's theory that whites were genetically superior to blacks.

Condi Rice was on her feet, telling the professor off.

"I'm the one who speaks French," she said. "I'm the one who plays Beethoven. I'm better at your culture than you are. This can be taught!" she said.

At Denver, Rice realized she would never climb to the pinnacle of the music world. In her senior year, she switched her major to international relations and was drawn to Soviet studies. After graduating *cum laude* and a member of Phi Beta Kappa, Rice enrolled at Notre Dame and obtained a master's degree, then a Ph.D. from the University of Denver, where her mentor was Josef Korbel, Madeleine Albright's father.

At age twenty-six, Rice became a professor at Stanford University. In 1986, Brent Scowcroft attended a dinner with arms control experts at Stanford when Rice—the only woman, the only black, and the youngest person there—asked a "brilliant question" involving international law. Scowcroft invited her to join a foreign-policy group at the Aspen Institute.

When Bush's father named Scowcroft as his national-security advisor, Scowcroft asked Rice to join him in the White House. As communism fell, she was the National Security Council's senior director for Soviet and East European Affairs. Rice returned to Stanford, where she was named provost at age thirty-eight. When they were both visiting the Bush family home in Kennebunkport in 1999, George W. Bush asked Rice to tutor him in foreign policy. That led to her position as his national-security advisor.

Rice's mother Angelina died of cancer in 1985. In December 2000, John Rice, weakened by heart disease, was on his deathbed at Stanford University Medical Center when his second wife told him the news that his daughter had been appointed national-security advisor, the first woman and the first African-American to be named to the post.

"Tears came down his cheeks," said Clara Bailey Rice.

Looking back, Rice would come to understand the paradox that American slaves used to sing, "Nobody knows the trouble I've seen—Glory Hallelujah!" For, she told a National Prayer Breakfast in February 2003, "nothing of lasting value has ever been achieved without sacrifice." It is, she said, a "privilege to struggle. A privilege to struggle for what is right and true. A privilege to struggle for freedom over tyranny. A privilege, even, to struggle with the most difficult and profound moral choices."

Rice's prestigious corner office was down the hall from the Oval Office. The White House front lawn and the Eisenhower Executive Office Building were framed in her picture windows. On her wall was a painting of a black revival meeting commissioned by the New Deal's Public Works of Art Project and on loan from the Smithsonian. The books on her shelves ranged from *The Prayer of Jabez* by Bruce Wilkinson and *Kaddish* by Leon Wieseltier to the *Official National Football League Record & Fact Book*. On the side of her highly polished desk, she kept a small vanity mirror.

In person, Rice is even prettier, more charming, and more composed than she appears on TV. She maintains constant eye contact, gesturing with her hands as she makes her points.

I asked Rice, who is single, if she dated.

"The one thing I don't do is talk about my personal life, but let me tell you this: I'm not a workaholic, I have friends," she said. "I do other things besides work, and I wish I had time to do more other things."[128]

About once or twice a month, at 5:30 P.M. on Sundays, Rice played the piano with a chamber group at her apartment. Her favorite composer was Brahms. A Russian speaker, she occasionally read a Russian-language newspaper. She liked any sport that "ends with a score."

The fact that Rice, a black, held one of the most powerful and sensitive positions in the administration in itself refuted liberals' stereotype of Bush as a right-wing racist. But in Rice's view, Bush did not give it much thought.

"I think he really tries to look at people as people," Rice told me. "But it's a funny thing that it is this president and this Republican administration in which the two highest foreign-policy positions are both held by blacks. I've always kind of sensed that it doesn't really occur to him that that is the case. Sometimes we'll joke about it. I kidded him that his father's immigrant ship was the *Mayflower*. I said my ancestors were probably below," she said. "He's not uncomfortable with race. He doesn't say it doesn't matter. But it never occurs to him to think it remarkable that his national-security advisor and secretary of State are black."[129]

With Bush, Rice said, "The worst thing you can do is tell him you're going to do something and then not do it." The next worst thing is to waste his time beating around the bush.

"He is very straightforward himself and tends to like straightforward people," Rice said. "You don't want to spend a long time constructing a baroque argument for him. I've watched him with more foreign leaders than I'd like to remember, some of them multiple times. His best relationships with foreign leaders are when he feels they are being as straightforward with him as he is with them. He can do that past language barriers. He can sense the body language."

Rice cited Bush's relationship with Prime Minister Junichiro Koizumi of Japan, who understands some English but does not speak it. At their first meeting at Camp David in June 2001, they tossed around a baseball. In his remarks to the press, Koizumi said he was surprised that, at their meeting, they had established a warm relationship of trust. Rice said Bush applies the same directness to his speeches and policy declarations.

Almost everyone recognized the need for a Palestinian state, but the issue was so politically charged that no president prior to Bush had come out and said it. When government officials discussed the issue, they used vague terminology to refer to such a state.

"Presidents used to mumble when it got to the question of a Palestinian state," Rice told me in her office one Saturday morning. "They couldn't bring themselves to say 'Palestinian state.' In preparing a speech to the UN, he said, 'There's going to be a Palestinian state, so let's say that. What will it be called? It will be called Palestine. If that's the case, let's call it Palestine.' "

On November 10, 2001, Bush told the UN, "We are working toward a day when two states, Israel and Palestine, live peacefully together within secure and recognized borders as called for by the Security Council resolutions."

On any given day, Bush conferred with Rice constantly. He often invited her to dinner with Laura. Bush suggested books like *Paris, 1919* or Edvard Radzinsky's biography of Joseph Stalin for her to read, and he would discuss them with her. Before Rice could get through one book, Bush would recommend another. When Rice, with her academic background, used a fancy word, Bush would pretend he didn't understand it.

Despite their closeness, going back to the General Electric analogy, Rice was like the head of a division. Her chief role was to solicit and convey to Bush the views of what are called the national-security principals, ranging from Cheney to Powell and Rumsfeld. Once Bush made a decision, she would go back to them and work to get them on board and make sure the policy was implemented.

"She fixes things," an aide said. "When there seems to be a disconnect between a few Cabinet colleagues, or something the president wants done that isn't being done, she will get on the phone, find out what the problem is, identify it, and solve it."

At interagency meetings, Rice rarely expressed her own views, but, as Bush's confidant, she came up with her own ideas and told him what she thought. Yet the direction was Bush's.

Bush "allows his principal advisors freedom to present all sides of an argument," Colin Powell told me. "He allows us to debate amongst ourselves and debate as a group within the principals' committee meeting. And he then lets, if necessary, the debate continue in front of him as National Security Council chief, and he encourages us to discuss with one another, debate with one another, and disagree with one another. And he then works hard to draw out the best ideas from everyone, makes his decision, and then moves on."[130]

While there was a "fondness for writing about what, oh, Powell thought, or Don [Rumsfeld] thought, or Dick [Armitage, the deputy secretary of State] thought," Powell said, "it's what the president thinks that counts, and what he decides that we do." Powell said that contrasted with Clinton, where, "There was a great deal of debating and discussion in almost seminar fashion, and you didn't always have a clear idea of what had been decided or not decided and what was still open."

As Bush headed for a showdown with Saddam Hussein, Stephen J. Hadley, Rice's deputy, began to see the pattern in his thinking.

Born in Ohio, Hadley attended Cornell University and Yale Law School. He worked for the Nixon administration, first in the Defense Department and then at the NSC, continuing into the Ford administration. He was assistant secretary of Defense for Bush's father and became a partner in Shea & Gardner, a Washington law firm, and a principal in Scowcroft Group, an international consulting firm headed by Brent Scowcroft. Rice called Hadley, who was low-key and well organized, her alter ego.

"I don't think people really understand very well who this president is," Hadley told me in Rice's well-appointed office. "One of the things I think people don't understand is the extent to which he sees himself as a change agent. That is, somebody who really wants to step up to problems and try to solve them. He wants to leave the situation better than he found it. If you look at his speeches, he says it. In his inauguration speech, he said, 'We must show courage in a time of blessing by confronting problems instead of passing them on to future generations.' He has said that all the way through. Nobody recognizes it."[131]

Particularly after 9/11, Hadley came to realize that the statement Bush made most often was, "We gotta think differently." The second most common command was, "Get after it."

"He is always looking for new opportunities and prodding people to do more," Hadley said. "He is prepared to make a revolutionary change through a phrase. The decision to say, 'If you harbor a terrorist, you'll be treated like a terrorist,' was his. It's become the defining principle of the war on terror, but it really came just from him. He has, I think, a good sense of where there is a strategic opportunity to make progress or change the way an issue is framed."

Besides Bush's approach to Iraq, Hadley cited two examples: his position on Palestine and his reaction to North Korea's development of nuclear weapons. Bush had an unerring ability to size up people. He invited Russian President Vladimir Putin to his Crawford ranch because "the best diplomacy starts with getting to know each other. And I want him to know my values, and I want to know his values."

Bush concluded that Yasser Arafat was a hopeless case, someone who had little interest in helping his own people and who was an impediment to the peace process. Instead of pretending that he was relevant, in April and June 2002, Bush began saying that Arafat was part of the problem.

"Arafat put his own personal power above the interests of his people," Hadley said. "He had an opportunity to achieve peace and did not take it. He is not delivering; he is not a partner for peace. Who are we kidding? Let's move on. Everyone had focused on territory and borders. The president said that was the wrong starting point. Let's focus on building the institutions of a Palestinian state. That means new leadership that is not committed to terror, that is in fact committed to fighting terror, and that is committed to true democracy. Let's start talking about a constitution and a state that Israel would be willing to have as a neighbor."

"I had warned Arafat twice that it was about to come to an end, that I could no longer deal with him if he didn't do something about terrorism," Powell said. "And he didn't, so we then came up with the twenty-fourth June speech that said we can't work with this guy; the Palestinian Authority has to reform itself, and that it has to be done quickly; and we'll wait for a new Palestinian Authority leadership to emerge, and we are looking for a Palestinian state, a two-state solution."[132]

In the case of North Korea, in 1994 the Clinton administration negotiated a nonproliferation treaty that the Koreans violated. Bush saw no point to negotiating a new agreement, one that the Koreans would only break. As in the case of the Kyoto Protocol on global warming, which only one country would ratify, Bush was not willing to participate in a charade, pursuing process for its own sake and ignoring reality. Given that North Korea possibly already had a few nuclear weapons, Bush decided that the only pressure North Korea would respond to was from her neighbors.

As Hadley described it, Bush said, "This is a strategic opportunity. We have to approach this on a regional basis. We have to get Russia, China, South Korea, and Japan in on this. We have to make them realize they have a stake in it. A nuclear North Korea is not in their interests. We have to get them to step up and solve the problem. If North Korea proceeds with its nuclear program, Russia and China will be mad at them, not just the U.S."[133]

"The president was the one who said he has to nail down the Chinese as true participants," Rice said. "He figured out they were the ones with influence over North Korea. You had the vice president, secretaries of Defense and State, and national-security advisor all with lots of foreign-policy experience, and it didn't occur to us."[134]

The new approach brought derision from pundits, editorial writers, and European leaders, who said any agreement had to be between the United States and North Korea. Over time, Hadley said, "People began to recognize that his position made sense."

By the end of 2003, Kim Jong Il, North Korea's leader, had moved from a defiant stance to an agreement in principle to restart international negotiations aimed at ending the country's nuclear program.

"The regional approach has become the new paradigm," Hadley said. "It takes tremendous strength to do what he did." As

Hadley saw it, Bush "has a way of planting the flag way out there, often to the dismay of foreign-policy professionals. He has a vision, and he holds to it. Over time, events tend to confirm the vision. The rest of the world tends to come around to it. You've seen that with North Korea and the Middle East."

Similarly, Bush's reference to the "axis of evil" in his January 2002 State of the Union address created consternation, particularly among European leaders. Referring to Iraq, North Korea, and Iran, Bush said in his address, "States like these, and their terrorist allies, constitute an axis of evil, arming to threaten the peace of the world. By seeking weapons of mass destruction, these regimes pose a grave and growing danger. They could provide these arms to terrorists, giving them the means to match their hatred. They could attack our allies or attempt to blackmail the United States. In any of these cases, the price of indifference would be catastrophic."

The early drafts of the speech mentioned only Iraq.

"Condi and I felt it needed to be more than just Iraq or it would look as if we were preparing to go to war in Iraq," Hadley recalled. "So we said to include North Korea and Iran, even though they were a little different. Then we said maybe we should drop Iran," Hadley said. "It has some elected institutions and some active dissent. The president said, 'Leave it in. I want to send a message that we support the people in Iran who favor freedom against those people who do not.' So Mike Gerson and I came up with a statement that 'Iranians, like all people, have a right to choose their own government and determine their own destiny—and the United States supports their aspirations to live in freedom.'"

Bush said, "I want to focus on these three states," Hadley said. "I want to call them the axis of evil. I want to highlight the intersection of rogue states working to acquire weapons of mass destruction and supporters of terror. That is the new nexus that is a threat to national security."

Contrary to press reports, Bush was never opposed to obtaining UN approval for going into Iraq. "People like to write about that," Powell said, "but when I first raised the issue directly with the president in early August of 2002, I told the president that if we're going to solve this problem, there are two ways to do it: getting the broadest international coalition and concurrence, or at least authorization for it; or just doing it unilaterally, and if we did it unilaterally, we would have difficulty getting willing partners in a coalition. And since it was UN resolutions that were being violated, I believed he had to go back to the UN." Bush was "attracted to that argument, and a week or so later, he asked me at an NSC meeting to present the argument, and I did," Powell said. "And Vice President Cheney and Don Rumsfeld agreed."

While there were "varying degrees of skepticism, strong differences with respect to whether the UN would play a useful role and whether or not it would be helpful to go up to the UN, there was no disagreement about going to the UN," Powell said. "Nobody said, 'Don't do it, Mr. President.' "[135]

Contrary to what the critics said, Bush supported "multilateralism and getting our friends and neighbors involved," Powell said. The United States worked with other countries on solutions to weapons-of-mass-destruction programs in North Korea, Iran, and Libya.

"We might have done a better job in letting the world know we were about to make the Kyoto decision," Powell said. "But the decision was the right one. It was early in the administration, and we weren't sensitive enough to the need to, you know, precook these things and tell our friends what's coming so that they don't immediately knee-jerk respond."

While Powell got unanimous consent to Resolution 1441, which said Iraq was in "material breach" of previous resolutions and gave Baghdad a "final opportunity to comply with its disarmament obligations," France, China, and Russia insisted on another resolution before war could be authorized. France then declared that it would veto any such resolution, and Bush abandoned the effort.

"A lot of people say, 'Well, you failed to get the second resolution,' " Powell said. "We never thought we needed the second resolution, and, in fact, we had no desire for a second resolution. But our British friends and our Australian and Spanish and Italian friends needed a second resolution, they said, for their domestic political requirements."[136]

Despite his UN efforts, Bush lacked a "sense of diplomatic finesse," complained Donald McHenry, a U.S. ambassador to the UN during the Carter administration. Bush agreed that he was not a diplomat. His concern was what four airplanes did to America and the potential for another surprise.

"Most people don't pay attention to the oath they take when they serve the government," Andy Card said. "The oath the president takes is the simplest one of anybody in government. It's in Article Two, Section One, Clause Eight. His only obligation is to preserve, protect and defend the Constitution. Not if a majority of the people agree with you, or if the UN ratifies it, or if the French are with you."

Hadley recalled a conversation between Bush and the leader of a major ally about how to hold an alliance together. The other person said, "I think the way you do it is you consult, you show you are willing to listen to other points of view, and you try to reach a consensus."

"I agree with that," Bush said. "But I think the way to do it is to show strong leadership. You identify important issues, you are on the right side of those issues, you take a firm position, and you show you are willing to see it through. They see that confidence, it inspires them, and they come with you."

"Texans admire directness," Gonzales told me. "In briefings, the president likes you to get to the bottom line. If you can communicate in that fashion, he really appreciates it because he has information thrown at him all day long. Some people mistake directness for being a cowboy. It's actually sort of polite. It doesn't waste people's time. I think he realizes this is the only superpower in the world," Gonzales said. "If you're not going to use that power to make a positive difference, what's the point?"[137]

On February 5, Tenet sat behind Powell in the UN as the secretary of State presented the case against Iraq. He displayed images from U.S. spy satellites that had caught apparent "housecleaning" efforts at close to thirty suspected sites for making biological or chemical weapons. Just before inspectors arrived, decontamination vehicles that would be used if anything went wrong were moved. Powell played intercepts of Republican Guard officers instructing Iraqi soldiers not to refer to "nerve agents" and to hide "forbidden ammo." A "modified vehicle," according to another intercepted conversation, "should not be seen" when weapons inspectors arrived.

While Powell did not claim Iraq had nuclear weapons, he said it had been working actively to acquire them and had two of the three necessary ingredients: a bomb design and a cadre of nuclear scientists. He said Hussein was working on obtaining the last requirement, sufficient fissile material to create a nuclear explosion.

Powell pointed out that Iraq had refused to permit U-2 surveillance flights over the country and had prevented inspectors from having unfettered access to Iraqi scientists. In December 1998, UN weapons inspectors withdrew from Iraq because of its refusal to cooperate. Hussein warned scientists that they faced execution if they cooperated with inspectors, Powell said. And Powell pointed out that Iraq had not accounted for known weapons produced in the past, including an estimated 25,000 liters of anthrax and between 100 and 500 tons of other chemical weapon agents. When given a chance to declare the material, Hussein failed to do so. The concealment and deception documented by Powell led to a simple question: Why would anyone go to so much trouble to hide something unless they had something to hide?

With Rumsfeld's prodding, General Tommy R. Franks conceived a brilliant, flexible plan using the Army, Navy, Marines, Air Force, and special forces in parallel, to quickly overrun Iraq. Like Cheney, Rumsfeld had wide experience in government and in the private sector, having been a member of Congress, chief of staff in the White House, and the youngest secretary of Defense in history from 1975 to 1977. He became CEO of G.D. Searle & Co., a pharmaceutical company, and then of General Instrument Corp., a broadband transmission company.

The idea of the Iraq battle plan was to stay a step ahead of Hussein and overcome his defenses before he could issue instructions or figure out his next move. The plan relied on intelligence and technology that had not existed or was just being developed in the first Gulf War. In Desert Storm, only twenty percent of air-to-ground fighters could deliver a laser-guided bomb. In Operation Iraqi Freedom, all fighters possessed that capability. In Desert Storm, it took up to two days to photograph a target, confirm its coordinates, plan the mission, and transmit the information to a bomber crew. In the more recent conflict, with near-real-time imaging, photos and coordinates of targets were e-mailed. Using the CIA's Predator drone aircraft and other reconnaissance techniques, commanders could view the battlefield and communicate with each other in ways never experienced in the history of war.

During the planning, Hadley said, Bush pointed out that in Iraq, because it would be a liberation rather than an occupation, and because modern warfare had evolved in terms of intelligence and the accuracy of weapons, "We could hold the pillars of the regime at risk with military force and spare the civilian population. We wanted to send a message that we were liberating them from the real oppressor rather than attacking them and that we wanted to get a democratic Iraq up and running."

The plan employed just half the number of troops from coalition countries—the United States, Great Britain, Australia, Denmark, and Poland—as had been used in the first Gulf War, when 550,000 soldiers were deployed to achieve the more limited objective of expelling Iraq from Kuwait.

According to Rumsfeld, in briefings on the plan, Bush would frequently say, "Excuse me," and then bore in on something: "What about this? What about that? If this occurs, what would the approach be?" Rumsfeld said that in probing for answers, Bush "pushes people to think about things that he does not know whether or not they have thought through." As a result, Bush was prepared for complications, mistakes, and losses.

"He's a very quick study," Rumsfeld told me in his Pentagon office one Saturday afternoon. "He has an excellent sense of humor. He's rooted. He knows who he is. He's comfortable with himself. He works his way through problems with a whole lot of questions. He arrives someplace and then stays there. He doesn't waiver with the wind and how things are blowing every five minutes."[138]

At the same time, Rumsfeld said, Bush was comfortable hearing dissenting views. "I'll send things like [articles challenging his positions] to him from time to time, and he'll read them, and he'll comment on them and ask me what I thought about points in them," Rumsfeld said.

Rather than being a lackey of Cheney or Rove, Bush came up with his own ideas and ways to deal with problems relating to "the entire span" of issues at the Defense Department, Rumsfeld said.

"The press would have you believe NSC meetings are run with Rumsfeld and Powell presenting their views, and the president picks which view he favors," Steve Hadley said. "There are many times when the president comes in and says, 'We're having a problem. Let me tell you how I see this issue.' He will lay out his approach. That basically ends the discussion, and it becomes a matter of how to get it done. Or he'll listen to folks around the table and sometimes articulate a view that wasn't brought up. For the next thirty minutes, we discuss who is going to execute his policy."[139]

The policy disagreements and leaks tended to come in the execution phase, particularly at the lower levels, Hadley said. In that case, "We get them in and say, 'This is what the president wants. Let's try to resolve this.' "

Contrary to the impression conveyed by the media, "This is a guy who is very much in charge," Hadley said. "He gets a lot of input from a lot of sources, knows what he thinks, and is not shy about laying it out. The media asked if he knew by heart the names of foreign leaders of the world. Is that what you want the president to bring to foreign policy? Experts we got. What he does is bring a set of principles and convictions and the ability to see strategic opportunities and give a sense of priorities."

18

"MR. BUSH OKAY!"

On Wednesday, March 19, 2003, the CIA received information from an Iraqi agent that Saddam Hussein and his two sons would be at a compound in Baghdad called Dora Farms that night. With blue lights flashing on his security detail's SUV, George Tenet, the director of Central Intelligence, sped to the Pentagon to discuss the intelligence with Donald Rumsfeld and General Richard B. Myers, the chairman of the Joint Chiefs of Staff.

General Tommy Franks got the same heads-up from CIA officers in the field. In case Bush were to order a strike, Franks sent two F-117A stealth fighter–bombers aloft. By 3:40 P.M., Tenet, Rumsfeld, Myers, Powell, Cheney, Rice, and Andy Card had convened in the Oval Office to discuss the risks of the operation. Tenet brought with him CIA officers who briefed the president on the reliability of the Iraqi agent.

As they discussed the plan, more details came in from the Iraqi agent.

Bush had already given Franks orders to proceed with the invasion at a time of his own choosing. Now the question was whether to speed up the plans. The debate centered on the veracity of the information and the propaganda value to Saddam Hussein if the tip proved wrong.

"I was hesitant at first, to be frank with you," Bush told NBC anchor Tom Brokaw, "because I was worried that the first pictures coming out of Iraq would be a wounded grandchild of Saddam

Hussein . . . that the first images of the American attack would be death to young children."

By 7:15 P.M., Bush decided it was worth the risk. The day before, after playing cat and mouse with UN weapon inspectors for months, Hussein defiantly had rejected Bush's ultimatum that he leave the country within forty-eight hours. Calling that Hussein's final mistake, the president said, "Go."

At 9:33 P.M.—5:33 A.M. Baghdad time—two satellite-guided one-ton bombs hit the Dora Farms bunker. Warships and submarines in the Persian Gulf and Red Sea fired thirty Tomahawk cruise missiles at the compound as well. Forty-five minutes later, Bush addressed the nation from the Oval Office. "On my orders, coalition forces have begun striking selected targets of military importance," he said.

While Saddam survived, the strike was a psychological blow. The regime's command and control began to crumble.

"We went right to the heart of their inner being," Tenet told me. "Psychologically, that had to have a big effect."

Bush knew that his political career would rise or fall on the results of the war. Yet it was one of the few decisions he made without consulting Karl Rove, his political guru.

"Karl will participate in many types of decisions by giving strategic and political advice," Gonzales said. "For example, Karl may tell the president this is what we believe will be the public reaction in certain parts of the country to a particular decision. However, the decision to go to war was not driven by Karl's political advice. That's a decision the president has to make based upon what he believes is best for the national-security interests of America. In fact, I remember that in one meeting close to the time that hostilities began, there was some staff discussion in the Oval Office that we have not done a good enough job of explaining to the American people why force might be necessary in Iraq," Gonzales said. "This was based on recent polls. Someone said that we shouldn't take any action until we accomplish that goal. The president said, 'I don't care if it's twenty percent in favor and eighty percent against. We may need to do this to protect America, and if we have to do it, we're going to do it.' Taking bold and decisive action that you believe is required by circumstances no matter how unpopular is the true test of leadership and is a hallmark of this president."[140]

The danger of waiting was illustrated by what American troops found in Afghanistan.

"If we had had to wait going into Afghanistan, in all likelihood in six months or a year, al Qaeda would have had the capability of launching a chemical or biological attack," FBI Director Robert Mueller told me. "We found a nascent effort to develop a biological or chemical weapon in a Kandahar camp. Had we not gone in then, they would have had no compunction about using the weapons against women and children. Not that al Qaeda isn't seeking weapons of mass destruction in other countries. They are."

When Bush entered the White House, he began to put on a few pounds eating the desserts turned out by pastry chef Roland Mesnier. His favorite was coconut cream pie. Besides eating his own dessert, he would, if he could, snatch Condi Rice's, Andy Card's, Karen Hughes's, or Dan Bartlett's. When the war started, Bush cut out sweets and coped with the anxiety by exercising and praying.

"He knows that we're all here to serve a calling greater than self," Bush's friend and Commerce Secretary Don Evans said. "That's what he's committed his life to do. He understands that he is the person in the country, in this case really the one person in the world, who has a responsibility to protect and defend freedom."

In the final analysis, the tyranny upon which Iraq was built was its undoing. Having seen colleagues executed for giving Hussein bad news, commanders were loath to tell him the Americans were wiping out Iraqi forces. Soldiers whose motivation to fight was based on fear posed little threat. Since commands came only from Hussein, his personal secretary, his son Qusay, or his cousin Ali Hassan Tikriti, Americans' ability to wipe out military communications meant that Hussein's forces were paralyzed. Citizens who had been intimidated into turning out to cheer on Hussein's birthday were only too happy to see him go.

On Wednesday, April 9, after a series of increasingly aggressive armed reconnaissance missions through nearly every quarter of Baghdad, Iraqis in Firdos Square were the first to visibly defy the regime. As TV cameras recorded the scene, an Iraqi took a sledge hammer to a towering bronze statue of Saddam Hussein. Others pounded the statue with the soles of their shoes, a sign of disrespect in the Arab world. That gave other Iraqis, who had lived in fear of Saddam Hussein, the courage to begin trying to tear down the statue.

A Marine tank recovery vehicle finally toppled the statue of Hussein, and a young boy sat on its head as Iraqis dragged it away. The episode demonstrated that the Iraqis had been liberated. After three weeks, the war, for all practical purposes, was over. As Cheney had said, it would take weeks, not months, to topple Hussein. But the rapidity of the victory surprised everyone.

Overjoyed Iraqis welcomed the Americans. "Thank you, Mr. Bush. Thank you, Mr. Bush. Mr. Bush Okay!" an Iraqi said over and over on television. "Human Shields Go Home," a homemade sign said, referring to antiwar protesters who had gone to Baghdad hoping their presence would deter an attack. Women asked American soldiers to kiss their babies. Iraqis danced in the streets.

The critics had predicted tens of thousands of American casualties during the war. The Vietnam War took 58,000 American lives. By comparison, American troops suffered 139 casualties during the Iraq war and another 643 in the ensuing years. The critics had claimed Iraq would attack Israel and that going to war would lead to immediate terrorist attacks on the United States. When the objections proved wrong, the critics then questioned whether Iraqis—whose homeland was the cradle of civilization— could govern themselves democratically. Since diplomacy had not worked, the critics blamed Bush.

"I'm saddened that the president failed so miserably at diplomacy that we are now forced to war," Senate Minority Leader Thomas A. Daschle, a Democrat from South Dakota, said. "Saddened that we have to give up one life because this president couldn't create the kind of diplomatic effort that was so critical for our country."

Yet diplomacy had as much chance of working with Saddam Hussein as it had with Hitler. Like Bush, British Prime Minister Tony Blair had risked his political career on the decision to go to war. Acutely aware of how Neville Chamberlain, the British prime minister at the start of World War II, had naively appeased Hitler, Blair drew a line in the sand, later revealing that he had been prepared to quit his position if Parliament failed to support him.

While going into Iraq may have appeared to well-intentioned people who opposed the war to be a preemptive strike, it was a continuation of the Persian Gulf War, when the United States agreed to a cease-fire only on condition that Saddam Hussein disarm. In contrast, the United States under Clinton had used force in Bosnia, Haiti, and Kosovo without going to the UN first. No one complained. Nor did anyone mind that Hussein was sending his planes into the no-fly zones and firing on U.S. planes protecting those zones hundreds of times a year.

As in Afghanistan, just before American victory, the media and Democrats declared the United States to be stuck in a "quagmire." When victory was achieved, they said the fight had been too easy and compared American forces to bullies crushing a feeble foe. Remarkably, even after Operation Iraqi Freedom had proven successful, the critics ignored not only the traditional concerns of conservatives about protecting American security but liberals' traditional concerns about protecting human rights. Some on the far left compared Bush with Hitler.

"In maddened corners of the internet and at swastika-choked antiwar marches, Bush is shown with a Nazi uniform or a Hitler mustache," John Leo wrote in the conservative *Front Page Magazine.com*. "But does everyone on the far left believe this? Not at all. Some think that Dick Cheney is the real Hitler . . . Others think Don Rumsfeld is Hitler (both men favored mountain-top retreats, the Action Coalition of Taos points out). These comparisons are still being argued. Air Force veteran Douglas Herman, writing an op-ed piece in Florida, says Rumsfeld is more like Goering, since both men were fighter pilots, while Lyndon LaRouche decided that Cheney isn't just Hitler—he's Lady Macbeth as well."

Leo continued, "Many on the left believe that either Ari Fleischer or Karl Rove is Nazi propagandist Joseph Goebbels. Or maybe Richard Perle is related to Goebbels. The September issue of *Vanity Fair* suggested that Perle could be Goebbels' twin . . ."

But, Leo wrote, "The common charge that Bush is Mussolini is controversial—many leftists insist that the Mussolini role is reserved for Tony Blair, the junior partner of Bush's Hitler. Cartoonist Aaron McGruder said on TV that Condoleezza Rice is a murderer but failed to give her any Nazi designation—a big mistake by prevailing standards."

When asked if Iraqis were better off after the war than under Hussein, who had ordered the execution of an estimated 300,000 of his countrymen, Democratic presidential hopeful Howard Dean said, "We don't know that yet." In making such statements, Dean and other critics brushed aside the fact that liberation meant that Iraqis would no longer undergo torture by having electric prods attached to their genitals or by being given acid baths, having holes drilled into their ankles and skulls, being left naked in refrigerators for days, having their tongues cut out and their ears cut off, or being forced to watch gang rapes of their wives and sisters.

"I have absolutely no regret about my vote on this war [opposing it]," said Nancy Pelosi, the Democratic House minority leader from California. "The same questions remain: The cost in human lives; the cost to our budget, probably $100 billion. We could have probably brought down that statue for a lot less. The cost to our economy. But the most important question at this time, now that we're toward the end of it, is: What is the cost to the war on terrorism?"

Even as Pelosi spoke, the CIA was interrogating Khalid Shaikh Mohammed, bin Laden's operations chief, and rolling up dozens of al Qaeda operatives as a result. Among them was Walid Ba'Attash, one of bin Laden's top lieutenants who was believed to have played a crucial role in the bombing of the *USS Cole* and the attacks of 9/11. Less than a week later, the CIA and Pakistani authorities stopped an al Qaeda plot to fly an explosive-laden plane into the U.S. consulate in Karachi, arresting two al Qaeda members who had had roles in the September 11 plot and the bombing of the *USS Cole*.

Based on information from the CIA's interrogation of Mohammed, the FBI secretly arrested Iyman Faris, an Ohio truck driver, for plotting with al Qaeda to bring down New York's Brooklyn Bridge by cutting its suspension cables while launching a simultaneous unspecified attack on Washington. Faris, a Kashmir-born naturalized American citizen, met with bin Laden and transported cash, cell phones, and other supplies for al Qaeda. After performing surveillance of the bridge, Faris determined that security was too tight and that trying to sever the bridge cables with cutting torches was not feasible. He sent a coded e-mail message to al Qaeda saying, "The weather is too hot."

After his arrest, Faris agreed to plead guilty to providing material support to a terrorist organization. He got twenty years in prison. The arrest demonstrated both the success of the war on terror and the impact of increased domestic security.

19

SIXTEEN WORDS

On May 1, 2003, Bush donned a military flight jacket and landed on the deck of the aircraft carrier *USS Abraham Lincoln* to proclaim victory in Iraq and to thank the troops. To Bush and the military, it was a patriotic gesture, one that came from the heart. Just as he showed appreciation to the Secret Service agents, military aides, and maids and butlers around him, Bush became overwhelmed with emotion when he thought of the sacrifices American men and women were making to defend the American way of life. Bush constantly visited troops in the United States to show his gratitude for their efforts.

But to Democrats and liberal critics, Bush's well-orchestrated landing on the carrier was an exploitation of the war for the "momentary spectacle of a speech," as Senator Robert C. Byrd, a Democrat from West Virginia, put it. Byrd pronounced himself "deeply troubled" by Bush's "flamboyant showmanship."

If the Democrats were "tone deaf," as a *Washington Post* editorial described them, Bush remained unfazed by the criticism. "It was," Bush said afterward, "an honor for me to go on the *USS Abraham Lincoln*. I appreciate the chance to thank our troops. It was an unbelievably positive experience."

On the carrier, Bush warned that "difficult work" remained. That would prove to be an understatement.

"There were obviously some things that surprised us," Steve Hadley said. "We had planned to use some Iraqi army units to rebuild the country and help provide security. But the army melted away. Most of the Iraqi military equipment got taken or looted.

There was extensive looting. That was a surprise." The fact that the country only had half the electrical generating power it needed was also a surprise.

At the same time, without being clairvoyant, the Bush administration had no way to foresee every problem that Iraq would pose after the war. The press covered the aftermath like a political campaign, focusing on setbacks and charges and countercharges. Reporters loved to try to put Bush on the defensive by prefacing their questions, "What can you tell the families of the soldiers who have died?" A variant was: "What can you tell the American people about how many American soldiers will die?"

Unlike the Vietnam war, the war in Iraq was fought by soldiers who volunteered to serve. They understood what they were fighting for and strongly supported Bush. Bush's response to the loaded questions was always the same: "We will stay the course until the job is done."

While problems remained, when most people in Iraq were asked whether life had improved since the war, they would answer that, of course, things were better.

"Policy experts say the Middle East is an exception to the notion that people desire democracy," Hadley said. "The president says he doesn't believe that. It's like the soft bigotry of low expectations about whether blacks and Hispanics can learn to read. It's unseemly and wrong."[141]

After a dinner with Japanese Prime Minister Junichiro Koizumi in Tokyo in October 2003, Bush turned to Rice and said, "I was thinking that had we not gotten it right after World War II and managed to build a strong democratic partnership in Japan, that conversation about how to manage international policies in partnership with Japan would never have taken place. One day an American president is going to be talking with an Iraqi president about how to manage some problem in the world. They will both be really glad that we did what we did in creating a democratic Iraq."

As problems in Iraq continued and American soldiers were being killed, the media portrayed the Bush White House as dysfunctional, with the staff feuding and Rumsfeld and Powell sparring with each other. Inside, it was a different story.

"I've never been more optimistic," Bush told Margaret Spellings in the Oval Office one day, as the media was busy portraying the reconstruction effort in Iraq as hopeless. "We're doing great."

If Rumsfeld and Powell were at war, nobody had told them. Every morning at 7:15, they held a conference call with Rice.

"My husband and I went to a small dinner at the Rumsfelds' home," Margaret Spellings said. "Powell was there. They very much like each other. They just have a different worldview on a lot of things and a different portfolio. The president is perfectly comfortable with having all points of view represented. I think there are people who view everything that is going on in this administration with a different shade of lens."[142]

"We are all strong personalties," Rice told me. "We have strong views. These are hard issues where the answers are not always self-evident. We have really great and robust debates. But there is one thing that everyone on this NSC understands: there is one president. When the president has decided what he wants to do, we stop debating it, and we start doing it."[143]

Illustrating the point, Powell pointed to a report by author Peter Stothard, who had been granted real-time access to Tony Blair for four weeks. In his book *Thirty Days*, Stothard, former editor of *The Times* of London, recounted exchanges between Bush and Rice following a summit meeting on postwar Iraq between Bush and Blair in Belfast, Northern Ireland, in April 2003. Blair wanted to describe the UN role as being of "vital importance." Bush agreed to say the UN would play a "vital role." In the ensuing news conference, Bush mentioned "vital role" eight times.

"You were brilliant," British Foreign Secretary Jack Straw told Bush after the news conference.

But Rice thought Bush might be going overboard. In his book, Stothard said, "Rice begins gently to suggest to her boss that some of their colleagues back in Washington might not be best pleased. When she becomes more vigorous," Stothard wrote, "Bush leads her away from the crowd. He looks at first concerned, then a bit frosty." Later, at a photo session, "Rice continues her commentary on the excess vitality of the press conference," Stothard wrote. " 'Ease it, Condi, ease it,' says the president. The dispute ceases."

Rice got the message. Shortly thereafter, she was sitting on a bench under a large tapestry of Don Quixote tilting at windmills. She was talking on her mobile phone to Washington.

" 'Yes' she says firmly, 'a vital role for the UN. I just want to make sure that the DOD [Department of Defense] doesn't say anything wrong about this. Yes, it's important that we all use the same language.' "

"Are there bureaucratic disagreements? Sure," Powell said. "There have always been bureaucratic disagreements in every administration I have served in. And there have been some stiff ones in this administration because it is a conservative administration, and there are those in the administration who are conservative, there are those who are very conservative, and there are those who might be considered conservative but more toward the moderate side, and that would include me. I have tended to be the one who talks about reaching out and being inclusive, and sometimes that causes debates, but nothing . . . the president doesn't resolve."

"The president talks about how people often come into the Oval Office and stammer and can't say anything," Gonzales said. "He says it would be disastrous if his staff were like that. There has to be a variety of viewpoints. It's healthy."

With the war over, the media began running a barrage of stories questioning the rationale for going to war. Many of the stories relied on the selective use of facts. Instead of connecting the dots, the articles presented them dot by dot, as though the entire reason for toppling Saddam Hussein rested on a single element of the case for war. For example, stories that questioned whether Hussein had tried to buy uranium from Niger did not say that Hussein already possessed enough uranium to build a hundred nuclear bombs or point out that, since the end of the war, an Iraqi scientist led CIA officers to buried components needed to produce the only missing ingredient for making a nuclear bomb—fissile material. Experts said the buried cache would have allowed Hussein to cut years from the time needed to reconstitute his nuclear-weapons program.

The biggest flap arose over Bush's sixteen-word statement in his State of the Union speech that British intelligence believed Saddam had been trying to buy uranium from Niger. To be sure, George Tenet, as director of Central Intelligence, did not believe the information was solid enough to include in Bush's speeches. Tenet had succeeded in cutting a reference to the British report from a presidential speech in October 2002, but the reference slipped into Bush's State of the Union address on January 28, 2003. Yet when Bush said, "The British government has learned that Saddam Hussein recently sought significant quantities of uranium from Africa," the statement was true.

In fact, MI6, the British intelligence service, still believed that its intelligence about Niger was correct. Contrary to news reports, its information did not rely on bogus documents. Nor did Powell mention Niger eight days after the State of the Union in his formal presentation to the United Nations. Few news stories mentioned these points. Yet Democratic presidential candidates and those who had opposed the war pounced on the reference in the State of the Union address as evidence that Bush was purposely fabricating intelligence to support going to war. A Democratic attack ad declared that "It's time to tell the truth" and ran a video clip of Bush's sentence, omitting the critical words: "The British government has learned that . . ."

Tenet stepped up to the plate and said he took overall responsibility for the fact that, when reviewing drafts of the president's speech, his agency did not object more vigorously to citing the Niger report. Then Steve Hadley took the blame, saying that when he approved the material used in the State of the Union speech, he had no memory of the previous two CIA memos saying the evidence on the Niger claim was weak. Thus including the reference to Niger was an error, much like errors large and small that were corrected daily by the same papers that trumpeted what the *Wall Street Journal* called Bush's "non-lie" as the most important story of the day.

"Don't worry," the author e-mailed a senior CIA official during the flap. "If Britney Spears admits she slept with a second guy, the media will lose interest in the sixteen words."

"If she does admit it, we'll take responsibility," the official e-mailed back.

The *Washington Post*, in a June 5, 2003, story by Walter Pincus and Dana Priest, created an entirely new controversy when it said visits by Cheney and Lewis "Scooter" Libby, his chief of staff, to the CIA to question analysts created "an environment in which some analysts felt they were being pressured to make their assessments fit with the Bush administration policy objectives." However, the third paragraph of that same story said, "Other agency officials said they were not influenced by the visits from the vice president's office, and some said they welcomed them." Nor did the story claim that the alleged pressure actually changed any CIA assessment.

If the lead of the story had honestly said, "Some CIA analysts felt pressure from visits by Vice President Cheney to make their assessments fit with the Bush administration's policy objectives, while other analysts said they were not influenced by the visits and welcomed them," the story, which ran on page one, likely would have been laughed out of the paper.

Even though Hill staffers interviewed more than a hundred analysts after the war, none ever came forward to say he or she had felt any pressure. By questioning analysts, Cheney was doing his job, making sure he and Bush understood the intelligence before going to war. Yet the claim that the Bush administration had politicized CIA intelligence and lied about the reasons for going to war became accepted truth in liberal circles.

Not to be outdone, the *New York Times*, in a June 9, 2003, page-one story by James Risen, said that two of the highest-ranking al Qaeda leaders in American custody, Abu al-Zarqawi and Khalid Sheikh Mohammed, had said the terrorist organization "did not work jointly with the Iraqi government of Saddam Hussein." The implication was the Bush administration had lied again. In fact, the administration never said bin Laden and Hussein were working jointly. Rather, at the UN, Powell said, "Iraq today harbors a deadly terrorist network headed by Abu Musab al-Zarqawi, an associate and collaborator of Osama bin Laden and his al Qaeda lieutenants." While the section of Iraq where the associate operated was outside Hussein's control, it was under the control of one of his agents, who had allowed al-Zarqawi to train terrorists in the use of poisons and explosives at the camp. This bin Laden associate allegedly masterminded the assassination of American diplomat Lawrence Foley in Amman in October 2002.

Nor, in addressing the terrorism issue, did the media refer to the fact that, on the outskirts of Baghdad, a Marine unit found a terrorist training camp operated by the Palestine Liberation Front. Documents showed that Iraq had sold weapons to the terrorist group as recently as January. Other troops found eight hundred black leather vests stuffed with explosives and ball bearings. Empty hangers suggested some of the lethal vests were already on the backs of would-be suicide bombers.

Going after Saddam Hussein was indeed part of the war on terror.

If there was any question about media bias, it was dispelled when the British House of Commons Intelligence and Security Committee reviewed the MI6 intelligence about the Niger claim and concluded in September 2003 that, based on the information MI6 gathered, the finding was "reasonable." Moreover, the committee, which is well-regarded by members of Parliament, also said MI6 was justified in continuing to claim that the intelligence was credible.

The story reporting the committee's conclusion appeared in the United States as a separate story in only one paper—the *Wall Street Journal*. The *Washington Post* devoted one paragraph to the conclusion near the end of a twenty-two paragraph story. The *New York Times*, which had run fifty-six stories mentioning Bush's State of the Union address and the Niger claim, had no story on the British Parliament report. It was as if Soviet-style press censorship had been imposed on the country—except pro-government news rather than antigovernment news was being suppressed.

Other stories portrayed the intelligence leading up to the war as flawed simply because it was not evidence that could be presented in a court of law. Intelligence is information gleaned from spies, surveillance satellites, and interceptions of communications. To make sense of it, analysts often must draw conclusions based on clues that point in a particular direction. If the information were solid evidence—say, a videotape of Saddam Hussein unleashing anthrax on a neighboring state—there would be no need for intelligence in the first place.

Al Gore chimed in with a speech in which he "validated just about every conspiratorial theory of the antiwar left," as a *Washington Post* editorial put it. While Gore had previously described Iraq as a "virulent threat in a class by itself," now he said that Bush designed the war "to benefit friends and supporters." He said the war was waged in part to secure "our continued access to oil," a claim later echoed in a December 2003 tape by bin Laden himself. And Gore said the war was started because of "false impressions" that Hussein was "on the verge of building nuclear bombs," that he was "about to give the terrorists poison gas and deadly germs," and that he was "partly responsible for the 9/11 attacks."

The "impressions" were, in fact, misimpressions. To be sure, a majority of Americans thought that Bush had said Saddam Hussein was involved in the September 11 attacks. But they confused Bush's simple point that, after 9/11, America must never again be in the position of passively waiting for an attack by a country like Iraq. It was like a homeowner whose friend has been burglarized and decides to have a security alarm installed for himself. The fact that he took action to protect himself does not mean that he thinks he was burglarized.

"After September 11, the doctrine of containment just doesn't hold any water, as far as I'm concerned," Bush said with typical bluntness. "We must deal with threats before they hurt the American people again."

Nor had Bush said that Hussein was "on the verge of building nuclear bombs" or was "about to give the terrorists poison gas and deadly germs." In fact, it was Al Gore who said in September 2002 that, based on what he had learned as vice president, Hussein had "stored secret supplies of biological and chemical weapons throughout his country."

In his interim report, David Kay, the leader of the United States hunt for Iraq's weapons of mass destruction, concluded that, rather than having been reconstituted, Saddam's nuclear weapons program was rudimentary. Rather than still producing deadly chemical agents, such as mustard and VX, Kay reported that Iraq did not have a large, centrally controlled chemical weapons program after 1991.

But Kay also found significant illegal weapons programs that were not discovered by UN inspectors, demonstrating that Saddam was aggressively violating UN Resolution 1441, which offered him a "final opportunity" to voluntarily disarm. Kay said his team "discovered dozens of WMD-related program activities and significant amounts of equipment that Iraq concealed from the United Nations during the inspections that began in 2002." They included a "clandestine network of laboratories" suitable for producing biological weapons; a prison lab that may have been used to test biological agents on humans; strains of biological organisms concealed in a scientist's home; and documents and equipment hidden in scientists' homes for enriching uranium. Interviews with Iraqi scientists and other government officials revealed that Saddam remained intent on resuming nuclear-weapon development at some future point. Finally, the Kay report said the team discovered extensive Iraqi programs for producing banned long-range ballistic missiles, some of which continued even while inspectors were in Iraq, along with programs to produce unmanned aerial vehicles that could be used to disperse biological or chemical agents. At the same time, Kay found extensive efforts to erase evidence of weapon programs from hard drives and to sanitize equipment to remove traces of proscribed weapon development.

Given Saddam Hussein's history of using weapons of mass destruction and invading Iraq, those findings alone were enough to require military action. By waiting, the United States would have faced the certainty that Iraq would be further along in its weapons-of-mass-destruction program. Yet, rather than focusing on the dozens of new programs Kay had discovered, the media emphasized the fact that no stockpiles had been found, which at that point was not news.

After resigning in January 2004, Kay morphed into a talking head, displaying an astounding ability to provide ammunition to both sides of the debate. On the one hand, Kay said, "We were almost all wrong" about Saddam's capabilities before the war. He called for an investigation of the CIA, which he said was responsible for the failure. On the other hand, on National Public Radio, he said essentially what he had said in his interim report: that Saddam remained intent on developing weapons of mass destruction, that he had a "large number" of "substantial" programs to do so, and that he could quickly have "resumed large-scale production" of weapons like mustard gas. While he said he thought it was unlikely stockpiles would be found, Kay said he did not know if that was because they did not exist or because records had been destroyed or stockpiles were contained in shipments to Syria before the war. It was possible, Kay said in other interviews, that small caches of weapons were hidden in Iraq and will never be found. Iraqi generals all thought Saddam had chemical weapons and that they would be used against American troops, Kay said.

In some cases, Kay said, Iraqi scientists misled Hussein into thinking they were working on weapons-of-mass-destruction programs, when, in fact, the money had been corruptly diverted to other uses. But Kay said that Saddam was a threat, and he did not disagree with the decision to go to war. In fact, Kay said, near the end of the regime, Saddam was so out of touch with reality that Iraq was even more of a threat because terrorists could have more easily appropriated ongoing weapons programs, such as production of ricin, a deadly chemical, or mustard gas.

"I think it shows that Iraq was a very dangerous place," Kay told the *New York Times*. "The country had the technology, the ability to produce, and there were terrorist groups passing through the country—and no central control."

The press corps, located under the nose of the White House, usually did not have the foggiest idea what was going on inside the West Wing. Instead, reporters often created impressions that bore little relation to reality. Yet those same members of the media castigated the CIA for not knowing more about the state of Iraqi weapons than Saddam and Iraqi generals themselves did in a country where cooperating with the CIA resulted in execution.

Still, the failure to find weapons of mass destruction initially was embarrassing. After Kay's publicity blitz, Bush decided to appoint a bipartisan presidential commission to study not only the intelligence on Iraq but how intelligence on other emerging threats could be strengthened.

In assessing what happened in Iraq, Richard J. Kerr, a former deputy director of Central Intelligence, was in a unique position. He headed a panel of four former senior CIA officials chosen, at Rumsfeld's suggestion, months before the war started. The job of the panel was to evaluate retrospectively what CIA and military intelligence got right and what they got wrong, with the purpose of improving intelligence and its use by policy makers.

"Based on what I saw in the intelligence from the beginning of the war, they had intelligence that went back into the Gulf War and when inspectors were there, but it continued to be reinforced by more current information," Kerr told me. "It was less firm but it certainly reinforced the earlier judgments that programs were under way. There was no evidence to the contrary. There was no evidence that would alert someone or even hint that the programs had been stopped. So it would have been hard to conclude other than that the programs were continuing. I believe the information was strong enough to make those judgments."[144]

Kerr said the fact that Iraqi generals expected that chemical weapons were going to be used was significant. It may have meant that the Iraqis had chemical weapons but chose not to use them, or that they destroyed them as the Americans advanced. The CIA had judged that Iraq had a hundred to five hundred tons of chemical weapons—enough to fill a swimming pool or a warehouse. Enough biological weapons to kill tens of thousands of people could be contained in a vial. Finding such items in a country larger than California, when Iraqis were still afraid of coming forward, was difficult at best. Millions of documents still had not been reviewed.

"There was some initial reporting that they dumped them in the river to try to get rid of them," Kerr said. He said it was also possible that Iraqi scientists, to curry favor, lied to Saddam Hussein about the extent of the programs.

"They were quite good at deception and denying information," he said. "That led us to the conclusion they were carefully covering up the programs they had under way. They ran away and concealed things, as Powell said at the UN. But what they were covering up may not have been as significant as we thought."

On the one hand, Kerr said, the analysis was sound. On the other hand, there was not enough information to pinpoint the extent of Saddam's weapon programs. One reason was that Clinton insisted that spy satellites focus primarily on military targets instead of tracking Hussein's program to develop weapons of mass destruction. The president wanted to protect U.S. planes, which the Iraqis were trying to shoot down in "no-fly" zones, the areas of southern and northern Iraq where Hussein's planes were prohibited from flying. The restriction had been imposed to keep Iraq from attacking opposition Kurdish and Shiite Muslim groups from the air.

"The no-fly effort made tracking Iraq's weapons of mass destruction difficult indeed," James Simon, the former CIA assistant director for administration, said. "The Clinton administration told the military to take no, repeat no, chances of losing a pilot. So every effort was subordinated to that goal. The consequence was years of indifferent coverage of Iraqi WMD. We all knew that, sooner or later, this would be the issue and we would never make up for the lost opportunities. We needed more SIGINT and IMINT [signal and image intelligence] from satellites to do the job with confidence. There was outrage throughout the intelligence community at an administration that seemed not to be able to set clear priorities."

After Bush became president, he approved Tenet's proposal to reallocate satellite coverage to track Iraq's weapon programs. Yet because of cutbacks proposed by Senator John F. Kerry and other Democrats in the 1990s, the CIA's budget was eighteen percent lower after inflation than it had been a decade earlier. The cutbacks decimated the CIA's ability to penetrate rogue states and terrorist organizations with human spies. The number of CIA clandestine officers had been cut by twenty-five percent. That cut was on top of severe cuts previously made in the clandestine service by Stansfield Turner, Jimmy Carter's CIA director. At the same time, Democrats in Congress and John Deutch, Clinton's director of Central Intelligence, were imposing a risk-averse culture on the CIA.

"Lack of enough information is not unique in intelligence programs," Kerr said. "That is the nature of intelligence. It is never perfect. But given what was known, coming to the alternative conclusion that Saddam was not a threat was not an acceptable option. He clearly had weapons programs and clearly harbored terrorists."

20

BUSHIE

By June 2003, the name George W. Bush inspired caricatures far beyond the domain of political cartoonists. According to presidential scholars attending a conference at Princeton University, Bush was a right-wing cowboy and religious zealot who appealed to "Joe Six-Pack" types who don't read newspapers or magazines. In the jargon of substance abuse treatment, Bush was described as a "dry drunk" who substituted a child-like Christian faith for what he really needed, a twelve-step program. At a similar conference at the University of London, attendees portrayed him as a scheming warmonger who was refashioning America into a "garrison state."

The caricatures amazed and perplexed Bush's friends. Unlike other recent presidents, who were surrounded by new-found friends and hangers-on, Bush had dozens of genuine, close friends going back to childhood.

Bill Clinton surrounded himself with Hollywood stars like Barbra Streisand and Tom Hanks and turned the White House into a fund-raising machine. He often gave receptions for as many as 650 guests, mostly potential contributors. Clinton averaged more than six state dinners a year. In contrast, in the first three years of Bush's presidency, Bush gave four state dinners for no more than 130 guests. These were in honor of Mexican President Vicente Fox, Polish President Aleksander Kwasniewski, Philippine President Gloria Macapagal-Arroyo, and Kenyan President Mwai Kibaki.

Bush and Laura preferred private dinners with old friends like

Clay Johnson and his wife Anne. The only people Bush invited to sleep over at the White House and Camp David were family members, true friends, and dignitaries Bush felt comfortable with, like Tony Blair.

Bush defined a friend as "someone who is loyal. An acquaintance is someone who might not be loyal. Loyal means that I'm with you when times are good or times are bad." While some became campaign contributors, Bush's friends had known him long before anyone dreamed he would become president. Most were from Texas or Yale.

If Bush were the hayseed the media portrayed, he had fooled all the sophisticated and accomplished people who remained loyal to him over the years. As Cervantes wrote in *Don Quixote*, "Tell me thy company, and I'll tell thee what thou art." Bush's friends from Skull and Bones alone represented a *Who's Who* in their respective fields. There were, for example, Dr. Rex Cowdry, a former acting director of the National Institute of Mental Health, whose wife Donna Patterson had been a deputy assistant attorney general in the Clinton administration; Dr. G. Gregory Gallico, a surgeon and associate professor at Harvard Medical School who invented synthetic skin used on burn patients; Robert D. McCallum, Jr., a Rhodes Scholar who was the associate attorney general; and Don Schollander, an Olympic swimming champion.

After succeeding in their fields, some of Bush's friends had taken public-interest jobs. Dr. Cowdry became medical director of the National Alliance for the Mentally Ill, an advocate for people with severe mental problems, such as schizophrenia and bipolar illness. Clay Johnson, after finishing Yale, obtaining a master's degree in management from MIT, and being president of Horchow Mail Order, became chief operating officer of the Dallas Museum of Art.

Having been offended by what he saw as its liberal orthodoxy and intellectual snobbery, Bush had had no relationship with Yale after his graduation until his friend Roland Betts, a Yale board member, began working on a rapprochement. When a Yale classmate asked him to contribute to the twenty-fifth reunion class book, Bush responded, "I don't have such great feelings about the place right now." When he was Texas governor, Bush turned down a prestigious Chubb Fellowship from Yale. But Bush finally agreed to give the 300th commencement address at the university in May 2001. Bush was proud that his daughter Barbara was going to Yale. The night before the commencement, he donned a tuxedo for a dinner given by Yale President Richard C. Levin.

"He was returning to an estranged family," Betts said. "It's hard to do. Of course Bush was nervous."

When Bush began speaking to the students at 12:05 P.M. on May 21, he reflected on receiving his degree thirty-three years earlier.

"Just barely!" a heckler shouted.

Protesters waved signs: "Execute Justice, Not People" and "Got Arsenic?" But Bush plowed ahead and won over the students with his self-effacing humor.

"To those of you who received honors, awards, and distinctions, I say, well done," the president said. "And to the C students I say, you, too, can be president of the United States," he said to laughter and applause. "A Yale degree is worth a lot, as I often remind Dick Cheney who studied here, but left a little early. So now we know—if you graduate from Yale, you become president. If you drop out, you get to be vice president."

Bush looked at Levin and said, "I want to give credit where credit is due. I want the entire world to know this: Everything I know about the spoken word, I learned right here at Yale." Even some of the protesters laughed.

Bush noted that this was his first time back in quite a while. "I'm sure that each of you will make your own journey back at least a few times in your life," he said. "If you're like me, you won't remember everything you did here," he said to laughter. "That can be a good thing. But there will be some people, and some moments, you will never forget."

As a student, Bush said, "I tried to keep a low profile. It worked. Last year, the *New York Times* interviewed John Morton Blum because the record showed I had taken one of his courses. Casting his mind's eye over the parade of young faces down through the years, Professor Blum said, and I quote, 'I don't have the foggiest recollection of him.'" But, Bush said, "I remember Professor Blum. And I still recall his dedication and high standards of learning."

On May 30, 2003, Bush held a reception at the White House for five hundred of his classmates as part of the thirty-fifth reunion of the Yale Class of '68. The reunion was supposed to be on the South Lawn, but rain forced it inside. On the menu were filet mignon, gulf shrimp with mango jalapeño salsa, bay scallops from Connecticut, and hominy and poblano casserole.

Bush reveled in greeting his classmates, who were impressed that he remembered their names. The event was supposed to end at 9:00 P.M., but Bush stayed up beyond his bedtime and continued the party until just before eleven.

Clay Johnson, who remembered how his roommate at Yale would select his dress for the day from dirty T-shirts on the floor, noticed that since becoming president, Bush had upgraded his suits. Now many were tailored. Johnson figured that Bush considered dressing well part of the job. Other than that, Bush seemed to be the same person he knew at Andover and Yale.

"My roommate was Don A. Barrows, a Yale fullback and Ivy League Player of the Year," said Tomlinson G. Rauscher, one of the guests. "He had cancer and couldn't go to the reunion. After the reunion, I wrote a letter to Bush to thank him. I said, 'By the way, could you send a photo to Dan?' He died three weeks later. I spoke at his memorial service. It turned out Bush had written a handwritten letter to him. He wished him the best. His family was so appreciative. Bush did not know him personally. It shows he has lot of character."[145]

Because they were from out of town, Bush invited seven of his close Yale friends and their wives to stay over that night at the White House. The next morning, they had breakfast with Bush and Laura. The guests illustrated both the caliber and diversity of Bush's friends. One of them, lawyer Roland Betts, was a former Democrat. After graduating from Yale, he worked for five years as a teacher at P.S. 201, a public school in central Harlem under local control. Betts became an assistant principal and also headed a not-for-profit teacher-training program, which recruited Lois Phifer, an African-American teacher. After several months of having coffee together, they began dating and eventually married, to their parents' initial distress. They lived in a basement apartment on West 102nd Street in Manhattan.

In 1975, Betts left Harlem and wrote *Acting Out*, a book about the frustrations of working in a big urban school. On his wife's salary, he attended Columbia Law School and negotiated his own book contract. That led him, upon graduating, to become an entertainment lawyer with Paul, Weiss, Rifkind, Wharton & Garrison. Leaving to finance movies, he started his own company, Silver Screen Production, which devised a new strategy for pooling the resources of many investors. The company attracted the attention of Disney Co. executives, and Disney and Betts's company wound up producing seventy-five films. Betts made sure his company retained the rights to the films, which included blockbusters like *Pretty Woman, Beauty and the Beast*, and *The Little Mermaid*. When Disney severed its ties to Betts's company in 1991, it bought back the rights to the films, and Betts and his partner split $100 million. They created Chelsea Piers, the sports and entertainment complex on Manhattan's West Side. When Bush wanted to take over the Texas Rangers, Betts became its largest investor.

Now Betts and his wife own the building where they once lived in the basement, as well as other homes in Connecticut, Wyoming, and New Mexico. Betts was one of the original Pioneers who raised more than $100,000 for Bush's presidential campaign.

Donald Etra, another guest at the White House after the Yale reunion, was a lawyer in Los Angeles whose clients have included actors Eddie Murphy and Fran Drescher. An orthodox Jew, Etra was a liberal Democrat who coauthored the 1974 book *Citibank* when he was a Nader's Raider. Another guest, Robert Dieter, was a professor at the University of Colorado Law School and a former Democrat. Bush appointed him to the board of the Legal Services Corporation, which provides legal assistance in civil cases to low-income individuals. Muhammed Saleh, a Timex vice president, was a Moslem from Jordan. Clark "Sandy" Randt, Jr., a lawyer, was a Foreign Service officer and fluent speaker of Mandarin. Bush named Randt, an expert on Chinese law, ambassador to China. Dr. Kenneth S. Cohen was an Atlanta dentist. In addition, Bush invited the reunion chair, William H. Baker, to stay over.

Many of Bush's friends had views that were polar opposites to

Bush's on particular issues. Betts, for example, supported abortion rights, while Bush was antiabortion.

"I think he really enjoys [the conversations]," Betts said. "I think he enjoys somebody who is not saying the same thing [as he]."

As a criminal defense lawyer, Etra was opposed to many of the provisions of the Patriot Act. Several times since 9/11, Etra had discussed his reservations with Bush. Etra said he thought that, rather than authorizing the FBI to wiretap an individual at any phone, a judge should have to approve each telephone number to be tapped.

"He listens carefully, and we agree to disagree," Etra, a former assistant U.S. attorney in Los Angeles, told me. "That doesn't inhibit our friendship. I'm a liberal Democrat. I was a Nader's Raider. But he's never held that against me."[146]

Etra attended Bush's wedding in Midland, and Bush attended Etra's wedding in Los Angeles. They toured the Holocaust Museum together, and two years later, Bush named him to the U.S. Holocaust Memorial Council.

Like other Bush friends, Etra suffered with forbearance the portrayal of Bush in the press, a reflection of Bush's own posture.

"He knows that in certain journalistic circles, he will never come out well," Etra said. "That's the nature of politics. You don't want to see a friend hurt. But that's part of the territory. His concern is accomplishing what he wants to accomplish."

Because of the way they felt the press treated Bush and twisted their comments when he first became president, Bush's friends rarely talked about him to the media unless urged to do so by the White House.

When Etra stayed at the White House, Bush made sure he was served kosher food. Back when Bush's father was vice president, Etra was to attend a wedding in Washington on a Saturday. Bush invited him to stay at the White House so he could walk to the wedding. Orthodox Jews do not drive on the Sabbath.

"My four kids were his guests at the White House for dinner," Etra said. "It was just our family and Craig Stapleton, who is ambassador to the Czech Republic and is married to Bush's cousin Debbie. The president engaged the children, who ranged in age from nine to fifteen, in subjects from appreciation of art to Midwest politics to the joys and travails of public service."

On a different occasion, at a lunch of pizza and grilled-cheese sandwiches at the White House, Bush turned to Etra's eleven-year-old daughter. Addressing her as Anna, he asked her opinion on the subject they were discussing. When Laura pointed out that the girl was Dorothy, not Anna, Bush said, "I am so sorry, Dorothy. I hope you won't take offense that I called you by your sister's name."

Dorothy responded: "Mr. President, would you mind if I called you Jeb?"[147]

Etra's acquaintances sometimes tried to take advantage of his special access.

"People say, 'Could you tell him this?' " Etra said. "I explain I am not the president. He is president. All we are is friends."

"I've seen friends come to Camp David or for dinner at the White House," Clay Johnson said, "and they will engage him on some policy issue, a bill or a foreign matter. He'll stop sometimes and say, 'Are you lobbying me?' So I never initiate anything unless I declare up front, 'I have a suggestion for you.' If he wants my opinion, he'll ask it. You don't take advantage of the relationship. He's very sensitive to what people's motivations are," Johnson said. "He doesn't want to be used."[148]

"People in that position need friendships that are nonpartisan," said Dr. Cowdry, the psychiatrist who was Bush's friend from Skull and Bones. "I don't offer political opinions unless asked. But he always makes time for friends. In the busiest times, he'll take time to call friends who have been hospitalized or had accidents. Being president is a preposterous way to live. That's why he goes to Camp David and Texas."[149]

"He realizes that he lives in a bubble and that the position of president of the U.S. is quite awesome and is off-putting and scary to many people," Etra said. "He tries to overcome that and make it clear to his friends he is the same person he was before he was president, and he hopes to be that same person when he is no longer president."

Since Bush does not use e-mail, friends keep in touch by phone.

"Most White House e-mail is a presidential record, and he

made a decision that he did not want to have an e-mail record of communications likely to be very deliberative or personal," Alberto Gonzales said. "Communications to his two daughters, for example, would not be presidential records and therefore would be exempt from disclosure. But he decided he didn't want to mess with it. He said, 'I don't want to worry about what a presidential record is and what it is not.' "150

"I call Ashley Estes [Bush's secretary], or he'll call here at home," Terry Johnson, his Yale roommate, said. "Or I send e-mail to him through her. When he calls me at my home, it's, 'How many fish have you caught?' "151

Bush's Midland friends, Dr. Charles Younger, an orthopedic surgeon, and Robert McCleskey, an accountant, were used to seeing Bush drive around his Crawford ranch in a pickup truck, his jeans dirty, his T-shirt ripped, wearing a grimy baseball cap. But when they attended the brunch at the White House after the inauguration, they made up their minds they would call their friend "Mr. President."

"You've got your friend that happens to be president," McCleskey said. "But the enormity of that office—it's hard to connect it with him. We made up our minds that when he's coming through the [greeting] line, we were going to say, 'President Bush,' but we all said 'George.' It's just going to take a while to train ourselves."152

Laura Bush called her husband Bushie, and he called her Bushie as well, symbolizing an equality in their relationship. Like everyone else around Bush, Laura was direct. They discussed issues, and she would occasionally look at a speech and say, "Oh, I don't think you ought to say that."

"Laura is his greatest sounding board," Gonzales said. "She doesn't have an agenda other than being a good spouse and supporting the president. Obviously, like other first ladies, she has projects she is interested in, such as promoting literacy and libraries."

"She's a good barometer," Clay Johnson said. "She offers advice. When he said bin Laden is wanted 'dead or alive,' she said, 'Whoa, Bushie!' But she is not a meddler."

Laura did not pretend to be in lockstep with her husband on

214 / A MATTER OF CHARACTER

every issue. On abortion, "If I differed with my husband, I'm not going to tell you," she once said. Several times, Laura Bush has hinted at a strain of pacifism. After 9/11, she said, "I knew the president would do the right thing, but like a lot of women, I was hoping that was going to be nothing." More recently, she said the decision to go to war in Iraq was "wrenching" but necessary to protect U.S. security.

"Laura reins him in," Terry Johnson said. "She is a good foil for him. He is active and assertive and go-get-'em."[153]

Unlike Hillary Clinton, who made a disparaging remark about being a homemaker and baking cookies, Laura cooked chili and shared her cookie recipes, which appeared on the White House website—www.whitehouse.gov. Her rich recipe for Cowboy Cookies included cinnamon, vanilla, coconut, pecans, oats, and chocolate chips.

In private, Laura wore blue jeans. In public, she wore suits designed by Michael Faircloth of Dallas, who met her when she was campaigning for her husband's first term as governor. For formal White House events, she wore gowns designed by Arnold Scaasi. Her hairstyle has remained the same over the years.

"I've never really been that interested in clothes," she has said.

Bush called Laura a great political wife—the "perfect complement to a camera hog like me." While she was often described as shy, Laura was, in fact, a skillful, articulate host who made people feel comfortable. She liked to tease and make subtle, one-line comebacks, delivered with a wry smile. She preferred to be called by her name rather than the first lady. Asked by Larry King what the role of the first lady is, she said, "I think the role of the first lady is really whatever the first lady wants to do."

Each first lady has had her own personality, and each has taken on a project. Lady Bird Johnson promoted a campaign to improve America's landscape. Pat Nixon talked up volunteerism. Betty Ford spoke out in favor of liberalized abortion laws and promoted aid to the handicapped and retarded. Nancy Reagan supported a program against drug abuse among the young. Barbara Bush helped promote adult literacy programs. Only Hillary Clinton assumed an operational role, tackling reform of the health care system.

Among other projects, Laura Bush helped to promote reading, libraries, and particularly Bush's education initiative. When Bush traveled without her, he was not as chipper as usual. In contrast, Clinton would come into the office in a happy frame of mind only to have his mood "darken" after receiving a call from Hillary, Clinton aide David Gergen wrote in *Eyewitness to Power*.

A former smoker of Kent cigarettes, Laura liked salt-rimmed margaritas. She performed traditional first-lady duties, like working with White House Executive Chef Walter S. Scheib III on White House events. For the dinner for Kenyan President Kibaki, Scheib and Laura devised a menu of grilled halibut with bay scallop risotto and lobster sauce served with Shafer Chardonnay Red Shoulder 2001; roasted rack of lamb with wild mushrooms and Armagnac sauce and sweet-potato flan and autumn vegetables, served with Soter Pinot Noir Beacon Hill 1999; and avocado and heirloom tomato salad with toasted cumin dressing. For dessert, guests were served Arabica ice cream and coffee liquor parfait and caramelized banana and pineapple served with Honig Sauvignon Blanc Late Harvest 2002.

But Laura Bush's real interest was reading novels—her favorite was Fyodor Dostoevski's *The Brothers Karamazov*. Laura's literary salons brought together conservative authors, like George Will and Tom Clancy, as well as gays and leftist black historians. While Karl Rove devoured historical works—even reading them between plays at football games—Laura was the top fiction maven in the Bush White House.

"The first lady undoubtedly is the most literate person in President Bush's inner circle," *Business Week*'s Thane Peterson wrote. "Those who snicker 'that isn't saying much' may not realize she's one of the most literate people associated with any White House in decades. Jackie Kennedy seems like a dilettante by comparison." Laura Bush "has spent her life plunging passionately—and privately—into American and world literature ... Anyone who doubts Mrs. Bush's passion for literature could listen to an interview she did two years ago with Susan Stamberg of National Public Radio. Stamberg asks her to read a few lines, and the first lady thumbs through a well-worn copy of *The Brothers Karamazov* held together with a rubber band. As she reads and they talk, it's quite clear she knows the dense and difficult eighty-page Grand Inquisitor section of the novel and its surrounding chapters almost by heart. You get the impression she would just as soon dispense with the small talk and keep on reading. I doubt that many literature professors know it as well."

Bush was an avid reader as well. During the campaign, Frank Bruni of the *New York Times* wrote in the paper that Bush was not a great reader of books. When Bush next spotted Bruni—whom he called Panchito, a Spanish derivative of Frank—in a parking lot, Bush drove his sport utility vehicle over to him. After rolling down the window, he asked how he was.

"Tired," Bruni said.

"I got up early," Bush said, "because I was in the middle of a really good book." He snapped off a "touché" and drove off.

After that encounter, Bush would brandish books like *Titan*, a biography of John D. Rockefeller, and show how far he had read. He and Bruni exchanged recommendations on novels, including *In the Lake of the Woods* by Tim O'Brien (Bush's) and *The Concrete Blonde* by Michael Connelly (Bruni's). Based on Bush's reviews of those books and others, Bruni concluded that Bush was, in fact, a "pretty steady consumer of books" and that his report in the *Times* had been wrong. In fact, Logan Walters, his personal assistant, said Bush was a "voracious reader" who constantly read books during his free time on planes, at night, and on weekends. They were a mix of nonfiction—usually history—and mystery novels. Often, Karl Rove recommended the history books.[154]

At the same time, as someone who rarely watched TV and never read magazines like *People*, Bush was not up on pop culture. He did not know what the TV show *Friends* was or who Leonardo DiCaprio was.

To the extent he could, Bush guarded his personal life. In the Clinton administration, the White House likely would have leaked the identities of the friends who had stayed over for the Yale reunion, appealing to Jewish or Moslem voters. In the Bush administration, such details were off-limits, especially the lives of the Bushes' twin daughters.

Bush, when he was governor, provided a rare glimpse into his parental philosophy when he spoke of frustrations familiar to most fathers.

"They're interested in things foreign to me: bands I've never heard of and TV shows that disgust me," Bush said of the twins, who were thirteen. "I'm constantly at war with them over that 90748," he said, trying to come up with the zip code in *Beverly Hills 90210*. Bush told a reporter, "I don't want my daughters listening to songs that demean women or have ugly words. Garbage is not allowed in our house. I'm sure garbage worms its way in, but a parent has to be a censor."

Bush said he felt an obligation to force them to go to church.

"Certain Sunday mornings, it's a struggle," he said.

Looking back at his own upbringing, Bush said he survived his wilder years in part because his parents never withheld love when they were disappointed in him.

"The greatest gift a parent can give is unconditional love," he said. "As a child wanders, finding his bearings, he needs a sense of absolute love from a parent."

Bush took the same approach to bringing up his two daughters.

"You never see the president's eyes light up quite so much as when he is with Jenna and Barbara," said Mike Wood, Bush's Andover and Yale friend.

The Bushes admired the way the Clintons tried to shield Chelsea from undue press scrutiny. When the Bush twins had a few brushes with underage drinking laws when they were younger, the White House made no comment. After Barbara had been ticketed for possessing a margarita at the age of nineteen, a reporter demanded that the White House talk about it because, after all, the press had reported it. But Ari Fleischer refused to take the bait. Exasperated, the press finally resorted to demanding that the White House critique the media's coverage of the June 2001 episode, according to the pool report.

"Can you tell us if you believe that coverage of the episode yesterday is a legitimate occupation for the press?" a TV correspondent implored.

"I am not going to deem to tell the press at this juncture what the press should or shouldn't do," Fleischer said. "I think that's why you're here. You're here to make those judgments, and you're the White House press corps. And I think you're set apart from most press corps in America in terms of exercising that judgment. You're not the internet."

But Bush was happy to talk about Barney the dog, whom he described as "the son I never had." Barney's biographical information, complete with his favorite food, appeared on the White House Web site.

21

MALLEABLE FACTS

During the campaign, reporters got to know Bush and like him. He had a habit of invading other people's space, leaning into them and touching them. He would pinch reporters' cheeks, or gently slap them, or playfully grab for a reporter's throat from behind.

On one flight, Bush pretended to be horrified that sushi was being served. Like a trophy, he held up his peanut-butter-and-jelly sandwich on white.

"This is heaven, right here," he said.

Coming up to a few reporters on the plane, Bush said proudly, "I don't read half of what you write."

"We don't listen to half of what you say," shot back a wire service reporter, thinking he had had the last word.

That was apparent, Bush said, in the half of their coverage he did read.

Bush handed an ad torn from an airline magazine to an ABC correspondent who was a Harvard graduate. The ad was for audio tapes that would give anyone "a Harvard graduate's vocabulary in just fifteen minutes a day!"

"I have just ordered several," the presidential candidate had written across the page. "What do you think? Do I have a chance?"

On the last flight of the campaign, Bush thanked the reporters and went up and down the aisle, shaking everyone's hand. Returning to his seat, he instructed the flight attendants to play a *Saturday Night Live* videotape of skits that ridiculed him for being vacuous and Gore for being overbearing during the debates. Bush joined in the laughter that filled the plane.

After 9/11, Frank Bruni, who covered the Bush campaign for the *New York Times*, began to wonder if Bush's critics had sold him short, and whether he had. It was the closest a political reporter will ever come to admitting he may have been wrong. In his book *Ambling into History*, Bruni brilliantly described the kind of group-think that nourishes the caricatures of Bush in the media. At one point, Representative Ray LaHood, an Illinois Republican, told reporters that many members of Congress thought Bush's tax cut proposal was too big and wouldn't fly. There had been a dip in the polls, and Bush was mangling his speech, referring to terrorists holding America "hostile" rather than "hostage" and saying "terrors" when he meant "tariffs."

Since Mike Allen of the *Washington Post* was new to covering Bush, he was not aware that Bush's run-ins with the English language tended to go in cycles. He wrote a page-one story, saying that "after five months in firm command of the presidential race, George W. Bush suddenly finds himself on the defensive, behind in some of the polls and struggling to fend off attacks." The claim that Bush was on the defensive was based on the fact that Al Gore was criticizing Bush's position on tax cuts but would not make himself available to reporters. Bush did make himself available and defended his tax cut.

"Ergo, Gore was not on the 'defensive,' while Bush was," Bruni said.

Allen followed the story with one headlined, BUSH'S GAFFES ARE BACK AS DEBATE NEARS. The story mentioned Gail Sheehy's bogus claim that Bush was dyslexic and cited choice Bushisms: Bush said, "More and more of our imports come from overseas." He promised "a foreign-handed policy," meaning an even-handed foreign policy. And he said he has "ruled out no new Social Security taxes."

Ironically, the story had to be corrected. It was Gore, not Bush, who referred to Michael Jordan as Michael Jackson, the correction stated.

Other papers quickly followed the lead of the *Washington Post*, which, along with the *New York Times*, was the media's compass. Initially, writing for the *New York Times*, Bruni resisted saying Bush was on the ropes. But a few days later, he followed the herd and toughened his language because the assertion that Bush was in trouble was "so rampant in newspapers and newscasts that it had transmogrified into the fact that Bush was flailing," Bruni wrote in his book.

Bruni wasn't sure if "this logic was pretzel or circular, but I knew it was pathetic," he wrote. "So much of campaign coverage—and of political journalism in general—carried this strain of dishonesty . . ."

Bush, having seen the pack mentality devour his father when he was running for a second term, thought he understood the press and how to deal with it.

"He knows that they are there to stir things up," Clay Johnson said. "If there is not a disagreement, they will dig a little deeper until they find one. Someone described to Karen Hughes what political reporters do: They promote fights. They like controversy and differences of opinion."[155]

In earlier years, the press covered up for presidents, failing to write about matters that might be embarrassing. The fact that Franklin Roosevelt was crippled from a bout with polio came as a shock to most people because the press had gone along with his wishes to keep it quiet. Thomas P. "Tip" O'Neill, the former Speaker of the House, recalled how amazed he was when, as a college freshman, he met Roosevelt in the White House.

"When I saw the president sitting in a wheelchair, I was so shocked that my chin just about hit my chest," he said. "Like most Americans, I had absolutely no idea that Franklin Roosevelt was disabled. It's hard to imagine in this day of television, but in those days the president's handicap was kept secret out of respect for the office."

President Johnson's dissembling about the war in Vietnam, the CIA and FBI abuses portrayed in the Church Committee hearings, and the cover-ups by President Nixon during Watergate changed press coverage of the White House forever. But by 2003, the pendulum had swung so far away from reverential coverage that any journalist who said something good about a president was considered by his colleagues to be either naive, a wimp, or a prostitute.

"Journalism has changed over the years I've been doing it," said one reporter who has covered the White House for years. "It's more adversarial, more edgy, and we are less inclined to just report things straight. There is pressure from editors to not just write wire stories. In press conferences, reporters want to provoke because that gives you a good headline. Atmospherics and mood are more dominant than they were in the past. Now we compete with the cable TV outlets. Everyone is trying to find ways to distinguish themselves, for better or worse. I'm not sure how happy readers are with that kind of coverage, either."

Nervous about editors' reactions, the reporter did not want to be quoted.

Bush's response was to stay on message, batten down the hatches, and joke around at press conferences.

"Can you finally offer us some definitive evidence that Saddam Hussein was working with al Qaeda terrorists?" NBC's Campbell Brown asked Bush in August 2003.

"Now," Bush said, "I know in our world where news comes and goes, and there's this kind of instant—instant news, and you must have this done, you must do this yesterday, that there's a level of frustration by some in the media." Looking at the alluring correspondent, Bush said, "I'm not suggesting that you're frustrated." The reporters tittered. "You don't look frustrated to me at all." The press corps roared with laughter.

"In many ways, he's got our number," said Mark Knoller, a veteran White House correspondent for CBS. "More than we often realize, he understands how we do our job—and our vulnerable underbelly."

For all its faults, the press more than any other institution has kept presidents accountable. Having initially accepted Lyndon Johnson's justification for the Vietnam War, the *New York Times* and later the *Washington Post* in 1971 published the secret Defense Department analysis that became known as the Pentagon Papers, which revealed that the government knowingly misrepresented the war to the American people. Those revelations fed growing opposition to the war, leading to Johnson's decision not to seek reelection. By revealing the progress of the FBI's investigation of

Watergate and conducting their own sleuthing, Bob Woodward and Carl Bernstein of the *Washington Post* made sure that Nixon could not suppress the investigation. By exposing the illegal surveillance of Americans by the FBI and CIA, the press was a catalyst for reforms and more oversight of both agencies.

But most presidents came to hate the press and became paranoid about leaks. Nixon tried to block publication of the Pentagon Papers and ordered illegal wiretapping of his national-security staff to try to uncover leaks. Clinton spent much of his time privately cursing the press, according to a Secret Service agent.

Leaks of information about pending developments—as opposed to genuine abuses—usually come from high-level political appointees who use the press to try to manipulate policy decisions or bolster their own positions. Besides impeding his efforts to govern, Bush saw leaks as a sign of disloyalty.

"If someone is leaking, he is not a good member of the team," Clay Johnson said.

With Karen Hughes, Bush crafted a strategy meant to prevent leaks and present a unified message. Hughes graduated *summa cum laude* from Southern Methodist University, where she majored in English and journalism and was inducted into Phi Beta Kappa. She became a reporter at KXAS-TV in Dallas and Fort Worth. In 1984, she left journalism to become Texas press coordinator for Ronald Reagan's presidential campaign. In 1992, she became executive director of the Texas Republican Party. Two years later, she began working for Bush during his first race for governor.

"I can read a speech and say, 'There's no sound bite here,' " she said. "I don't know if that's a very valuable skill, but it seems to come in handy around here."

Dana Milbank, who covered the Bush and Gore campaigns, described the six-foot-tall Hughes as being so on message that "I'm sure if you woke her up in the middle of the night, she would read you from paragraph three of the press release on the Bush tax plan."

But like the rest of Bush's close aides, Hughes had a sense of humor and was not prissy. When Milbank commented one day on how nice her shoes were, Hughes said she had trouble finding large enough shoes in Austin but finally found a store that stocked her size.

"You know, I usually have to go to Dallas to find shoes. How come you have these?" Hughes said she asked the clerk.

"Well, we stock these for the transvestites," the clerk replied.

Better than anyone else, "Prophet," as Bush called her, was able to understand and communicate his positions. But as senior counselor to the president and communications director, she had a much broader role, helping to shape policy. When naming her to the position, Bush said he wanted her "in every meeting where major decisions are made."

Like the rest of Bush's top aides, Hughes was exceptionally smart and had a balanced outlook. When I asked her about press attacks on Bush, she said, "I think most reporters try to be fair. I think they also don't recognize that they fall short of that."

Early on, Hughes became the enforcer of the no-leak strategy.

"The president saw from his father's administration what he considered to be disloyalty," Hughes told me. "A lot of people in 1992 were promoting themselves rather than fighting for the president when they thought the ship was going down."[156]

The downside of Bush's strategy was that it would frustrate reporters in search of exclusives and inside tidbits.

In the initial months after Bush took office, the generally favorable coverage of Bush during the campaign continued. The *New York Times* said Bush had "presided over one of the most orderly and politically nimble White House transitions in at least twenty years." The *Los Angeles Times* said that "all along Bush vowed to reach out to Democrats and, starting on day one, he did so with vigor."

White House aides attributed the initial positive coverage to the fact that many of the reporters had been with Bush during the campaign and had come to like him. But as other reporters replaced them, and press access to now President Bush diminished, the tone started to change. Leading the charge was Dana Milbank. During the campaign, Milbank wrote edgy features for the *New Republic* and then the Style section of the *Washington Post*. As Bush was to take office, the paper assigned the thirty-two-year-old reporter to cover the White House for the national staff. Weeks before the inauguration, Milbank told NPR's Terry Gross that the Bush press policy was "creating quite a bit of ill will, and when things get rough, they're not going to have a lot of friendship and goodwill in the press corps."

Along with Mike Allen, who was also assigned to the White House beat, Milbank did his best to support his own prediction. Going back many years, the *Washington Post* had a distinguished history of fair, incisive White House reporting. Milbank, on the other hand, was a caricature of a political reporter. A 1990 Yale graduate, he was Bush's idea of an elitist snob, commenting on whether a steward on Al Gore's campaign plane pronounced "merlot" with a silent "t" in the French manner. The well-fed Milbank devoted an entire column to an evaluation of the food served to the press on the campaign trail. Perhaps to his credit, Milbank would admit that the high quality of food the Bush campaign served the press—at one meal, striped lobster ravioli with red salmon caviar, Beef Wellington and cheesecake—probably influenced his coverage.

Unlike Woodward and Bernstein, who worked until midnight knocking on people's doors, Milbank's idea of investigative reporting and "making the White House accountable" was to whine publicly about his lack of access, to try to find conflicts in administration statements, and to ask gotcha questions at press conferences. If Milbank wrote about policy, it was purely accidental.

Milbank's pool reports reflected his attitude. After Bush paid a visit to the House Republican caucus, Milbank reported that Bush told the pool, "We're going to get a lot of things done for America." Sarcastically, Milbank wrote, "The president and the caucus got so many things done for America so quickly that the hour-long meeting lasted forty-five minutes." The "big news of the day," he wrote, "was when our protagonist spoke about education. He declared that education is 'a passion for me.'" Milbank called this a "startling revelation" from "our hero."

Any high-school paper would have fired Milbank for his insolence and unprofessionalism, but complaints from the White House made the *Post* more determined to keep him in his position.

Other White House reporters muttered to the White House Correspondents Association that by complaining, the White House was trying to "intimidate" them.

"They wanted us to do something," said Carl M. Cannon, a board member who became president of the correspondents' association. "I said, 'We dish it out. We have to take it.' "[157]

At the same time, Cannon learned that Terrence R. McAuliffe, the chairman of the Democratic National Committee (DNC), had decided that Bush's greatest appeal to voters was his credibility. Even if they disagreed with many of his policies, voters felt he was honest. McAuliffe, who was the Clintons' most frequent companion, played loose with the facts himself. Without any evidence beyond some missing records, he later declared that Bush had been AWOL from the Texas Air National Guard, a crime that the military prosecutes. The guard's records at the time were kept chaotically. If Bush had not fulfilled his duties, he would not have learned to fly a fighter jet, nor would he have received an honorable discharge.

During Clinton's impeachment, McAuliffe couldn't have been more dismissive of the notion that Clinton's perjury was an issue. But after Bush became president, the DNC began a campaign of ads and e-mails to the media drawing attention to the slightest wrinkle in administration statements.

Milbank was one of the first in the mainstream media to challenge Bush's credibility.

FOR BUSH, FACTS ARE MALLEABLE, said the headline on Milbank's October 22, 2002, story. Milbank questioned how the White House could say that Saddam Hussein's unmanned aerial vehicles threatened the United States when their range was limited. Milbank cited Bush's statement, made in response to a question at a news conference with Tony Blair, that the International Atomic Energy Agency (IAEA) said Iraq was "six months away from developing a [nuclear] weapon," when the agency had made no such statement. And he questioned Bush's statement that because of labor union objections to having customs officials wear radiation detectors, the policy of wearing the detectors was delayed for "a long time."

Milbank called Bush's statements "dubious, if not wrong." But it was Milbank's facts that were squishy. Bush made the statement about unmanned aerial vehicles targeting the United States because UAVs could be launched against America from a ship or brought into the country on a truck to disperse chemical or biological weapons. The complete text of Bush's speech, which Milbank did not quote, suggested that.

"We're concerned that Iraq is exploring ways of using these UAVs for missions targeting the United States," Bush said.

Before Milbank's story ran, the White House told him that Bush simply misspoke when he attributed the statement about Iraq and nuclear weapons to the IAEA. He meant to say the International Institute for Strategic Studies [IISS]. As for the union, it had objected to radiation tests as Bush had said. It did not withdraw its objection until three months later. But the Customs Service said it would override the union's objections.

Milbank either ignored the White House explanations or cited them further down in the story about Bush's alleged malleable facts. If they had been presented fairly with each alleged misstatement, Milbank would not have had a story. Either his facts were wrong or the discrepancies were so trivial that nobody would have cared. Like the paper's story that Cheney's visits to the CIA constituted pressure, Milbank's story would have been laughed out of the paper if the facts had been presented honestly. Nonetheless, Milbank compared Bush's statements with Clinton's perjury under oath about his relationship with Monica Lewinsky and denials by the Nixon White House about criminal involvement in Watergate.

Just as other papers followed the *Post* after Mike Allen wrote during the campaign that Bush was on the defensive, Milbank's story emboldened the rest of the press to go on the attack. Democratic National Committee spokeswoman Jennifer Palmieri sent out an e-mail to all White House correspondents.

"As noted by a major national newspaper earlier this week, President Bush is fond of malleable facts," she wrote. "For the remainder of the campaign, the DNC will provide a 'Whopper Watch' service for the traveling White House press corps, to help keep the facts stratight [*sic*]."

While Milbank's story did not equate Bush's credibility with

Hillary Clinton's, a comparison would have been instructive. When it came to dissembling, Hillary was in a separate class. Trying to engender sympathy, Hillary told NBC's Jane Pauley on September 17, 2001, that when the two airplanes hit the World Trade Center, Chelsea was at Battery Park near the towers. "She'd gone for what she thought would be a great jog," Hillary said. "She was going down to Battery Park, she was going to go around the towers. She went to get a cup of coffee—and that's when the plane hit."

"She was close enough to hear the rumble," Pauley said.

"She did hear it. She did," Hillary said.

"And to see the smoke . . ."

"That's right," Hillary responded, saying she did not locate her daughter until two hours later.

"At that moment, she was not just a senator, but a concerned parent," Katie Couric said the next day on *Today*.

It was a great tale, but Hillary had made it up from whole cloth. Her arrogance was so profound that she did not coordinate the story with Chelsea, who wrote an article for *Talk* in which she described what she *had* been doing that day. According to Chelsea, she wasn't jogging at the World Trade Center. Rather, she was miles away in a friend's apartment on Park Avenue South. She watched the events unfold on TV. Hillary told the story with as straight a face as her husband had when he said on TV that he "did not have sex with that woman," referring to Monica Lewinsky.

In contrast to that kind of fabrication, the closest the press came to genuinely nailing the Bush White House for knowingly lying—as opposed to being mistaken—was a press release issued by the Environmental Protection Agency just after the September 11 attacks. A confusing report by the EPA inspector general said the White House had softened the statements in the release about the possible health effects of the dust and debris from the World Trade Center. But a subsequent *New York Times* examination concluded the entire matter had been blown out of proportion. Reviewing the EPA news releases, a new, relatively low level public-relations official at the Council on Environmental Quality within the Executive Office of the President removed some scientific caveats and cautionary notes. The removal of the cautionary notes had little effect on the message New Yorkers received. Because of daily statements by EPA officials in New York, news stories conveyed a number of precautions. But as the November 30, 2003, *Times* story noted, the inspector general's report did not conclude that the EPA was wrong in saying that the air in Lower Manhattan was "safe to breathe." Rather, the report said that at that point, the scientific evidence was inadequate to make such a broad generalization largely because only tests for asbestos had been done. Later tests for PCBs and toxins largely validated what the EPA had said. So the press releases that allegedly constituted White House lies turned out to be right.

In fact, the Bush White House was so ethical that when Karen Hughes wanted to run a White House photo of herself with Bush in the Rose Garden on the jacket of her book *Ten Minutes from Normal*, the White House counsel's office would not bend its policy against using such photos on book jackets. Hughes was said to be most unhappy.*

In obtaining cooperation from the Bush White House for *A Matter of Character*, the biggest obstacle as the book progressed—after the usual penchant for secrecy—was the fact that it would reveal inside information about the Clintons and criticize some Democratic presidential candidates. Even though he knew that the author had his own Secret Service and other sources outside the administration for the critical items, or would be expressing his own opinion, Dan Bartlett expressed concern that the public and the media might think those who participated were criticizing the Clintons or Democratic candidates. After the author shared some of the critical items with Clay Johnson, he suggested that a few of them might be perceived as being unfair to Hillary Clinton or to particular candidates. In at least two cases, the author agreed with him and dropped the items.

Honest mistakes by the administration became grand conspiracies. The initial reports that Army Private Jessica Lynch fought

---

* The policy is based on the belief that running a photo on a book jacket is commercial use. In fact, book jackets are as commercial as the covers of news magazines or the front pages of newspapers and have the same First Amendment protections. The policy only applies to specially requested photos and not to those made available on the White House Web site or distributed to wire services.

fiercely and was stabbed and shot while being captured by Iraqis were based on U.S. military interception of Iraqi radio reports. One of them referred to a blond soldier who went down shooting. It turned out he was Private First Class Patrick Miller. Either the radio report mistakenly used the word "she" instead of "he" or an American had mistranslated the personal pronoun, leading to the belief within the Pentagon that the courageous soldier in question was Lynch rather than Miller. War critics claimed the Bush administration had made up the story of Lynch's bravery and circulated it to stir patriotism and support for the war. The Web became cluttered with sites devoted to "Jessica Lynch lies." Lynch herself fed the conspiracy theories.

"They used me as a way to symbolize all this stuff," Lynch told Diane Sawyer in an ABC interview. "It hurt in a way, that people would make up stories that they had no truth about."

Many stories targeting the Bush administration relied on slanted leads to make their point. When Cheney said on NBC's *Meet the Press* in September 2003 that he had no financial interest in Halliburton Co., Senator Tom Daschle, the South Dakota Democrat, asserted Cheney needed to reconcile his statement with the fact that he continued to receive hundreds of thousands of dollars in deferred compensation from his former employer. In response, Cheney's office said the vice president had taken out a $15,000 insurance policy that would guarantee the deferred payments even if Halliburton went under. Cheney was donating the deferred compensation, after taxes, to charity. Cheney also legally assigned his Halliburton stock options to a charity. Thus, he had no financial interest in Halliburton's fortunes.

The news was that Cheney had taken out the insurance policy. Any cub reporter on a minor paper would have learned from his city editor to identify that as the lead of the story. Instead, nourishing the conspiracy theories about Cheney and Halliburton fostered by the Democrats, the lead of a September 17 *Washington Post* story by Mike Allen and Dana Milbank said Cheney "defended" his assertion that he had no financial ties to Halliburton "even though he still receives deferred compensation from the Houston-based energy conglomerate."

By March 2003, Milbank was telling NPR that it's just "not

possible to procure information from this administration." Given Milbank's hostile coverage of the administration, that hardly came as a surprise. Any reporter knows that he closes off cooperation by writing slanted stories. Nor was that all.

"Pretend, just for fun, that you're a White House correspondent and you get invited to the president's ranch for an off-the-record dinner," wrote Joseph Curl, a *Washington Times* White House correspondent, in the privately owned *White House Weekly* newsletter. "The terms are straightforward: No quoting or paraphrasing the president. Period. So, whaddya do? If you answered: 'Hell, I'll just write it up and ship it in,' welcome to the White House press corps."

Curl cited Milbank's story about an off-the-record barbecue Bush gave for the press in Crawford.

"Bush, with his choice of a half-dozen tables, sat down with the camera crews," Milbank wrote in the August 29, 2003, *Washington Post*. "Though what they discussed cannot be divulged, the talk after Bush left focused on bass fishing and the Big Twelve conference."

After Milbank's story ran, an AP reporter decided to try the same underhanded method for broadly conveying what was discussed, violating the spirit if not the letter of the ground rules.

"Enjoy the account of the OTR [off-the-record] dinner," Curl wrote. "After the way reporters breached the rules, there isn't likely to be another."

But even that example of journalistic malpractice was dwarfed by a prediction Milbank made to Chris Matthews on NBC about finding weapons of mass destruction in Iraq just before the 2004 election.

"Don't be surprised," Milbank said on February 8, 2004, "if there is an October surprise, perhaps a finding of a small vial, another piece of equipment that we didn't have before that adds more of a solid case behind Bush's claim."

"Oh," Matthews said, for once speechless.

The implication was that Bush would either order weapons of mass destruction planted or, if they were found, would reveal their existence just before the election to acheive the greatest political impact.

Aside from such embarrassments to journalism, the Bush White House's buttoned-down strategy clearly contributed to the negative press Bush began to receive.

"You can't walk the halls of the White House," said Carl Cannon, who has covered the White House since 1993, first for the *Baltimore Sun* and then for the *National Journal*. "They work all the time. You can't find them off premises. You have men with Uzi submachine guns guarding the principals."

During the Clinton administration, reporters covering a Rose Garden event could pull George Stephanopoulos aside to "get a little more on their thinking," Cannon said. "Not to get leaks. With Bush, people like Karl Rove will stand in a guarded area. Then they'll go back inside with Bush. They act like it's beneath them to mingle with the press. Then they wonder why they don't get the benefit of the doubt or an explication of their views."

Cannon said the White House says that Bush presents his positions fully in his speeches. But, he said, "Reporters need more. They like to be able to question and examine."

Despite his frustration, Carl Cannon, for one, wrote his stories straight. Those reporters who wrote their stories straight managed to gain trust and more access. One of them, Judy Keen of *USA Today*, said, "The PR operation is very disciplined, and that's very frustrating and has created some bad feelings in the past." But, Keen said. "I think we've all now gotten kind of used to it. That's just the way they operate. Things have loosened up a bit in the last year and a half, but it's a very tight operation. It takes a lot of work to rise above it. It takes finding people who are willing to talk. The circle of people who know what's going on is fairly small. They've all been told to stick with the message."[158]

"That's what people don't understand about him," Bush's cousin John Ellis said. "They don't understand how tough he is."[159]

While some negative coverage may be attributable to frustration over access, "There is also great skepticism about a Republican president among some in the media," said Keen, who has been covering the White House since 1991.

After Bill Keller replaced Howell Raines as executive editor of the *New York Times*, the paper's coverage became more fair and thoughtful. As a result, David E. Sanger, Richard W. Stevenson, and Elisabeth Bumiller obtained greater access and were able to present more informed coverage than the *Washington Post*.

Sometimes, the *Times* simply covered groundbreaking speeches that the *Post* ignored, like Bush's November 6, 2003, speech at the Commerce Department on the twentieth anniversary of the National Endowment for Democracy. There, Bush asked, "Are the peoples of the Middle East somehow beyond the reach of liberty? Are millions of men and women and children condemned by history or culture to live in despotism? Are they alone never to know freedom, and never even to have a choice in the matter? I, for one, do not believe it. I believe every person has the ability and the right to be free."

While Bush had sounded similar themes before, this was the first time he singled out countries that were not sufficiently democratic, suggesting they need to change. Besides Iraq, Bush named Iran, the Palestinian Authority, Saudi Arabia, Egypt, and Syria.

The difference in approach between the *New York Times* under Keller and the *Washington Post* could be seen in the way both handled former Treasury Secretary Paul H. O'Neill's controversial assertions on *60 Minutes* and in a book, *The Price of Loyalty*, by Ron Suskind. O'Neill claimed that Bush began planning to invade Iraq as soon as he took office and wanted the NSC to "Go find me a way to do this." O'Neill, a member of the NSC who did not see the most sensitive intelligence, also said he never saw any "evidence" that Iraq had weapons of mass destruction.

The claim that Bush came into office with his mind made up on Iraq and planning war was absurd on its face: Planning for the war required the participation not only of the NSC and its staff but the Defense Department and CIA, each of which is subject to leaks. To keep such alleged planning secret would have required a vast conspiracy involving tens of thousands of government employees, many of whom have since left the government and are now free to talk. Especially in light of the later controversy over justifying the war, such a conspiracy would have had to have been bigger than all the JFK assassination theories put together.

Regime change in Iraq had been U.S. policy since the Clinton administration, but it was not until after 9/11 that Bush began seriously to consider the need to deal with Saddam Hussein. Based on extensive access to administration officials, Bob Woodward, in his book *Bush at War*, wrote that after 9/11, Deputy Defense Secretary Paul D. Wolfowitz urged action against Iraq because of its links to terrorists. But, Woodward wrote in an epilogue, "After Bush's initial decision not to attack Iraq immediately following the September 11 terrorist attacks, the issue had continued to percolate in the war cabinet—actively for Cheney and Rumsfeld, passively for Powell, who was not spoiling for another war."

Contrary to O'Neill's claim, planning for the war began slightly less than a year before the invasion, according to CIA officials interviewed by the author. Even as the invasion approached, Bush gave Saddam a chance to avoid war by disclosing Iraq's weapons programs or by leaving the country.

That same record refuted charges made by former White House counterterrorism coordinator Richard A. Clarke in his book *Against All Enemies* that, a day after the 9/11 attacks, Bush tried to push him into finding a connection between al Qaeda and Iraq. At that point, no one knew for sure who had perpetrated the attacks. Unlike the attack on Pearl Harbor, the hijackers who flew planes into the World Trade Center and the Pentagon were not wearing military uniforms or flying the planes of another country. As commander in chief, Bush had the responsibility of asking if Iraq, a sworn enemy of the United States, had been behind the attacks.

If Bush wanted to invade Iraq, he did not need a connection between Iraq and the attacks of 9/11: Iraq had been violating United Nations mandates to disarm since the first Gulf War. If Bush was intent on going after Iraq after 9/11 no matter what, why did he decide against it six days later, waiting a year and a half to do it? Even Democrats like Senator Joseph Lieberman said he saw "no basis" for Clarke's claims.

Clarke's assertion in his book that, prior to 9/11, the Clinton White House saw al Qaeda as a more urgent priority than did the Bush White House had even less credibility. In a background briefing with reporters in August 2002, Clarke himself said that a more comprehensive strategy for dealing with al Qaeda had been "on the table" in the Clinton White House from 1998 until Clinton left office. When Bush took over, Clarke said, his administration pursued the Clinton's administration's existing strategy but also beefed up CIA resources for undertaking covert action five-fold and began developing a "new strategy that called for the rapid elimination of al Qaeda."

In retrospect, prior to 9/11, neither the Clinton nor the Bush administrations took the al Qaeda threat seriously enough. Nor did members of the congressional intelligence committees, who saw most of the intelligence the presidents saw. But al Qaeda's initial attacks on U.S. interests had occurred on Clinton's watch. Unable to focus on a problem longer than the next news cycle, Clinton, in his eight years in office, had done nothing more than lob Cruise missiles into bin Laden's tents. In contrast, two months after taking office, Bush, saying he was tired of "swatting flies," recognized that the Clinton approach was not working. He had Condoleezza Rice develop a more aggressive strategy, which was approved on September 4. But that strategy would not have stopped the 9/11 attacks. By June 2001, sixteen of the nineteen hijackers were already in the country. Only the sight of body bags, as Clarke correctly said in his testimony before the 9/11 commission on March 24, 2004, would likely have been enough to create enough public and congressional support for the steps Bush took after 9/11 to go after al Qaeda.

Demonstrating his one-sided approach, Clarke was dismissive of Bush's efforts after 9/11, saying they were mostly obvious. On the other hand, in an interview on PBS's *Frontline* in March 2002, Clarke said that while the Clinton administration should have destroyed al Qaeda terrorist camps in Afghanistan, "There was the Middle East peace process going on. There was the war in Yugoslavia going on. People above my rank had to judge what could be done in the counterterrorism world at a time when they were pursuing other national goals." Clarke was referring to the same Clinton administration that he claimed in his book treated the al Qaeda threat as a top priority.

Clarke, who had been turned down by the Bush administration for a top job at the new Homeland Security Department, appeared to think that the measure of success in the war on terror was how many meetings the National Security Council held on the subject. That was despite the fact that Rice warned him several times about his failure to appear at her senior-staff meetings.

In focusing on meetings, Clarke ignored the fact that, in contrast to Clinton, who read the President's Daily Brief but did not receive daily CIA briefings, Bush met every morning with George Tenet, and, after 9/11, with Robert Mueller as well. Essentially, Bush ran the war on terror himself and did not need NSC meetings on policy. Rather than being obvious steps, Bush's approach to the war on terror was muscular and innovative, provoking incessant criticism from Democrats and the media.

Within the FBI and CIA, where Bush was viewed as a hero, there was tittering as reporters went on television to claim that counterterrorism experts within the government secretly agreed with Clarke. Many of the reporters who defended Clarke had been fed tidbits by him over the years.

"We can only shake our heads and hope America will see through this grandstanding," a high-ranking FBI official said.

As Clarke basked in the limelight, his attacks on the Bush administration became even more personal. He told Larry King that if "Condi Rice had been doing her job and holding . . . daily meetings," information the FBI held about two of the would-be hijackers who had been able to enter the country because the CIA had failed to place them on a watch list "would have been shaken out" from the FBI.

To those who know how unfocused and hopelessly bogged down in paper the FBI was prior to 9/11, that claim, like most of Clarke's other claims, was ludicrous. Championing himself as a hero who was the only one in government who knew the answers, Clarke presented a distorted, fun-house portrait of the problems prior to 9/11. Those problems related primarily to the fact that the Clinton administration had cut the CIA's budget and had made it so risk averse that it was unlikely to be successful in pinpointing bin Laden and penetrating the plot.

Unlike Clarke, after his allegations created an uproar, Paul O'Neill began retracting each one, just as John J. DiIulio, the former director of the Office of Faith-Based Initiatives, did after Suskind quoted him in *Esquire*. Two days after the *60 Minutes* interview aired, O'Neill said on NBC's *Today* show that his comments had been misinterpreted, and that Bush's position on Iraq when he took office was the same as Clinton's.

"You know, people are trying to make the case that I said the president was planning war in Iraq early in the administration," the former Alcoa CEO told Katie Couric with a straight face. "Actually, there was a continuation of work that had been going on in the Clinton administration with the notion that we needed regime change in Iraq."

O'Neill told Couric that while he saw no "concrete evidence" of weapons of mass destruction—something the CIA never said it had—there was intelligence pointing to their existence. He said he wished he had never characterized Cabinet meetings with Bush as a "blind man in a room full of deaf people." Finally, he said he was not against the decision to remove Saddam Hussein and would probably vote for Bush.

"I don't see anybody that strikes me as better prepared and more capable," O'Neill said, expressing amazement that anyone thought he had participated in painting an unflattering portrait of the president.

O'Neill "has made a total fool of himself," William J. Bennett, Ronald Reagan's education secretary, observed on Fox TV.

Retracted or not, O'Neill's original story was seized on by the Democrats. Representative Dennis Kucinich cited the Ron Suskind book as evidence of Bush's deceit.

"Now we find from Secretary O'Neill that the president was planning on attacking Iraq before 9/11 and that the American people, in effect, have been misled by this," Kucinich said. Retired general Wesley K. Clark said O'Neill's claims confirm "my worst suspicions about this administration." Months later, cable news talking heads were still parroting O'Neill's original allegations. Suskind, ignoring his multiple recantations, told Chris Matthews that O'Neill is "Mr. Evidence. The guy doesn't say anything unless he can back it up."

As the appointment of O'Neill demonstrated, personnel selection is not a science. On his first week on the job, O'Neill, a friend of Cheney's but not part of Bush's inner circle, derided Wall Street traders as "people who sit in front of a flickering green screen" doing jobs that he could learn "in about a couple of weeks." Like a ten-year-old, when he didn't get his way, he would threaten to quit.

"At the White House, your day is a series of meetings," Karen Hughes told me. "They have to be regimented or you wouldn't get anything done. We had a legislative strategy meeting where the purpose was to discuss the economic stimulus plan. Secretary O'Neill started talking about development of water resources in rural Africa. All of us started looking at each other. I remember Andy Card finally had to say, 'We need to get on the subject.' Water development was important, too, but that was not what the meeting was about."[160]

Media reports at the time had it that Bush pushed out O'Neill and Lawrence B. Lindsey, the economic advisor, because they did not come across well on TV. But Bush had decided that they were not coordinating and carrying out economic policy well. O'Neill's arrogance also was a factor.

"Paul is no longer a member of the team, and maybe he's demonstrating why," said Clay Johnson after the furor erupted.[161]

In journalism, any claim by a fired employee is suspect and normally requires corroboration before it is used. While O'Neill's previous position as treasury secretary made his statements newsworthy, that did not mean they should go unchallenged. In reporting O'Neill's bizarre claims, Dana Milbank quoted Bush in the January 13, 2004, *Washington Post* as saying that when he became president, he was focused on Iraqi flyovers rather than with invading Iraq. But Milbank made no attempt to cite a wealth of independent evidence demonstrating that O'Neill's claim was fiction. The *New York Times* story by Richard W. Stevenson, on the other hand, sought to balance O'Neill's assertion by citing statements Bush made to others early on in his administration. Based on those comments, the *Times* story said, "Mr. Bush did not sound like a man who had decided to mount an invasion of Iraq."

Yet neither paper ran O'Neill's retraction of his own claims. In fact, in its January 14 story by Milbank and Vernon Loeb, the *Post* repeated O'Neill's original claim about Bush and Iraq without referring to the fact that he had since admitted his claim was untrue. Nor was that an oversight: The story quoted from other parts of O'Neill's interview with Katie Couric.

The *Post* took the same one-sided approach in covering the controversy touched off by DNC Chairman Terrence McAuliffe, who claimed Bush was AWOL when he transferred to an Alabama National Guard unit in 1972. After running two-dozen stories saying records of his service were missing during 1972 and 1973, the paper quoted John B. Calhoun, an officer with the Alabama Air National Guard, as saying he had seen Bush sign in at the guard in Montgomery eight to ten times from May to October 1972. Calhoun recalled that Bush used to sit in his office and read flight manuals and magazines during his duty in Alabama. But the *Post*'s story, by Mike Allen and Lois Romano, buried Calhoun's comments in the eleventh paragraph of a February 13, 2004, story headlined, AIDES STUDY PRESIDENT'S SERVICE RECORDS; WHITE HOUSE WON'T RELEASE MORE DOCUMENTS NOW BUT IS AWAITING ANOTHER BATCH. In another article, Milbank, having contributed to the feeding frenzy, snickered at the White House for notifying reporters with an electronic page that records of Bush's dental exam at the Dannelly Air National Guard Base in Alabama in 1973 were being released.

While the White House policy of secrecy undoubtedly contributed to negative coverage, that was not enough to explain or excuse the kind of slanted stories the *Post* and many others in the media routinely turned out. Nor was the unfair coverage confined to the White House beat. Invariably, when the media wrote about criticism of Bush's decision to detain al Qaeda and Taliban prisoners at Guantanamo Bay without right to legal counsel, the press would say the United States was not following the Geneva Convention, without pointing out the reason: Only lawful combatants who conduct their operations in accordance with the laws of war are entitled to rights under the Geneva Convention. By deliberately attacking civilians, terrorists and those who support them put themselves beyond the Geneva protections.

A December 14, 2003, *Washington Post* story by Walter Pincus reported that the UN's top weapon inspector said the UN knew before the invasion of "most" of the weapon-related equipment and research that has been "publicly documented" by the U.S.-led inspection team in Iraq. Not until the tenth paragraph did the story reveal that the UN official, Demetrius Perricos, was flat-out ignoring the discovery since the war of dozens of additional weapon programs by the U.S. inspection team led by David Kay.

The reason was that even though Kay publicly listed the weapon programs he found, Perricos did not have access to the "full progress report." Therefore, he claimed, the UN could not assess the findings. If that fact had been in the lead of the story, the absurdity of Perricos's declaration would have been exposed, and the paper never could have run the story.

Under the guise of news stories, Pincus regularly turned out other diatribes against the administration's reason for going to war in Iraq. So extreme was his bias that when Bush told Tim Russert in an Oval Office interview on February 8, 2004, that Saddam Hussein was "paying for suicide bombers" to go to Israel, Pincus tried to undercut his point by writing that "many experts agree those funds . . . were not the motivation for the attackers."

In the same vein, a November 23, 2003, *New York Times* story reporting on an FBI law enforcement bulletin contributed to the mythology that the Bush administration was violating individual rights. The story by Eric Lichtblau said "civil rights advocates, relying largely on anecdotal evidence, have complained for months that federal officials have surreptitiously sought to suppress First Amendment rights of antiwar demonstrators . . . The FBI memorandum [bulletin], however, appears to offer the first evidence of a coordinated, nationwide effort to collect intelligence regarding demonstrations." But a reading of the two-page October 15 bulletin makes it clear that the FBI was saying nothing of the sort. Rather, the bureau was alerting local law enforcement to tactics used by demonstrators who engage in violence, urging them to report "any potentially illegal acts" to the FBI. That was exactly what the FBI was supposed to be doing. If the story had honestly reported what the bulletin said, the item could not have been run because it was not news.

Cassandra M. Chandler, the FBI's assistant director for public relations, wrote a letter to Bill Keller, the paper's executive editor, whose effort to make the paper more responsible apparently had gone unnoticed by Lichtblau. Chandler said the bulletin in question was "not focused on political protesters or others who exercise their First Amendment rights to protest the policies of the government, but simply cites the fact that anarchists and others have used violent tactics to disrupt otherwise peaceful demonstrations." The FBI posted the letter on its Web site.

Nonetheless, civil liberties groups and members of Congress opposed to the Patriot Act jumped on the story as proof that the FBI had returned to the illegal surveillance tactics conducted under J. Edgar Hoover. In liberal circles, it became an article of faith that the FBI was targeting antiwar demonstrators to intimidate them.

"This report suggests that federal law enforcement may now be targeting individuals based on activities that are peaceful, lawful, and protected under the Constitution," said Senator John Edwards, the North Carolina Democrat running for president. "What kind of McCarthyism is that?"

Without tips and cooperation from citizens, the FBI was almost useless. Untrue stories like Lichtblau's eroded trust in the bureau and diminished that cooperation. Yet when another terrorist attack occurred, the *New York Times* editorial page would be the first to jump on the FBI for failing to protect the country.

22

A LEAK

After Karen Hughes announced in April 2003 that she was returning to Texas, Dan Bartlett replaced her as communications director. Hughes continued to talk with Bush several times a week and with Bartlett about once a week. She also continued to help shape many of Bush's major speeches, often traveling with him. Because she was outside of Washington, Bartlett thought she had a better perspective on how the president was playing to the rest of the country and what was needed to sharpen his message.

Even his worst enemies in the press said Bartlett was a nice guy. It was just, as he put it with a sigh, that he had a "tough account." Prematurely gray, Bartlett, thirty-two, had a boyish face, an open manner, and a self-deprecating sense of humor. A native of Waukegan, Illinois, he grew up in Rockwall, Texas. While attending the University of Texas at Austin, Bartlett began working for Karl Rove's direct-mail business in 1992.

"My first day on the job, thirty minutes after I got there, the guy next to me picked up the phone and said, 'The president of the United States is on the phone for Karl.' All of a sudden, I was very interested in knowing who this guy was," Bartlett said.

Still taking courses at the university and working for Rove, Bartlett became one of Bush's two paid employees in November 1993, working on Bush's fledgling campaign for governor at the age of twenty-two. He would become Bush's longest continually serving employee. Bush called him Barty or Danny.

"Of all the people in the presidential universe, he is the one most like the president in demeanor, character, and wit," said

Mark McKinnon, who was a Bush media advisor at Public Strategies in Austin.

During Bush's 1998 reelection campaign and 2000 presidential race, Bartlett was charged with learning all there was to know about any sensitive personal issues, like Bush's National Guard service and his 1976 arrest in Maine for drunk driving. If the issues needed to be addressed, Bartlett would be prepared with the facts and an explanation. When the DUI story broke in the last week of the presidential campaign, "I said to myself, 'No! This is not happening,' " Bartlett told *Texas Monthly*. "I remember going into a room where [campaign chairman] Don Evans was talking to Karl. I closed the door and told them, and there was just silence. Then I called Karen and the governor, who were traveling. I had never seen Karen speechless before."

Bartlett began calling the press, and Hughes held a news conference. She pointed to an article in the *Dallas Morning News* in 1996 in which Bush said in a response to a question about whether he had ever been arrested for drinking, "I do not have a perfect record as a youth." Hughes said that was the only time she believed he was asked that specific question. She said he had not disclosed the incident previously out of concern for his twin daughters.

"He has always been very forthcoming in acknowledging that he drank too much in the past, before he quit drinking fourteen years ago," Hughes told reporters. "He had made a decision as a father that he did not want to set that bad example for his daughters or for any other children."

Bartlett's White House shop had fifty-two employees. They handled the thousand reporters who covered the White House, wrote Bush's speeches (Bush made more than six hundred public appearances a year, and most entailed giving a speech), and ran the White House Web site, which received fourteen million hits a day. Bartlett's job was to look at the "big picture," planning overall strategy for three to six weeks in advance. He also gave briefings and talked with reporters by phone on background, a task that took thirty percent to forty percent of his time. The "senior administration official" quoted in news stories was often Bartlett.

"What makes Dan Bartlett good is that he gets the game,"

Time White House correspondent John Dickerson said. "For Karen, this wasn't natural. Dan's relationship with the press is much better. I call him to get the real take on what is going on, and he does it without giving away stuff that will hurt him or his boss."

"We respect the press and the job they have to do," Bartlett told me in his second-floor West Wing office. "But the way we go about our job—and it's something I learned from Karen—is that we try as much as possible to treat all reporters fairly and equally. We're not going to play favorites. We are not going to pit one reporter against another or play one publication off against another."[162]

In contrast to the administrations of Clinton, Reagan, and Bush's father, "We do not have as many of the people in the West Wing litigating their differences with other members of the administration through the press," Bartlett said. "You could make an argument that they are still doing that in the State or Defense Department. But we have a team that appreciates that decisions ought to be made by the president, and that it's not fair to the president, the administration, or the country to not allow him to make a decision because outside forces put pressure on him because staffers are leaking information."

Because of cable news and the Internet, the Clinton and Bush administrations were the first to face a round-the-clock news cycle. As news outlets have proliferated all over the world, the pressure has intensified. At the same time, journalists have become more adversarial. While they have always tended to be liberal, what has changed is that many journalists increasingly target anyone in the establishment and are unwilling to listen to the other side and present a fair, honest account. The Bush press strategy was designed to counter that trend, giving reporters less opportunity to play one administration official off against another.

"I think of the Clinton people as day traders in the market," Bartlett said. "We are like long-term investors," he said. "If there was something in the news, they would jump in and try to win every news cycle. We take a different approach. We have a strategic plan, an objective to reach in communicating to the public.

When we make that plan, all our communications are going to support those specific objectives. When something appears that is inconsistent with that, we have to show discipline and not let the rudder start moving different ways to whatever is in the news cycle. That is frustrating to reporters. They want to go where the news is and be on the evening news or the front page."163

Looking back, the White House decided it had strayed from that approach in handling the flap in July 2003 over the sixteen words about Niger in Bush's State of the Union address. At the time, Bush was in Africa, discussing a $15 billion commitment over five years to fighting AIDS. Bartlett was with him. George Tenet, the CIA director, was on the West Coast. Other key aides were on vacation. Bartlett specialized in crisis communications. His approach was to release all relevant information quickly and accurately. Then, like the flu, the frenzy would run its course. But with the Niger flap, because everyone was in different time zones, they could not all sit down in one room and figure out exactly who knew what when. As a result, the initial comments seemed defensive or were wrong.

"The knee-jerk reaction to the controversy was probably not the proper reaction," Andy Card said. "We said, 'We wish those words had not been in there.' The truth is the words were accurate, but they were not necessary, and it would have been better to leave them out. But the way we described them played into the misimpression that the president lied or was misleading. He didn't lie and was not misleading. We should have said the words were accurate, but they were not necessary to show that we needed regime change."164

For presidents like Johnson and Nixon, critical coverage magnified their paranoia, leading them to demand that the FBI or CIA engage in illegal surveillance or wiretapping to zero in on sources of the criticism or the leaks. Nixon was so far gone that he and aide Bob Haldeman interpreted a *Washingtonian* magazine article reporting on the sexual hijinks of John F. Kennedy and Lyndon Johnson as an implicit attack on Nixon for being "square."

Recognizing the article for what it was, Nixon muttered to Haldeman as they discussed it, "People on the other side are getting desperate." Nixon warned, according to a transcript of the August 2, 1972, Oval Office recording, "You never know—they may go after a number of things."

The contrast between the obsequious way people treated them in the White House and the criticism they saw in the press only served to unbalance such presidents even more.

"You walk in and see the president standing behind that desk," George Reedy, Johnson's press secretary, said. "There are flags of the Marines and Navy and Air Force behind him. All of a sudden your knees start knocking. This is your country. To be nasty or critical of him is almost like blowing your nose on the American flag. He is your country. Then when people get out of the White House, they get their nerve back."

Unless they are well grounded, the contrast makes presidents feel that everyone around them is duplicitous.

"Someone will come in and could not be nicer, and then go out and denounce the president," Reedy said. "That makes the president cynical and mistrusting."

Unlike any other White House in recent memory, Bush and his aides took it all in stride.

"Right after a reporter asked Bush to name the heads of Taiwan, Chechnya, Pakistan, and India, I was down in Austin at the governor's mansion," said Terry Johnson, Bush's Yale roommate. "He and I were sitting around chewing the fat. I said, 'Man, was that ever a cheap shot,' giving him a perfect opportunity to vent about the unfairness of the press and gotcha journalism."[165]

"No, not really," Bush said. "He had a right to ask that question, and I just didn't answer it very well. I'll do better next time."

"If they give opinions, that's fine," Clay Johnson said. "But I've seen him get perturbed if there is a misrepresentation of the facts. He will go to Dan Bartlett or Andy Card and say, 'This person is totally wrong. You need to get aggressive about correcting the facts.'"

Bush's equanimity went back to his balanced approach to life and to his job. In an interview during the campaign, Bush said, "I feel like saying, 'God's will be done. That if I win . . . I know what to do. If I don't win, so be it." Hopefully, he said, "I'll be able to survive all the gossip and slings and arrows and all the scrutiny and the discussions and the questions. And if it works, great. And I believe I can do the job. And if it doesn't work, that's just the way it goes, and I'll come back home and my wife'll love me, the dog'll love me, the cats will play like they don't, but they really will."[166]

A self-centered lot, reporters were sure that Bush and his aides spent their time worrying about what they were saying about them. But Bush's aides kissed off the critical coverage as "a Washington thing." Working fourteen-hour days, they had little time to tune in to what the media were saying about them. While their assistants kept their TVs on, many of Bush's senior aides kept them off.

Reporters reacted with stunned disbelief when Bush said he wasn't watching TV for news on the war in Iraq. At a press conference on December 12, 2003, Fox TV correspondent Wendell Goler asked Bush, "Mr. President, in light of the *New York Times* editorial today, tell me why—"

"Let me stop you, Wendell," Bush said. "I don't read those editorials," he said to laughter. "So you're going to have to—maybe you ought to ask the question not in that context, but in another context."

Bush's aides made the point that not everyone reads the *Washington Post* and the *New York Times*. More and more people get their news from their trusted local TV anchor or from the Internet.

"The president always has opponents," Andy Card said. "If he says, 'It's a beautiful day,' someone will say, 'Maybe to you it is, but . . .'"[167]

Even when interviews were approved, many Bush aides avoided appearing in print or on television, even if it could help correct the media caricatures. Instead of competing for media attention, as White House aides in previous administrations had done, they competed over who could be the most modest. The Bush people were like antimatter: Rather than having the normal inclination to feed their egos by garnering attention, they had the opposite orientation and were nearly impervious to press criticism.

"The press office and I have a deal," Margaret Spellings said.

"They don't do policy, and I don't do press. You never see Harriet Miers' name in the paper," Spellings said.[168]

Before becoming staff secretary and then deputy chief of staff in the White House, Miers—pronounced Myers—was comanaging partner of Locke, Liddell & Sapp in Dallas, a firm of 425 lawyers. Her clients included Microsoft and Disney. She was the first woman president of the Texas State Bar and the first woman president of the Dallas Bar Association. In 1997, the *National Law Journal* named her one of the Hundred Most Influential Lawyers in America, along with Lawrence H. Tribe, Robert M. Morgenthau, and William P. Barr. The publication also listed her as one of the Fifty Most Influential Women Lawyers in America.

Miers represented Bush's campaign committee, his transition committee, and his first inaugural committee. Occasionally, she did legal work for Bush personally.

As staff secretary, Miers controlled the paper flow to the president, making sure that briefing papers submitted to him were clearly written and timely and presented all sides of the issues. She also supervised the executive clerk and the records management and correspondence departments. While most people have never heard of the position, the job of staff secretary is critical. In the past, some staff secretaries have used their power to try to influence policy by skewing briefing papers in one direction or another. Jerry H. Jones, who was Nixon's staff secretary, said his job was to "kill ideas" if necessary.

"I know that sounds awful, but the problem with the White House is people come in with great ideas, and they don't understand the consequences of this brilliant idea," he once said. "And you have to send the genius idea to its natural enemies and test it and see if the natural enemy can kill it. If the natural enemy can't kill it, then it's worth going with."

In contrast, Miers, petite and soft-spoken, operated as an honest broker. She applied discipline even-handedly, telling aides that they had not gotten their papers in on time or had written a magnificent paper but it was not tight enough or did not have a bottom line.

In June 2003, Bush appointed Miers as one of two deputy chiefs of staff, replacing Josh Bolten when he became director of the Office of Management and Budget. Joe Hagin, the other deputy chief of staff, focused on the operations of the White House, including arrangements for out-of-town trips, buying supplies, and supervising White House security and construction projects. In her new job, Miers coordinated the development of policy. That meant she worked with Spellings, who was over domestic policy; Condi Rice, who was over international issues; Stephen Friedman, who was in charge of economic matters; and John Gordon, a former deputy director of Central Intelligence who was over homeland security issues, to ensure that they had well-reasoned, politically vetted, and timely policy recommendations. When Ari Fleischer announced Miers's appointment as deputy chief of staff, a reporter had to ask how to spell her name.

"She doesn't want to be in the paper," Spellings said of Miers. "She's all about the president. Will people think she is important and in the know for her next gig? I can tell you she is and she is. But everyone wanted to know about John DiIulio and David Frum."

The fact that Spellings and Miers, two of Bush's most powerful aides, were unknown to the media and the public was a measure of how successful the Bush White House was at maintaining secrecy. In Clay Johnson's view, their lack of a public profile was also emblematic of the kind of people Bush wanted around him—aides who were smart, hardworking, totally loyal, and had a good sense of humor but who also were focused on Bush instead of themselves and were "not interested in being heralded for their role."[169]

Besides keeping a low profile, eschewing leaks, and avoiding Potomac Fever, the Bush team was expected to present ideas to the president in a collaborative fashion.

"Directly lobbying for an idea that everyone else is against, i.e., taking advantage of a friendship or proximity, is not kosher," Clay Johnson said. "I have heard the president ask, not in an admonishing fashion but as a way of referencing the desired process, 'Are you trying to lobby me?' I've also heard him say that the person should make sure his or her opinions are understood by the appropriate policy people, again turning them back toward the process."

Those few aides who tried to make end runs around the process were admonished by Andy Card or Brett M. Kavanagh, who replaced Miers as staff secretary. A former law clerk to Supreme Court Justice Anthony M. Kennedy, Kavanagh had previously been a partner with the law firm of Kirkland & Ellis and then served as Bush's senior associate counsel.

Longtime Washington Republicans—not to mention Democrats—complained that the Bush White House did not consult them. But Karl Rove maintained an intricate system for obtaining feedback from political leaders throughout the country, from governors to members of local school boards.

"My perception is a lot of those people want to say, 'I was at the White House this morning,'" Spellings said. "They get to trade on that and have cachet. We're not here to puff up the reputations of people who want to trade on their access."[170]

In part, the caricatures played into Bush's hands, his aides believed.

"One of the best qualities in politics is to be misunderestimated," Bartlett said with a grin.[171]

The media reported on strategy sessions by Hughes, Bartlett, and Mary Matalin, the former CNN *Crossfire* cohost who was Cheney's press aide for two years. Hughes was said to be the protective nanny, shielding Bush from contact with the press. But the idea that Hughes called the shots was another myth. As was true of everything else that went on in his White House, the strategy was Bush's.

"Bush has a keen understanding of communications," Bartlett said. "He is like a CEO—somebody who sets goals and builds a team. He views communication the same way. He wants to know what are our objectives and what is our strategy for achieving those objectives. If I bring him a request for an interview, he says, 'You've told me our strategy is XYZ. How does that fit into our strategy?' You better have an answer that this reinforces our short-term or long-term strategy. He doesn't want me coming to him with an interview request from some reporter because I have a problem with that reporter and I want to fix it."[172]

Based on Bush's strategy, Hughes and Bartlett in the early days worked out a clear set of goals.

"We're not going to give a speech just because there was something critical in the paper that day," Bartlett said. "We're not going to be reactive. We're not going to talk about what we're against. What are we for? You can't lead America by saying America is going to hell in a handbasket." Instead, Bartlett said, "You have to lead by presenting an optimistic agenda set on principles and certain goals. That's why you find a lot of Americans who may not support everything the president is doing, but they still support him because this person knows where he wants to take the country, because the way he thinks is based on principle, because he has good character, and because they believe he may have more information than they do. They think, 'Maybe I should trust him in the direction he's taken us.' I think that's why we have maintained the support we have."

Thus, balancing the negative press the White House might get because reporters are frustrated by the secrecy policy against the positive effect of communicating Bush's message with a single voice, the White House decided that the benefits outweighed the drawbacks. But as Bartlett was quick to point out, even the Bush White House was not able to prevent all leaks.

On July 14, 2003, conservative columnist Robert D. Novak wrote a piece naming CIA employee Valerie Plame as an "agency operative on weapons of mass destruction." As he later wrote, while talking with a "senior administration official," Novak had asked why the CIA sent former ambassador Joseph C. Wilson IV to Niger to look into reports that Saddam Hussein had been trying to buy uranium from that country. Novak's source, whom he described privately as being in the White House, told him Wilson was sent because he was married to Plame, who worked for the CIA. Another official confirmed her CIA affiliation to Novak.

For months, Wilson had been using his role in the affair to attack the Bush administration. First without attribution and then publicly, Wilson accused the administration of "misrepresenting the facts on an issue that was a fundamental justification for going to war," as Wilson was quoted in the July 6, 2003, *Washington Post*. The same day, the *New York Times* published an op-ed piece by Wilson with similar charges.

Wilson said he had reported to the CIA that it was "highly

doubtful" that Hussein had tried to buy uranium from Niger. On the one hand, he told the CIA, one former Niger official told him in February 2002 that he was unaware of any contract signed while he was in office to sell uranium to any rogue state. On the other hand, Wilson said the former official told him that in 1999, a businessman approached the official urging him to meet with an Iraqi delegation to discuss "expanding commercial relations" between Iraq and Niger. The former official believed the overture was to discuss uranium sales.

The CIA considered the report inconclusive. While it was distributed, it was not given much weight and was not seen by those drafting Bush's State of the Union speech. But contrary to Wilson's claim, the Niger reference was never a major justification for going to war. The CIA never mentioned Niger in briefings to Congress. Colin Powell never referred to it in his presentation to the UN, George Tenet had little confidence in the Niger claim and wanted it out of Bush's speeches. The Niger reference made it into Bush's State of the Union address only because it was attributed to British intelligence.

Contrary to what Novak's source told him, the CIA had not asked Wilson to go to Niger because he was married to Plame. She was then working at CIA headquarters in an undercover role on weapons of mass destruction. She had previously worked overseas in an undercover role, both under diplomatic cover and without it. When working under nonofficial cover (NOC), she had sometimes used a phony name. Because she was in a covert role, disclosure of her identity could jeopardize agents she had recruited, leading the countries they had betrayed to investigate them as spies. Moreover, if her name were disclosed, she likely could not continue in covert work.

Novak's source did not tell him that Plame was working undercover and likely was not aware she was. Most people outside the intelligence world are not tuned in to the distinction. However, the fact that Wilson made himself a lightning rod for attacks on the Bush administration made it more likely that his wife's employment might start to circulate in Washington.

Before running the story, Novak called a CIA official and said he would be referring in his column to Wilson's wife. The official told Novak that using her name might create "difficulties" if she traveled abroad. He asked him not to name her. Novak did so anyway.

When the column appeared in July, the CIA prepared a report to the Justice Department, as it is required to do whenever classified information is disclosed. About once a week, the CIA makes such a report, prepared by a low-level lawyer in the counsel's office. Because the report is supposed to include data on how widely known the information was and what impact its disclosure would have, the CIA did not send the Justice Department all the pertinent information until late September. The Justice Department opened an investigation into the leak on September 26. After notification was sent to the intelligence committees on the Hill, Democrats tipped off the press that the Justice Department was investigating a leak from the White House.

Now that Plame was outed, Wilson and the Democrats claimed that the White House leaked her name to Novak in retribution for Wilson's attacks on Bush. Democrats said Bush was trying to stifle dissent and compared the leak to Watergate abuses. Other press reports said administration officials had called reporters to persuade them to use Plame's name. Since those reports were based on anonymous sources, their veracity remained in question.

Bush was concerned about the leak to Novak and made it plain that, if caught, the leaker would be fired if not prosecuted. However, since prosecution under the Intelligence Identities Protection Act of 1982 would require that the leaker was aware that Plame had worked undercover, it was unlikely criminal charges would be brought even if the leaker were identified.

Lost in the controversy was that the real culprit was Novak. If asked by the CIA not to use an officer's name, virtually everyone in the media would abide by the request. The CIA made such a request about a dozen times a year, and only once in recent memory had a journalist—David Wise for his book on FBI traitor Robert Hanssen—failed to honor that request. There was no legitimate reason to use Plame's name. The CIA had not engaged in any wrongdoing or abuse. Nor did using her name add anything to Novak's piece. Yet virtually no one in the media pointed out that, while the source should not have disclosed her name, Novak was the only person who was on notice that identifying Plame would be damaging. In this case, it was Novak rather than the source who was most to blame for revealing her identity.

Having taken on the Bush White House, Wilson became a media darling. He and Plame, an attractive blonde, showed up at parties given by Campbell Brown of NBC and by *Washington Post* vice president Ben Bradlee and his wife Sally Quinn, a *Post* reporter. At one event, Wilson became emotional when addressing his wife's exposure.

"I'm sorry for that," he said, looking at her and fighting back tears. "If I could give you back your anonymity, I would do it in a minute."

She sat quietly, wiping away a tear, as her husband added, "Frankly, frog-marching is too good for those who decided that their political agenda was more important than either American national security or your life."

It made good copy, but their claims to have been victimized by the Bush White House were destroyed when they agreed to be photographed sitting in their Jaguar for the January 2004 issue of *Vanity Fair*. Wilson claimed that the fact that his forty-year-old wife wore sunglasses and a scarf disguised her. But anyone she had dealt with overseas could clearly recognize her.

"The pictures should not be able to identify her, or are not supposed to," Wilson told Howard Kurtz of the *Washington Post*. "She's still not going to answer any questions, and there will not be any pictures that compromise her." The reason, he said, was that "she's still employed" by the CIA and "has obligations to her employer."

In fact, the CIA never would have given her permission to appear in a photograph. No doubt because of that, she never asked. Agency officials were stunned.

Once again, the press, which had pounced on Bush over the leak, applied a double standard. Not only had Wilson and Plame subverted their own posturing as victims of the Bush White House, they had undermined the integrity of the CIA's clandestine program to collect intelligence using covert officers. If a CIA officer took so lightly her duty to remain in a clandestine role, it could make agents leery of risking their lives to provide intelligence to other CIA officers trying to recruit them.

What's more, "They risked undermining any possible criminal prosecution by their public statements and appearances," said John L. Martin, who, as chief of the Justice Department's counterespionage section, was in charge of supervising leak investigations. "The scarf and the sunglasses worn in the *Vanity Fair* picture were a sham."

Yet the only editorial criticizing Wilson's and Plame's conspicuous hypocrisy appeared in the *Boston Herald*.

"They say opposites attract, but former diplomat Joseph Wilson and his wife, CIA operative Valerie Plame, are the exception to that rule," the editorial said. "These two phonies make the perfect couple."

23

BAGHDAD

In mid-October 2003, several of Bush's top aides were batting around ideas for future events when one of them suggested that the president visit the troops in Baghdad for Thanksgiving. It was not a novel idea. Presidents in the past routinely visited the troops, whether in Bosnia or Vietnam. What made this proposal different was that Baghdad was a far more dangerous place than the locations of other troop visits.

Andy Card presented the idea to Bush. The security of the trip would depend on how secret they could keep it. Bush was skeptical but agreed to it anyway. He told Laura about the plan, and Joe Hagin, the deputy chief of staff, began planning the operation. Dan Bartlett, who was in on the first meeting, was not told that Bush was actually going until the Tuesday before Thanksgiving, when Bush signed off on the plan.

The press would be told that Bush would be spending Thanksgiving at his Crawford ranch. Dick Cheney, Colin Powell, and Donald Rumsfeld were told of the plan, but even Secret Service agents were not clued in until the last minute.

On Wednesday morning, Bush held a secure videoconference from Crawford with Cheney, Andy Card, and Rice.

"The president went around and asked if we still thought we should go," Rice told me. "He was concerned about how many soldiers we would see. He didn't want a lot feeling left out. He was told the dinner would be for six hundred soldiers. He felt that would be representative. He also didn't want to be in the way. He wanted to make sure the command really wanted him to come. Then he asked us if we thought it was worth the risk, particularly because Andy and I would be on the plane. We said we thought it was what we should do."[173]

That afternoon, Bartlett began rounding up the thirteen pool correspondents who would accompany Bush to Baghdad. They were told not to notify their bosses or their families. While Bush told his daughters just before he left, he did not tell his mother and father, who were coming for Thanksgiving.

At 5:30 P.M., Bush and Rice got in an unmarked van with tinted windows. They were driven to a private airport near Waco for the first leg of the flight on *Air Force One*. Normally, the Secret Service and local police block traffic in advance of the president's motorcade. In this case, because the plans had to be kept secret, the van proceeded like any other vehicle and got stuck in pre-Thanksgiving traffic. Bush commented that "someone probably should have thought of this," according to Rice. Bush and Rice wore baseball caps that they pulled down to shield their faces.

"We looked like a normal couple," Bush later told reporters with a smile.

They landed at Andrews Air Force Base outside of Washington, where they picked up additional pool reporters. They took off for Baghdad in a second Boeing 747-200B used as *Air Force One*. The plane is equipped with the most sophisticated tactical countermeasures of any U.S. aircraft. It can fool heat-seeking missiles and take evasive maneuvers on autopilot, allowing it to withstand any in-air attack. It can also be refueled in air. But reporters were nervous. Five days earlier, insurgents using what were believed to be SA-7 shoulder-fired, surface-to-air missiles attacked a DHL cargo plane as it landed in Baghdad. A missile hit one of the plane's wings, but it landed safely. Everyone on board *Air Force One* wore flak jackets. They were told to keep their blinds down. If word of the trip leaked out, Bush said later, "I was fully prepared to turn this baby around and come home."

Fighter jets escorted *Air Force One* as it approached Baghdad. The cabin running lights and cabin lights were out. The only light,

Rice recalled, was from the glow of an illuminated clock inside the senior-staff cabin.

"We said a collective prayer just before landing," Rice said. "We asked for God's guidance and protection."[174]

Rice said she prays as many as ten times day.

"I'm a minister's daughter," she said. "It's the most natural thing in the world. Sometimes I pray to myself and sometimes, when I'm alone, I pray out loud."

The entire trip from Texas took seventeen hours.

Bush showed up in the mess hall at Baghdad International Airport, where soldiers from the First Armored Division and the Eighty-Second Airborne Division were to have Thanksgiving dinner.

"We knew there was a dinner planned with Ambassador [L. Paul] Bremer and Lieutenant General [Ricardo] Sanchez," an Army captain wrote to a retired military buddy. "There were six hundred seats available, and all the units in the division were tasked with filling a few tables. Soldiers were grumbling about having to sit through another dog-and-pony show, so we had to pick soldiers to attend. I chose not to go," the captain said.

At about 1500, a lieutenant, with a smile, asked the captain to come to dinner with him. He said to bring a camera.

"I didn't really care about getting a picture with Sanchez or Bremer, but when the division's senior intelligence officer asks you to go, you go," the captain said.

As the captain was seated in the chow hall, Secret Service agents showed up.

"Then Brigadier General Dempsey got up to speak, and he welcomed ambassador Bremer and LTG Sanchez," the captain said. "Bremer thanked us all and pulled out a piece of paper as if to give a speech. He mentioned that the president had given him this Thanksgiving speech to give to the troops."

Rather than reading the speech himself, Bremer asked if there was "anybody back there more senior than us" who could read it.

"Then, from behind the camouflage netting, the president of the United States came around," the captain wrote. "The mess hall erupted with hollering. Troops bounded to their feet with shocked smiles and just began cheering with all their hearts. The building actually shook. It was just unreal. I was absolutely stunned."

Soldiers were hollering, cheering, and a lot of them were crying, the captain wrote. "There was not a dry eye at my table," he said. "I could clearly see tears running down his [Bush's] cheeks. Here was this man, our president, came all the way around the world, spending seventeen hours on an airplane and landing in the most dangerous airport in the world, where a plane was shot out of the sky not six days before, just to spend two and a half hours with his troops. Only to get on a plane and spend another seventeen hours flying back."

Bush told the troops, "We did not charge hundreds of miles into the heart of Iraq, pay a bitter cost of casualties, defeat a ruthless dictator, and liberate twenty-five million people only to retreat before a band of thugs and assassins."

After Bush delivered his speech, he "stepped down and was just mobbed by the soldiers," the captain said. "He slowly worked his way all . . . around the chow hall and shook every last hand extended. Every soldier who wanted a photo with the president got one. I made my way through the line, got dinner, then wolfed it down as he was still working the room. You could tell he was really enjoying himself."

As the captain was having a photo of himself taken with Rice, Bush got closer to his table.

"I felt like I was drunk," the captain said. "As he passed and posed for photos, he looked me in the eye and said, 'How you doin', Captain?' I smiled and said, 'God bless you, sir.' To which he responded, 'I'm proud of what you do, Captain.' Then he moved on."

Just before takeoff, there was a delay as the plane waited for clearance. That was the only time Rice became really apprehensive, she said. She slept most of the way back.

After Bush left Baghdad, the White House let the rest of the media in on the secret. The story made an astounding tale on TV on the evening of Thanksgiving. The trip sent a message that Bush meant what he said when he vowed not to leave Iraq until it had been stabilized. It showed what a big heart he had. But to Bush, the meaning went far deeper. He was going to protect the United

States. The troops were part of that effort. He would do everything he could to support them and demonstrate the same loyalty to them that they demonstrated to their country.

While the Democratic candidates did not directly attack the trip, they made use of the event to say the war was wrong and the United States was failing in Iraq. Howard Dean said the president is "incapable" of winning international support for reconstruction efforts because "he managed to insult all the people whose help we need, gratuitously."

Other Democrats took to TV to say the Thanksgiving Day trip was a publicity stunt. Of course, any human endeavor can be cast in selfish terms: A Nobel-winning scientist did it for the money. A firefighter who ran into a burning building to save a child did it so he could become a hero. People who view the world through such a warped lens betray a lot about how they feel about themselves.

Soon the media took up the cause. They grumbled that they had been lied to about where Bush was on Thanksgiving. They tried desperately to find the slightest discrepancy in the account of the trip. And they asked gotcha questions at press briefings.

The *Washington Post* led the pack. Every reporter agreed that, if faced with the choice of participating in the secrecy required by security considerations or not going on the trip, they would choose to go. But Mike Abramowitz, the national editor of the *Post*, said he was "concerned that no one on the desk knew where a White House reporter was."

As national editor, Abramowitz was in charge of the coverage of not only the White House but the Defense Department, the CIA, and the FBI. The fact that he had trouble distinguishing between his need to know the location of one of his reporters and the need to protect the lives of the president and the journalists on the plane was disturbing.

Referring to the fact that radio and TV reporters were saying Bush was in Crawford when he was flying to Baghdad, Dana Milbank, at a press briefing, asked Scott McLellan, "So the White House has no compunctions about having misled the American people on this trip?"

"Look, I understand, and I appreciate the question you're asking," McLellan said politely. "But I think that the American people understand the security arrangements that we made so the president of the United States could go and thank our troops in person, on Thanksgiving, during a very special moment for them, while they were celebrating Thanksgiving Day."

"So did the president then—I mean, he made a decision that it was worth telling a white lie to accomplish this policy goal—or a political goal," Milbank said.

Professional journalists ask questions to elicit information. They do not use their positions to engage in harangues or launch ideological attacks. Milbank's questions and those of some other White House reporters did not constitute journalism. They were simply abuse.

It was ironic that under Fred Hiatt, the chief of the editorial page, the *Washington Post* ran thoughtful, informative editorials that generally supported Bush on foreign policy. The *Post* was one of the few major newspapers to support the Iraq war. The editorials reflected the views of Donald Graham, the chairman and CEO of the Washington Post Co., who had done a stint as a District of Columbia police officer and appreciated the need for security. But in its coverage of the White House, the news side of the paper resembled the liberal *Village Voice*, and the paper made little effort to keep editorial comments out of news stories. In one example, Milbank wrote about the trip: "While the troops cheered the moment, it was too soon to know whether the image of Bush in his Army jacket yesterday will become a symbol of strong leadership or a symbol of unwarranted bravado."

Not to be outdone, Milbank's colleague Mike Allen wrote that when Bush was photographed in Baghdad holding a platter with a roast turkey on it, the turkey was not to be eaten until later. As is routine at large catered events, the contractor had sliced the turkey beforehand for the troops and displayed a whole turkey as an ornament. Bush knew nothing about it. But in his December 4, 2003, story, Allen wrote that "the foray has opened new credibility questions for a White House that has dealt with issues as small as who placed the 'Mission Accomplished' banner aboard the aircraft carrier Bush used to proclaim the end of major combat operations in Iraq, and as major as assertions about Saddam Hussein's arsenal of unconventional weapons and his ability to threaten the United States."

The credibility question was one that Allen himself invented, based both on the fact that the turkey was not eaten at the dinner and the fact that there had been slightly varying accounts of an encounter in the air with another plane as *Air Force One* returned to Washington. To say that either one created a credibility question, a reporter would have to have paranoid tendencies.

In an effort to give them some color, Dan Bartlett relayed to reporters on the return trip an anecdote from an *Air Force One* pilot. To maintain security, the presidential plane was using a designation other than *Air Force One*. But the plane is unmistakable. According to what Bartlett told reporters, a British Airways plane flying part of the way with the president's plane saw it and radioed, "Did I just see *Air Force One*?"

Bartlett said the president's pilot radioed back, "Gulfstream V." Since the Gulfstream is a small plane, the response was taken as an inside joke. After a pause, the other pilot said, "Oh."

Bartlett thought the conversation took place between *Air Force One* and the other plane. Actually, it was a conversation overheard by *Air Force One* between another pilot and a British controller. Since the other pilot had a British accent, and a British Airways plane was in the vicinity of the presidential plane for a good portion of the flight, Colonel Mark Tillman, the *Air Force One* captain, and others in the cockpit assumed that the other pilot was a British Airways pilot. But after no British Airways pilot came forward to say he had asked the question about *Air Force One*, the British checked and said the conversation was between a "non-UK operator" and the British controller. What happened was that the other aircraft asked if the plane behind it was *Air Force One*. After consulting flight plans for the area, the controller radioed back that the plane was a Gulfstream V. For security reasons, *Air Force One* had filed a flight plan identifying it as a Gulfstream V.

Experienced reporters understand that relayed conversations are always subject to minor misunderstandings. If there was no motive for giving one account over another and no evidence of deception, they disregarded the discrepancy. Whether the conversation took place between a plane and a controller or between that plane and *Air Force One* did not alter the point of the story. But some White House reporters pounced on the differences as if they thought they were on to another Watergate. One actually asked Scott McLellan at a briefing if the different accounts had taken "some of the shine off the president's surprise visit to the troops." Once again, the *Washington Post* led the way.

"The White House yesterday made a third approach in its attempt to land the controversy about whether a plane spotted *Air Force One* on its secret flight to Baghdad on Thanksgiving Day," Dana Milbank wrote in a December 5 story.

Still, mysteries remained, Milbank maintained.

"Who was this 'non-UK operator'?" he asked. "And how is it that a British Airways plane could have been with *Air Force One* 'for a good portion' of the flight if the president's plane was averaging 665 miles per hour—far beyond the speed of commercial aircraft?"

As usual, it was Milbank's facts that were malleable. According to his colleague Mike Allen, who was on the trip, and the itinerary distributed to reporters, the average speed that was given applied to the trip from Texas to Washington, not from Baghdad to Washington. The speed from Baghdad was never given. Thus, Milbank's premise was wrong. But even if the speed of 665 miles per hour applied to the trip back from Baghdad, there are so many variables that go into a plane's speed that no conclusion can be drawn from the facts available to Milbank, according to commercial pilots.

Airplane speed is affected by the weight of the plane, how it is equipped, the cruising speed chosen in relation to the need to conserve fuel, and the temperature and wind conditions at particular heights and positions. Another plane flying with *Air Force One* could have been going faster or slower depending on what headwinds or tailwinds it was experiencing.

Referring to Milbank's story, Wayne Merrill, a senior Delta Airlines captain who regularly flies across the Atlantic, said, "He's trying to say something without knowing the facts. He doesn't know what he's talking about."

Steven Nehlig, a recently retired American Airlines captain who was a check airman, meaning he instructed other American pilots, said: "He is way off base. There's nothing sinister in the White House account."

24

LIBERAL ENDS,
CONSERVATIVE MEANS

From across the lobby of the West Wing, Karl Rove looks about as remarkable as your neighborhood druggist. He has flat features that make him appear cherubic, pale blue eyes, a pinkish complexion, and wispy white hair combed back from a receding hairline. Sitting at his conference table in his second-floor office in the West Wing, the fifty-three-year-old Rove looked more imposing. His glasses gave him an intellectual look. He missed nothing.

As senior advisor to the president, the amount of time Rove spent with him was matched by only a handful of Bush's other top aides, like Andy Card, Condoleezza Rice, Margaret Spellings, Harriet Miers, and Dan Bartlett. Rove, whose office had a view of the Washington Monument, began his day with a 7:15 A.M. meeting with Card, Dan Bartlett, Harriet Miers and Joe Hagin, the two deputy chiefs of staff. At 7:30 A.M., Rove sat between Condoleezza Rice and Margaret Spellings at the meeting of the senior staff, whose members make the top salary of $151,000. After Bush's 8 A.M. national-security briefings from George Tenet and Robert Mueller, Rove met with Bush, together with Andy Card, Dan Bartlett, and Vice President Dick Cheney.

Rove had the knack of absorbing mega amounts of information about a problem, boiling it down to simple terms, and illustrating issues with clear examples. He was famous for talking on the phone while at the same time sending e-mail on his Blackberry.

"He has more facts to bring to bear than most people," Clay Johnson said. "You want him at your table."

Rove churned out ideas that fit the compassionate conservative rubric. He picked the optimal moment to unveil them. In what he called "political heuristics," Rove would say that most people don't retain the details of the proposals but come away with a positive feeling about Bush.

"They get a sense of his values, of what kind of a person he is," according to Rove.

While Rove is feisty, those who know him laughed at the caricatures of him.

"Karl is kind, gentle," Margaret Spellings said. "Can he get mad? Sure. But the sort of evil Darth Vader image is ridiculous."[175]

Asked what he does, Rove told me, "I'm a generalist. I obviously pay attention to the politics," he said. "I look at a wide variety of issues and get educated and offer up perspectives."[176]

One of Rove's jobs was to manage expectations. No matter what election was coming up, he would say he expected a close race. When there was a victory in Iraq, he made sure Bush pointed out the difficult road ahead. Perversely, Rove was happiest when he saw Bush portrayed as a "miserable failure," as Democratic presidential candidate Dick Gephardt called him. It meant the president was being misunderestimated again.

"I can't explain why they underestimate him, but they do," Rove said. "Whatever the reason, I hope they keep doing it. I think it is because he is from Midland, Texas, and his idea of a vacation spot is Crawford rather than Hyannisport."

Fifty employees in four offices reported to Rove. The Intergovernmental Affairs Office kept in touch with governors, mayors, and school boards. The Office of Public Liaison explained Bush's programs and acted as an early warning system. The Political Affairs Office maintained liaison with state party officials and interest groups.

"It keeps us from being isolated," Rove said. "They find out how the realtors and title companies are going to respond to proposals to simplify real-estate closings."

The Bush people wanted to avoid the mistakes of Bush's father, who rested on his laurels after victory in the first war against Iraq and did not offer new initiatives in 1992. In that administration, one person was in charge of long-term planning.

"Andy said we can't duplicate what happened in the administration of Bush 41," Rove said. "They said, 'You're in charge of long-term planning.' Others said, 'I'm not part of that, so forget it.' Andy said we needed to have all major players participate."

The result was the Office of Strategic Initiatives, the fourth office reporting to Rove. Once a month, the office held what was called Strategery, a meeting of twelve principals who looked at the big picture. Under the rules, the principals cannot send a deputy to the meeting, which was held in room 208 of the Eisenhower Executive Office Building.

When Rove began working for him in November 1993, Bush was running for governor of Texas. He was talking about three issues: the need to improve reading instruction in the schools, the need to toughen punishment for juveniles who commit crimes, and the need to let welfare recipients know they will lose benefits if they do not make an effort to get a job.

As governor, Bush presided over Medicaid and became familiar with the inadequacies of the American health care system, including Medicare. Back in 1965 when Medicare was passed, doctors still made house calls, and the number of prescription medicines was limited. The concept of preventive medicine was in its infancy. In his presidential run, Bush made Medicare reform one of his six goals. In December 2003, Bush signed the Medicare Prescription Drug, Improvement, and Modernization Act.

To Rove, the bill embodied Bush's approach. On the one hand, it helped seniors, many with low incomes, by covering prescription drugs and checkups that were not covered before. While coverage would not start until 2006, a prescription discount card was to start giving seniors savings of ten percent to twenty-five percent in June 2004. On the other hand, by introducing competition, free enterprise, deductibles, and preventive health care, the new law used free market approaches of the private sector to keep costs in line.

The concept was the opposite of the Democrats' approach, symbolized by the health care package put together by Hillary Clinton when she was first lady. She wanted to create a Frankenstein of two hundred new regional health cooperatives run by 50,000 new bureaucrats to administer the program in the command-and-control style of the old Soviet Union. If passed, the program would have cost $1.6 trillion over five years.

In contrast, the Bush approach was to use elegantly simple market-based solutions to reduce costs. Under the old Medicare, "The federal government will not pay $500 for medications that will help keep you from developing ulcers," Rove said. "But it will pay $29,000 for treatment in the hospital. When Medicare was passed, there was no preventive care. Now when you are a senior and turn sixty-five, you will get a physical. Medicare can identify problems rather than waiting until you are seventy-five and they are more serious. Now a doctor can identify hypertension early on and give you the diet and exercise and medication to prevent heart disease."[177]

The bill was as desirable as apple pie. How could anyone be against giving the elderly prescription drugs that they did not have before? But the Democrats found a way to oppose the measure, saying vaguely that its passage would bring about the "beginning of the end of Medicare."

"It would be a dagger in the heart of Medicare as we know it," said Representative John Lewis, a Georgia Democrat. "This bill is a backdoor attempt by the Republican Party to privatize Medicare."

If that sounded like gobbledygook, it was. Seniors would either have drug coverage or they wouldn't. It was the same kind of doomsday argument liberals used to oppose Bush's efforts to improve reading instruction by imposing reading tests, saying testing will ruin the education system and drive away teachers. There was even a Students Against Testing organization on the web.

"I guess they are saying they are nervous about the government losing a monopoly and empowering people to make choices," Rove said. Under the new law, seniors will be able to choose between traditional Medicare and plans administered by private companies, which might offer a better deal because they are more efficient than the government-run plan.

"My dad is seventy-eight," Rove said. "He doesn't want to make any choices. He should have a system where he doesn't have to. But I want to be able to make the choice."

The bill "uses conservative means to achieve liberal ends," Rove said. "The liberal end is quality health care for seniors. The conservative means is we're going to use the market, choice, innovation, and empowerment of the individual and incentives for savings and for taking personal responsibility to try to achieve it."

Bush applied the same approach to the federal workforce. Since the private sector, because of the profit motive, inherently has more incentive to be efficient, Bush had the Office of Management and Budget work with agencies to pinpoint functions that were commercial in nature and could possibly be performed at lower cost by the private sector. Then agencies worked with employees to determine their most efficient organization and cost for a particular task, compared this to the lowest private-sector bid for the same work, and determined who could best perform the work for the taxpayers. Printing, automobile maintenance, and computer operations were examples of work that could be reviewed in this fashion.

At the same time, the OMB developed programs to improve the effectiveness and efficiency of government agencies and employees. The idea was to make employees and agencies more results oriented, using a scorecard system to evaluate accomplishments and progress toward great accomplishments. Asked in an online chat on the White House Web site what the penalty was for failing, Clay Johnson, as deputy OMB director, responded, "Public shame and humiliation and the opportunity to be questioned about it by the president."

In the same fashion, instead of signing on to the Kyoto Protocol, with its drastic mandatory cuts in greenhouse gas emissions, Bush developed a program of incentives and tax credits to stimulate research and encourage utilities and manufacturers to reduce emissions voluntarily. By proposing limits on noneconomic damages arising from lawsuits, Bush hoped to diminish the overall cost of the tort system on the economy and the negative impact it had on individuals, such as doctors. Going back to his days as governor, Bush had been concerned about physicians and surgeons— three of whom were his friends—being driven from practicing medicine because of the high cost of liability insurance and fear of frivolous lawsuits. The idea that someone else was always to blame, even if an individual spilled hot coffee on himself or failed to follow his doctor's instructions, sickened Bush.

"For the last thirty years, our culture has steadily replaced personal responsibility with collective guilt. This must end," Bush said in a speech when he was governor.

Besides fitting into Bush's compassionate conservative agenda, overhauling Medicare was an example of Bush's desire to tackle big problems that have significant impact.

"Health care accounts for one out of seven dollars of our economy," Rove said. "If I said the poll numbers show the most important thing you can do is call for school uniforms in public schools, I would get kicked out of the Oval Office on my fanny."[178]

Bush placed Stephen Friedman, who replaced economist Lawrence Lindsey as his economics advisor in December 2002, in charge of coordinating policy on the Medicare bill as it went through Congress. Friedman's office on the second floor of the West Wing was next to Rove's, who was on the Medicare team along with Health and Human Services Secretary Tommy G. Thompson and Thomas A. Scully, the administrator of the federal Centers for Medicare and Medicaid Services. A former chairman of Goldman Sachs, Friedman had impeccable credentials and the kind of low-key, team player approach that was a prerequisite to working for Bush.

Bush made it clear to his staff that he wanted them to get sufficient rest, to eat healthily, and to get regular exercise. To help in that regard, he added equipment to a health club on the ground floor of the Eisenhower Executive Office Building. Staffers compared notes on how much weight they had lost. Bush was said to have remarked that Lindsey needed to exercise. Friedman, sixty-six, had no such problem. At Cornell University and Columbia University's law school, Friedman had been a wrestler. In 1961, he was the Amateur Athletic Union National Champion. In 1993, he was inducted into the National Wrestling Hall of Fame. Friedman was fond of veggie burgers for lunch from the White House mess.

Friedman came to Bush's attention through Josh Bolten, another transplant from Goldman Sachs who was director of the Office of Management and Budget. A graduate of Stanford Law School who was previously deputy chief of staff, Bolten maintained a close relationship with Bush. He was also the unofficial White House expert on Judaism. On the evening before Chanukah, he appeared in a videotape on the White House Web site with two children to read bedtime stories about the holiday.

Like many of Bush's top advisors, the soft-spoken Friedman didn't need a job. When he came to the White House, he had to divest himself of $60 million in stocks, placing the money in Treasury bills and similar interest-bearing instruments. As a reminder of the more leisurely life he gave up, Friedman kept a photo over his sofa of his family taken at his vacation home in Wyoming, the mountains meeting the blue sky.

While Friedman gave background interviews, he was rarely quoted on the record. About every two weeks, he had lunch with Alan Greenspan, the chairman of the Federal Reserve Board, alternating locations between the White House and the Fed.

As chairman of the sixteen-member National Economic Council, Friedman provided Bush with advice on the economic impact of proposed programs, and he coordinated administration economic policy, a function similar to what the NSC does in the national-security area. The other top member of the economic team, Treasury Secretary John W. Snow, was both a lawyer and an economist who had been chairman and CEO of CSX Corp., the freight railroad. He was recommended by Dina Habib Powell, who, at age twenty-nine, was selected by Bush to head presidential personnel after Bush nominated Clay Johnson to be deputy OMB director.

Dina Powell was a highly respected and influential White House aide who was known for her candor but—like many in the Bush inner circle—never appeared in the media. Besides Snow, she recommended William H. Donaldson, co-founder and CEO of Donaldson, Lufkin & Jenrette, as chairman of the Securities and Exchange Commission. An Arabic speaker who was born in Cairo, Egypt, she immigrated to the United States with her family and settled in Texas when she was four. Powell had worked for Clay Johnson in the White House as well as for the Republican National Committee as director of congressional affairs and for Representative Dick Armey as member relations coordinator when he was House majority leader.

"She's not afraid to disagree with the president, albeit respectfully," Clay Johnson said of Powell. "He welcomes constructive debate and values those who are willing to engage in it with him. He does not want yes-men or women on his team."[179]

In pursuing the Medicare initiative, Friedman and his team kept in constant touch with Bush, first developing a framework for the bill and then keeping him informed on progress in Congress, asking where the president wanted to compromise to gain passage.

"The president is wise about choosing his battles," Al Gonzales said. "He knows the right battles to fight. He knows some battles are not worth it."

Contrary to Paul O'Neill's claim that Bush was like a "blind man" in meetings, Friedman found Bush's management style to be as effective as those of the top CEOs he had dealt with on Wall Street and in the corporate world.

"He has an exceptional instinct for getting to the nub of an issue and getting to it quickly," Friedman said. "He is also very curious. So when you prepare for sessions with him, you have to be on your mettle, thinking where his inquiry may go. He will have read the briefing material. He may see a direction you did not intend to pursue, and it may be very useful. He gives you clear guidance. He spends time talking philosophically about why he is where he is. So you pretty much know the direction he is going in."[180]

Rather than being the end of Medicare, Friedman said, "We believe the new law sustains it by bringing it into this century." At the same time, by providing preventive care, the new law could be expected to reduce costs incurred by long-term illnesses.

Contrary to the impression created by the media, Bush's long-term strategy was to reduce the deficit, Friedman said. "He has had a focus on deficit reduction, but also has a clear set of priorities," Friedman said. "One is that in time of war, he was going to spend more to make sure the military had what it needed. In times of economic adversity, the priority was stimulating the economy with tax cuts and getting people back to work. Once the economy is moving again through progrowth policies, he expects us to move on a glide path toward reducing the deficit."

Under Bush's projections, the deficit as a share of the gross domestic product was expected to shrink by more than half over the next five years.

While reforming Medicare and giving seniors drug benefits will attract votes, Bush did not tailor his programs to the polls. The best way to get an idea shot down, Rove would say, was to tell Bush it would sell politically. At the same time, if a program happened to snatch an issue away from the Democrats, Rove was glad to oblige.

"His thought is, the best way to get reelected is to do what you say you will do, be clear about what you want to do in the future, and do it," Rove said. "A president, if he is pursuing the right policy, can bring public opinion with him. His idea is if you are a leader, you must lead."

On signing the Medicare bill, which will cost $534 billion over ten years, Bush said, "Some older Americans spend much of their Social Security checks just on their medications. Some cut down on the dosage to make a bottle of pills last longer. Elderly Americans shouldn't have to live with those kinds of fears and hard choices."

But longtime Democratic strategist Harold Ickes, Clinton's former deputy chief of staff, said he was flabbergasted that key Democratic senators went along with the Bush plan. It was not that there was anything wrong with giving seniors prescription drugs. Rather, by giving Bush a win, the Democrats who voted for the plan had hurt fellow Democratic politicians. Thus, instead of being a dagger in the heart of Medicare, the bill was a dagger in the heart of the Democratic Party.

What was astounding was not that members of Congress wanted to help seniors by covering their prescription drugs, but that Ickes would openly give his reason for opposing the measure.

"It's totally beyond me," Ickes said, referring to the Democrats who voted for the bill. "I think it has seriously undermined our ability to change occupants of the White House next year. Republicans will make it sound like they invented Medicare. That's a big piece of political real estate to give up."[181]

25

THE CEO PRESIDENT

Five days after Bush signed the Medicare bill, Rumsfeld called Bush at Camp David. It was 3:15 P.M. on Saturday, December 13.

"Mr. President, the first reports are not always accurate," the secretary of defense began.

"This sounds like it's going to be good news," Bush said.

Rumsfeld said that General John Abizaid, who was the top military commander in Iraq, felt "confident that we got Saddam Hussein."

"Well, that is good news," the president said. "How confident is Abizaid?"

"Very confident," Rumsfeld replied.

Bush called Condoleezza Rice, who was preparing for a Christmas-caroling party to start at 5:30 P.M. at her apartment.

"Don Rumsfeld just called," Bush told her. "He talked to the command. They think they've got Saddam."

"Really?" Rice said.

"You know Don," Bush said. "He said first reports are often wrong."

Bush asked Rice to call Andy Card and Colin Powell and let them know. "Then we'll see," Bush said. "I'm skeptical. But we're not breathing a word of this."

"It's probably a double," Rice said.[182]

"I called Andy and Steve Hadley," Rice told me in her office. "They were both coming to my Christmas party anyway."

At five the next morning, the phone rang at Rice's apartment, waking her.

"We got him!" Paul Bremer, the presidential envoy to Iraq, told her.

Bremer described the capture: Outside a farm near Tikrit, an informant had directed a force of six hundred troops from the army's Fourth Infantry Division and Special Operations units to a Styrofoam trapdoor embedded in dirt and covered by a white rug. As soldiers prepared to drop a hand grenade inside, a pair of hands emerged, raised in surrender.

"I am Saddam Hussein, the president of Iraq," the man said, "I am willing to negotiate."

"President Bush sends his regards," a soldier responded.

The last refuge of the dictator was a dank crypt located about six feet below ground. Essentially a grave, it allowed Saddam to stand only directly below the shaft. It had an air pipe and fan but no plumbing. A light was not working, meaning Saddam had to lie in the hole in complete darkness.

"He was just caught like a rat," Major General Raymond Odierno, commander of the Fourth Infantry Division, said later. "When you're in the bottom of a hole, you can't fight back."

Rice called Bush. "I'm sorry to wake you, sir, but we got him."

"That's fantastic," Bush said. "Are you sure?"

"Yes," Rice replied.

Constantly on the run, Hussein had had little ability to direct the resistance in Iraq. But his capture had a psychological effect, both on Iraqis and on American public opinion. Confronted with photos of the disheveled tyrant looking like the evil person he was, Democrats and other critics found it more difficult to say that toppling the mass murderer was unjust or immoral.

Until they see threats like the ones posed by Saddam Hussein and Osama bin Laden, most people brush them aside. In fact, FBI agents who review bank security system photos of robberies often observe a bizarre sight: Some customers waiting in line actually smile as the robbers point guns at the cashiers, demand money, and even begin shooting.

Viewing a photo of one such customer, William J. Rehder, an

FBI agent in charge of bank robbery investigations in Los Angeles, told me, "The reactions of people inside vary from panic to—in this case, this guy is thinking that, 'If I do not acknowledge this, it's not really happening.' I've seen that in a number of takeover robberies," Rehder said. "He wants to continue on as if nothing is happening."

Firefighters see the same kind of denial. When people smell smoke or even see flames, they often do nothing, not trusting their own senses, afraid that others will think they have lost their cool, and hoping that if they pretend nothing is amiss, it will all go away.

"People don't want to face the fact that something is wrong," said Peter Vallas, a nationally known private fire investigator and decorated former firefighter. "They dillydally, and eventually it kills them."

In the same way, the United States, France, and Great Britain ignored the fact that Adolf Hitler was building up Germany's military in clear violation of the Treaty of Versailles. The result was World War II, in which an estimated fifty-five million soldiers and civilians lost their lives. Many more millions were left crippled, homeless, and impoverished. The U.S. military alone lost 291,557 in World War II.

George Bush saw the threat of al Qaeda and Saddam Hussein as a similar threat. Like Winston Churchill and Franklin Delano Roosevelt, he was willing to defy pundits and intellectuals who advocated appeasement. The fact that so many academics and other highly educated people did not see the threat was a commentary on higher education. People who are proficient at absorbing accepted knowledge and adopting existing conventions may not be as good at thinking originally and adapting to new conditions. Michael Dell and Bill Gates dropped out of college because they had little interest in tailoring their thinking to the prevailing wisdom.

"I took one course that was remotely related to business: macroeconomics," Dell has said. "One of the things that really helped me is not approaching the world in a conventional sense," he said. "There are plenty of conventional thinkers out there."

Bush's mind worked in the same nontraditional way. With

the rise of terrorism and the proliferation of weapons of mass destruction, Bush recognized that the accepted paradigms were no longer relevant. When a murderer like Saddam Hussein was avidly pursuing weapons-of-mass-destruction programs, Bush understood that containment and appealing to what has often amounted to an international debating society would not work. With terrorists willing to blow themselves up and kill thousands, conventional law enforcement deterrents were pointless. In a world with no margin for error, Bush was unwilling to roll the dice for the safety of America by letting dangers fester and waiting until a threat was "imminent," as Democratic candidate John F. Kerry has said he wished to do in Iraq.

If Bush's thinking was innovative, his competence in running the government was unparalleled. Most presidents were politicians who focused on enacting legislation. As the first president with an M.B.A., Bush led the government like a successful CEO. He selected talented, results-oriented aides to run a smoothly functioning White House and develop programs to make government more effective and efficient. In contrast to most recent presidents, Bush insisted on candor from his aides, insuring that he would get the best advice. His own irreverence and tendency to make fun of himself encouraged honesty. To prevent "White House-itis," Bush made it clear that anyone in his administration who developed Potomac Fever would find himself on the outside looking in.

Instead of trying to win each news cycle and poll, Bush had his eye on what America would be like long after he left the White House. In that respect, he was like multibillionaire Warren Buffett, who invested in companies he believed in for the long term and held on regardless of stock gyrations touched off by periodic setbacks in earnings and shortsighted analyst reports.

"The great difference between the real leader and the pretender is that the one sees into the future, while the other regards only the present; the one lives by the day, and acts upon expediency; the other acts on enduring principles and for the immortality," British statesman Edmund Burke said.

As someone who was centered and ethical, Bush did not engage in the kind of outrageous conduct of a Richard Nixon or Bill

Clinton. Regardless of whether one agreed with his policies, Bush was a model of how a president and his White House should operate.

"He knows who he is and is comfortable with who he is," Karl Rove said. "He doesn't need validation from the editorial pages of the *Washington Post* or the *New York Times*."

"My faith frees me," Bush said in his book *A Charge to Keep*. "Frees me to make the decisions that others might not like. Frees me to try to do the right thing, even though it may not poll well. Frees me to enjoy life and not worry about what comes next."

No one agrees with every position a president takes. Many Republican leaders opposed Bush's endorsement of a proposed constitutional amendment defining marriage as between a man and a woman. The amendment would not prevent state legislatures from allowing civil unions between gay individuals. But on most divisive issues, Bush tended to take the middle of the road. When the Supreme Court agreed to hear appeals on the University of Michigan's affirmative-action admission policies, deciding what position the U.S. government should take was "challenging," White House Counsel Al Gonzales said. "The president lived in, worked in, and ultimately governed a state with a great deal of diversity. He also believes in opportunity for everybody. He wants to use the majestic power of the presidency to create an environment where people will help other people. There are, for example a lot of different reasons people are given opportunities, and a lot of different reasons that people get into a college. It could be because their father went there, because they can run a hundred-yard dash in fewer than ten seconds, or because they can catch a football better than anyone in the state. But to not be able to consider a person's race caused this to be an issue he wrestled with. After all, in announcing my appointment to the Texas Supreme Court, he said that it did matter that I was Hispanic."[183]

Thus, Gonzales said, the decision on what course to take "involved competing core principles and providing a remedy to those who have suffered discrimination and providing equal opportunities to everyone, irrespective of skin color." In making the decision, Bush "would meet routinely with his advisors and get input. Then he would think some more about it. Ultimately," Gonzales said, "he made a decision based on what his gut told him was the right thing to do, and that was essentially to follow a middle course."

In a friend-of-the-court brief, the administration argued in the Michigan case that racial and ethnic diversity were important goals to pursue. But the brief said the university's undergraduate and law school programs were unconstitutional because race was an overwhelming factor in the admissions decision and because Michigan did not attempt a race-neutral means of achieving diversity first. The administration recommended adoption of policies like those at the University of Texas, which guarantees admission to the top ten percent of graduates at each high school in the state. Because many high schools are largely populated by minority students, the idea was that the proposal would increase minority representation.

The Supreme Court went further, saying affirmative action was permissible if it was one of the factors considered in admissions. But the justices struck down the undergraduate school's number-based scorecard program, in which every minority applicant automatically received bonus points.

When Bush thought the Democrats had a point, as when they pushed for a Department of Homeland Security, he was not afraid to reverse course and support the measure. At the same time, he rejected the idea espoused by Democratic candidate Senator John Edwards and others of creating a new domestic counterterrorism agency similar to MI5 in Great Britain. What has made the FBI effective and kept it from engaging in the abuses of the J. Edgar Hoover years is that, under the supervision of the Justice Department, it focuses on violations of criminal laws. If that standard for undertaking investigations were removed, investigators would lose their compass, straying into extraneous matters, such as political beliefs and associations, and forgetting what their real target was.*

When it came to the war on terror, there would be no middle ground, no compromise, no bending to the criticism of the Democrats or the media. Bush's resolve was as steely as Winston

---

* See the author's op-ed "No to an American MI5" in the January 5, 2003, *Washington Post*, page B7, and "Another Spy Agency? No Way," in *USA Today*, April 21, 2004, page 11A.

Churchill's during World War II. The objective, Churchill said in his first speech after becoming prime minister, was quite simple: "Victory: Victory at all costs. Victory in spite of all terror. Victory however long and hard the road may be: for without victory there is no survival."

"My job is to keep America secure," Bush would say. "I've got a solemn duty to do everything I can to protect the American people. I will never forget the lessons of September 11, 2001. Terrorists attacked us. They killed thousands of our fellow citizens. And it could happen again. And, therefore, I will deal with threats— threats that are emerging and real."

Liberal critics said that by going into Iraq, Bush had detracted from the war on terror. That was like saying that before the FBI tackles a kidnapping, child pornography, or spy case, it should first wipe out the Mafia. Unlike the war in Iraq, the war on terror was an invisible war. It was therefore easy for Democratic politicians to claim Bush had done little to prosecute that war. Unless one were part of the effort, it was difficult to know just how much Bush's leadership had done to make America safer. The fact that every morning he demanded to know what Robert Mueller of the FBI and George Tenet of the CIA were doing to prevent the next attack created pressure that focused and energized both agencies. Rather than worrying about what the critics and media were saying about him, Bush would sort through the threat list each day and make the tough decisions to try to thwart them.

If the efforts were secret, the results were not. Since 9/11, the CIA has rolled up more than 3,000 terrorists worldwide, usually with the help of foreign countries. Two-thirds of al Qaeda's leadership has been eliminated. Khalid Shaikh Mohammed, bin Laden's operations chief, has been captured. As other countries like Syria and Iran watched Saddam Hussein's regime topple, they themselves began to arrest al Qaeda members. In March 2003, as the United States began the invasion of Iraq, Libya approached the United States and eventually agreed to give up its weapons-of-mass-destruction program. By February 2004, North Korea was making a similar offer.

It was no coincidence that for an extended period after 9/11, America had not been attacked. While no one knew how many strikes might have taken place without that effort, hundreds of plots had, in fact, been thwarted. America clearly was winning the war on terror. Nor, with Saddam Hussein gone, would Americans have to worry about whether he might use weapons of mass destruction against his neighbors or against the United States, with or without the help of terrorists. For Bush, the decision to go into Iraq was akin to an FBI agent's response when confronting a serial killer he has stopped. If the agent orders the suspect to raise his hands, but instead the killer begins to reach into the back of his car, holding fire to see if the killer really has a gun would be foolhardy.

The same kind of myopia about the war on terror and the threat posed by Saddam Hussein prevented most liberals and academics from acknowledging the humanitarian aspects of Bush's policies. By getting rid of Saddam Hussein, Bush had saved the lives of Iraqis who would have been executed beyond the 300,000 the dictator already had killed. By creating another democracy in the heart of the Middle East, Bush was helping to spread freedom to the Arab world. By pushing phonics through the No Child Left Behind Act, Bush was making sure that millions of children, especially blacks and Hispanics, who otherwise would be illiterate, would learn to read. Through faith-based initiatives, Bush was helping the destitute who otherwise might not receive help. By placing blacks, women, and Hispanics in some of the highest and most sensitive positions in his administration, Bush had done more than any other president to send a message that, when it comes to accomplishment, skin color and gender were irrelevant. By giving seniors prescription drug coverage through Medicare, Bush helped some of the neediest and most desperate Americans.

The hypocrisy of the liberal position opposing the war was demonstrated when those who opposed it were asked if they thought Saddam should be restored to power. Without exception, they would say no. At the same time, they maintained the war was wrong. Thus, they wanted to have their cake and eat it, too. In the same way, liberal politicians and pundits were the first to castigate the government for failing to stop the attacks of 9/11. Yet they were the same critics who opposed measures like the Patriot Act that were needed to prevent another 9/11. In fact, Senator John F. Kerry maintained the war on terror should be handled primarily as an intelligence and law enforcement matter rather than as a job for the military. That was the same kind of wishful thinking that had allowed Osama bin Laden the freedom to attack in the first place. Rather than seeing the war on terror as his first priority, Kerry listed it as one of his last priorities after improving the economy, health care, education, and the environment. Yet without security, none of those worthwhile goals could be achieved.

Traditionally, liberals have been the champions of the underdog. Yet liberal politicians and educators were the ones who sneered at requiring regular reading tests in schools. They maintained that blacks and Hispanics, without the cultural advantages of whites, could be expected to fail reading tests. That attitude was what Bush called the "soft bigotry of low expectations." In Texas, Bush had proven them dead wrong. By introducing phonics and extra help, he brought the rate of third graders who could not read down from a scandalous twenty-three percent to less than two percent. As president, he was trying—despite resistance from Democratic politicians, education colleges, and teachers' unions—to do the same thing nationally. Rather than underfunding programs, as the Democrats maintained he was doing, since taking office he had increased federal spending on education by forty-nine percent.

"He saw children hurting," said Dr. Reid Lyon, Bush's reading advisor at the NIH. "He could have thrown money at the problem in a random fashion to please constituents, but he didn't. He knew that is what has always been done with little to no effect. Instead, he rolled up his sleeves, immersed himself in the scientific evidence about how kids learn to read, and for the first time held schools and teachers accountable for using the only reading method proven to work—phonics."[184]

In the 1960s, liberalism stood for the best in human values. On June 21, 1964, civil-rights workers James E. Chaney, Andrew Goodman, and Michael Schwerner were murdered near Philadelphia, Mississippi, because they were trying to help blacks register to vote before the presidential election. They were liberals who risked their lives to ensure that the statement in the Declaration of Independence that "all men are created equal" meant what it said. For all his faults, Lyndon Johnson pushed through the Civil Rights Act of 1964. One of the most important pieces of legislation in American history, it made discrimination in public places illegal and required employers to provide equal employment opportunities.

Today, liberal politicians and pundits live in a dreamworld, giving lip service to ideals they have always stood for and expressing pessimism about everything from the economy to the ability of Arabs to embrace democracy. More frightening, they refuse to learn the lessons of 9/11 and to face the reality of terrorism.

"Before the president even knows his opponent, his first political ad is blanketing Iowa today," Maureen Dowd complained in the November 23, 2003, issue of the *New York Times*. Dowd noted that the commercial ran Bush's statement in his State of the Union speech: "It would take one vial, one canister, one crate slipped into this country to bring a day of horror like none we have ever known." Contemptuously, Dowd wrote, "Well, that's a comforting message from our commander-in-chief. Do we really need his cold, clammy hand on our spine at a time when we're already rattled by fresh terror threats at home and abroad?"

That kind of denial was as shortsighted as the denial that firefighters and FBI agents encounter when people face danger. Bush was not willing to pretend that he did not see the smoke and flames, failing to connect the dots and letting the terrorists destroy America. The ability to foresee danger and to react to it was not taught at Harvard or Yale: It was innate horse sense, and Bush had it.

By refusing to look at Bush objectively, liberals engaged in the same kind of prejudice they have always abhorred. Bush may be helping minorities to read and seniors to get prescription drugs, but he wore cowboy boots, had a Texas accent, pronounced "nuclear" curiously, and mangled his words. According to the stereotypes, that meant he was slow-witted, and derision became the appropriate response to whatever he did. Just as academics tended to see the world from the confines of what they were taught, many liberals could not adjust to the fact that "Republican," which once stood for exclusion, had taken on a different meaning under George Bush. While "conservative" in the 1960s stood for southern sheriffs who egged on the Ku Klux Klan to commit violence against civil-rights activists, under George Bush it stood for using smart, market-based techniques to improve society.

The media abetted the distortions by downplaying progress in Iraq, brushing aside Saddam Hussein's atrocities, and ignoring what Bush has done to help kids to read and make a success of themselves. On November 8, 2003, the Associated Press reported that Sandy Hodgkinson, the top human-rights official in the U.S.-led Iraqi civilian administration, said that 300,000 Iraqis killed during Saddam Hussein's dictatorship were believed to be buried in 263 mass graves. It was the first time the number of graves was revealed, and the first time the number of executions was given with such authority. In light of that, the antiwar position that ousting Saddam Hussein was unjust appeared grotesque. But very few people ever saw the story. Only nine U.S. papers—including the *State* in Columbia, South Carolina, and the *Ledger* in Lakeland, Florida—ran it. The *New York Times* ignored the story, and the *Washington Post* referred to it in the last two paragraphs of a twenty-two paragraph article reporting that the International Committee of the Red Cross had decided to close its offices in Baghdad and the southern city of Basra.

Those same newspapers had run enough stories about the sixteen words in Bush's State of the Union speech to fill one of Saddam Hussein's palaces. Yet just as the American press initially buried stories of Nazi attacks on Jews in Germany, the media downplayed or disregarded stories that were not in line with the antiwar position.

As a boy, Bush had been too impatient to go fishing with his father for more than a few minutes at a time. He later imitated his boyish restlessness on fishing expeditions with his dad: "There are no fish! Take me in!"[185]

"I don't wait well," Bush would say.

Whether in Iraq or Afghanistan, whether in teaching kids to read or giving seniors drug coverage, Bush was not willing to wait. His dreams for America went far beyond the initiatives of his first term.

Because most people are afraid of change, great leaders are seldom fully appreciated while in office. Harry Truman was derided by many as a plain-talking Missouri farmer, yet he courageously made two of the most critical decisions in U.S. history—to end World War II by using the atomic bomb in Japan and to found the CIA and the national-security apparatus that were crucial to winning the cold war.

Like Bush, Truman thumbed his nose at elitist critics and pundits and placed his faith in the American people. Truman's plain, blunt speech played well with average voters. "Give 'em hell, Harry!" a man at a rally in Seattle yelled. Truman replied that he never deliberately gave anybody hell; he just told the truth, and the opposition thought it was hell. Today, Truman is viewed as one of the great presidents.

Before he was elected, the columnist Walter Lippmann dismissed Franklin D. Roosevelt as a "pleasant man, who, without any important qualifications for the office, would very much like to be president." In the years leading up to Pearl Harbor, Roosevelt was mercilessly attacked by isolationists opposed to his efforts to help the British, who were under siege by Hitler. By the time he died in office, Roosevelt was seen as a great president who had turned a provincial nation into a superpower.

Ronald Reagan was portrayed by the liberal media as a bellicose fool. When Reagan appealed to Soviet leader Mikhail Gorbachev to "tear down this wall," many liberals cringed. Yet Reagan's policy of dramatically increasing defense spending eventually convinced the Soviets essentially to give up, leading to a Russian democracy.

Despite the criticism, these leaders stayed the course. They understood, as country music singer Toby Keith sang in "American Soldier," that "freedom don't come free." They, like Bush, had character traits crucial to leadership, genuinely caring about the people around them and treating them with dignity and compassion.

"Reagan was such a down-to-earth individual, easy to talk to," a Secret Service agent said. "He was the great communicator. He wanted to be on friendly terms. He accepted people for what they were."

"Roosevelt would put you at ease," said William Hopkins, his executive clerk, who took dictation from him. "He asked if you wanted a cigarette or a glass of beer."

"Truman was one of the nicest people I ever met," said Charles Taylor, one of his Secret Service agents. "He treated the people around him as he would a member of his family."[186]

"He held to the old guidelines," David McCullough wrote in *Truman*. "Work hard, do your best, speak the truth, assume no airs, trust in God, have no fear."

Bush had those same values, learned in Midland instead of Independence, Missouri. Without publicity, Bush penned a note to the families of each soldier killed in Iraq and Afghanistan. Unlike the Clintons, he treated Secret Service agents, military aides, electricians, maids, and butlers with respect. Bush kept his friends, like his clothes, "for thirty years," as his friend Terry Johnson put it.[187]

In contrast, Al Gore showed his true character when he endorsed Howard Dean without first informing his former running mate, Senator Joseph I. Lieberman. Lieberman had delayed his own run for the Democratic presidential nomination to see if Gore would announce his candidacy.

John Kerry was a caricature of a politician, publicly claiming to support the troops and the war on terror while undercutting them by voting against funding to equip American soldiers and to enhance intelligence. A month before his vote against funding the military effort in Iraq, Kerry said, "I don't think that any United States senator is going to abandon our troops and recklessly leave Iraq to whatever follows as a result of simply cutting and running. That's irresponsible." He then did exactly that.

So intense was Kerry's desire to straddle every fence that after voting against the funding, he tried to explain away his vote with what amounted to gibberish: "I actually did vote for the $87 billion before I voted against it."

"The Secret Service has announced it is doubling its protection for John Kerry," late-night comedian Jay Leno said. "You can understand why—with two positions on every issue, he has twice as many people mad at him."

As a four-star general, former Democratic presidential candidate Wesley K. Clark was known as a brownnoser who would worry problems to death. General Hugh Shelton, who engineered Clark's firing as Supreme Allied Commander in Europe when Shelton was chairman of the Joint Chiefs of Staff, considered Clark a "nut." Even as Clark described how, without his knowledge, Shelton put through papers forcing his early retirement from the military, Clark insisted on MSNBC's Chris Matthews show that he had not been fired. With a similar degree of credibility, Clark claimed that if he were president, there would be no more terrorist attacks. Depending on what day it was, Clark espoused diametrically opposite positions on the war in Iraq. Asked by Paula Zahn after Saddam Hussein was captured if Saddam would still be in power if Clark had been president, the candidate said disingenuously he "would probably have been brought out of power in most likely a different process . . . we would have worked it through the United Nations, through that process."

Even when going after al Qaeda, Clark proposed setting up an international tribunal for prosecuting terrorism. The idea that America would be protected from terrorists in this way was laughable, yet it was typical of the leading Democratic politicians' shortsighted approach. They were willing to entrust the safety of Americans to international bodies with no interest in American security. The founding fathers did not pledge their lives, fortunes, and sacred honor so that America's fate would depend on the whims of other countries.

Former Democratic presidential candidate Howard Dean demonstrated how mean-spirited, unfair, and irresponsible he was by suggesting that Bush might actually have been warned by the Saudis about 9/11. Despite the fact that Osama bin Laden described on videotape how he sent nearly 3,000 people to their deaths, Dean said the terrorist should not be prejudged. When Dean spoke of wanting to be "the candidate for guys with Confederate flags in their pickup trucks," the Yale graduate and medical doctor betrayed an elitism and insensitivity toward blacks that was breathtaking. If Bush had said something similar, there would be rioting in the streets. Like Hillary Clinton, who made up the story about Chelsea's whereabouts on 9/11, Dean would invent facts as he went along. He claimed erroneously that Bush cut combat pay for soldiers in Iraq and Afghanistan when, in fact, Bush had just signed a bill to increase their pay.

Despite the fact that Bush signed the No Child Left Behind Act on January 8, 2002, because of foot-dragging by public-school systems, sixty percent of the public schools in the country still taught reading with the whole-language approach. Essentially, that meant that children were not being taught to read at all. Yet Senator John F. Kerry and other Democrats denounced the act and particularly the annual testing it requires. Displaying Bill Clinton's capacity to shift with the wind, Kerry supported and voted for the act but, seeking to appeal to teachers' unions in his run for the presidency, Kerry insisted the act had turned schools into "testing factories." He wanted testing curtailed, meaning schools would no longer be accountable. Dean said he would dismantle the No Child Left Behind Act entirely.

If that ever happened, it would be a devastating blow to America and its children. Just as slaves were not permitted to learn to read, millions of American children would be consigned to illiteracy and lives of failure if Dean, Kerry, and other Democrats got their way. Blacks and Hispanics would be the greatest losers. As it is, sixty-five percent of black fourth graders and fifty-nine percent of Hispanic fourth graders in America cannot read a simple children's book. Affluent children attending top private schools have no such problem: They are taught to read with phonics.

The irony was that liberals like John Kerry claimed to be reformers, yet when it came to America's most precious asset—its children—they stood for regression and policies harmful to those who were disadvantaged. Those same liberals thought of themselves as enlightened, yet many of them mocked Bush for the way he spoke and ridiculed him for demanding that the education establishment impose standards so it will stop turning out millions of illiterates.

In training new agents, the FBI Academy at Quantico, Virginia, teaches that the best predictor of future behavior is past behavior. Yet over and over, voters have ignored warning signs of poor character and candidates' track records and focused instead on their promises, their celebrity, and their acting ability on television. It was a blindness that they would never extend to choosing friends, car repair shops, or plumbers.

Each time, voters have regretted disregarding those clues to character. When he was a candidate for vice president, Richard Nixon became embroiled in an ethics issue when the *New York Post* revealed he had secretly accepted $18,000 from private contributors to defray his expenses. It should have come as no surprise that he would end up being driven from office by the scandal known as Watergate. Given Bill Clinton's flagrant, compulsive philandering while he was governor of Arkansas, it should have come as no surprise that he would turn out to be a spineless leader who was unwilling to deal effectively with al Qaeda but was willing to have sex with an intern in the Oval Office and to lie under oath.

Almost as if they feel they do not deserve decent, trustworthy politicians, Americans too often fall for the phony distinction that so long as they do not influence public acts, flaws in candidates' character should be disregarded. It was another display of denial. Human beings do not consist of two spheres, a public and a private one. Poor judgment, hypocrisy, deceit, arrogance, and corrupt tendencies displayed in one's personal life inevitably manifest themselves in public life.

The contrast between Hillary Clinton's nastiness in private and her Cheshire cat smile in public demonstrated both hypocrisy and an unbalanced personality. The fact that Hillary fired a White House usher who was the father of four children for trying to help a former first lady with her computer demonstrated ruthlessness and paranoia that could be expected to balloon if she were ever president.

"No man can climb out beyond the limitations of his own character," Viscount John Morley wrote. So long as Americans ignore that truism, they will continue to be surprised—for better or worse—by the candidate they elect as president.

"When I left here, I didn't have much in the way of a life plan," Bush told students when he returned to Yale in May 2001. "I knew some people who thought they did. But it turned out that we were all in it for the ups and downs, most of them unexpected. Life takes its turns, makes its own demands, writes its own story. And along the way, we start to realize we are not the author."

No one could have anticipated the peril that America would face during the presidency of George W. Bush. Yet no one could have been better suited to confronting that peril. It required vision, courage, patience, optimism, integrity, focus, discipline, determination, decisiveness, and devotion to America.

It was, in the end, a matter of character.

Notes

1. Franette McCulloch, July 25, 2003.
2. Former Secret Service agent, July 17, 2003.
3. Former Secret Service agent, June 30, 2003.
4. Andrew H. Card, Jr., September 15, 2003.
5. Nancy LaFevers, September 4, 2004.
6. Clay Johnson III, September 26, 2003.
7. Charles E. "Chuck" Taylor, June 21, 2003.
8. Kessler, *Inside the White House*, page 30.
9. Bertram S. Brown, M.D., February 24, 2004.
10. Martha Holton, August 31, 2003.
11. Barbara Bush, *Barbara Bush: A Memoir*, page 45.
12. George W. Bush, *A Charge to Keep*, page 96
13. Clay Johnson III, October 7, 2003.
14. Logan Walters, February 8, 2004.
15. Robert J. Dieter, November 7, 2003.
16. Clay Johnson III, September 26, 2003.
17. John E. Kidde, August 18, 2003.
18. John Axelrod, August 9, 2003.
19. Clay Johnson III, September 26, 2003.
20. Robert J. Dieter, November 7, 2003.
21. *Washington Post*, July 27, 1999, page A1.
22. Donald Etra, August 9, 2003.
23. Robert D. McCallum, Jr., December 16, 2003.
24. Clay Johnson III, September 26, 2003.
25. Frederick P. Angst, Jr., August 30, 2003.

26. David W. Heckler, August 31, 2003.
27. Frederick C. Livingston, September 2, 2003.
28. *USA Today*, July 28, 2000, page 8A.
29. *Time*, November 15, 1999, page 46.
30. "Born to Run," *Texas Monthly*, April 1994.
31. Ibid.
32. Collister "Terry" Johnson, Jr., October 16, 2003.
33. Andrew H. Card, Jr., September 15, 2003.
34. Walter Fiederowicz, August 30, 2003.
35. *Washington Post*, July 28, 1999, page A1.
36. "Junior Is His Own Bush Now," *Time*, July 31, 1989, page 60.
37. *Newsweek*, August 7, 2000, page 32.
38. *Washington Post*, January 22, 1989, page W21.
39. *Washington Post*, July 25, 1999, page A1.
40. *New York Times*, July 29, 2000, page A1.
41. *Washington Post*, January 22, 1989, page W21.
42. *Washington Post*, July 28, 1999, page A1.
43. *Washington Post*, July 28, 1999, page A1.
44. Clay Johnson III, September 26, 2003.
45. Ibid.
46. *Washington Post*, January 22, 1989, page W21.
47. *New York Times*, May 26, 2003.
48. Clay Johnson III, October 7, 2003.
49. Ibid.
50. *USA Today*, July 28, 2000, page 8A.
51. Clay Johnson III, October 7, 2003.
52. *Washington Post*, July 25, 1999, page A1.
53. *Houston Chronicle*, May 8, 1994, page A1.
54. Minutaglio, *First Son*, page 209.
55. *Washington Post*, July 25, 1999, page A1.
56. Ibid.
57. Minutaglio, *First Son*, page 210.
58. *New York Times*, September 11, 2000, page A1.
59. Clay Johnson III, September 26, 2003.
60. "Junior Is His Own Bush Now," *Time*, July 31, 1989, page 60.
61. Ibid.

62. Bruni, *Ambling into History*, page 117.
63. Karl Rove, December 5, 2003.
64. Clay Johnson III, September 26, 2003.
65. Barnett Alexander "Sandy" Kress, September 18, 2003.
66. Dr. G. Reid Lyon, September 9, 2003.
67. Ibid.
68. Margaret Spellings, November 12, 2003.
69. Beth Ann Bryan, September 22, 2003.
70. Clay Johnson III, September 26, 2003.
71. Clay Johnson III, January 5, 2004.
72. Clay Johnson III, January 12, 2004.
73. Clay Johnson III, September 26, 2003.
74. Alberto R. Gonzales, September 12, 2003.
75. Dr. G. Reid Lyon, October 11, 2003.
76. Clay Johnson III, October 7, 2003.
77. Collister "Terry" Johnson, Jr., October 16, 2003.
78. Karen P. Hughes, February 2, 2004.
79. Logan Walters, February 8, 2004.
80. Former Secret Service agent, October 20, 2003.
81. Kessler, *Inside the White House*, page 148.
82. Clay Johnson III, October 7, 2003.
83. Margaret Spellings, November 12, 2003.
84. Barnett Alexander "Sandy" Kress, September 22, 2003.
85. Dr. G. Reid Lyon, October 9, 2003.
86. Dr. G. Reid Lyon, September 9, 2003.
87. Karen P. Hughes, February 2, 2004.
88. Dr. Kenneth Goodman, October 9, 2003.
89. Karl Rove, December 5, 2003.
90. Margaret Spellings, October 9, 2003.
91. Howard Franklin, June 8, 2003.
92. Logan Walters, February 7, 2004.
93. Howard Franklin, June 8, 2003.
94. Former Secret Service agent, July 17, 2003.
95. Clay Johnson III, September 26, 2003.
96. Jim Savage, November 11, 2003.
97. Former Secret Service agent, May 8, 2003.
98. David Sibley, January 5, 2004.
99. Michael M. Wood, February 10, 2004.

100. Andrew H. Card, Jr., September 15, 2003.
101. Collister "Terry" Johnson, Jr., October 16, 2003.
102. Clay Johnson III, September 26, 2003.
103. Jim Towey, November 18, 2003.
104. Margaret Spellings, November 12, 2003.
105. Michael Alexander, M.D., August 15, 2003.
106. Clay Johnson III, October 7, 2003.
107. Andrew H. Card, Jr., September 15, 2003.
108. Clay Johnson III, October 7, 2003.
109. Margaret Spellings, November 12, 2003.
110. Charles E. "Chuck" Taylor, June 21, 2003.
111. Barnett Alexander "Sandy" Kress, September 22, 2003.
112. Frum, *The Right Man*, page 272.
113. Michael Gerson, November 15, 2003; Karen P. Hughes, February 2, 2003.
114. Margaret Spellings, November 12, 2003.
115. Clay Johnson III, October 7, 2003.
116. Alberto R. Gonzales, September 12, 2003.
117. Clay Johnson III, November 12, 2003.
118. Robert S. Mueller III, September 26, 2003.
119. Margaret Spellings, November 12, 2003.
120. Robert J. Dieter, November 7, 2003.
121. Rex W. Cowdry, M.D., September 6, 2003.
122. Kessler, *The CIA at War*, page 235.
123. Ibid., page 283.
124. Karen P. Hughes, February 2, 2004.
125. Andrew H. Card, Jr., September 15, 2003.
126. Alberto R. Gonzales, September 12, 2003.
127. Rex W. Cowdry, M.D., September 5, 2003.
128. Dr. Condoleezza Rice, January 31, 2004.
129. Ibid.
130. Colin Powell, December 22, 2003.
131. Stephen J. Hadley, October 18, 2003.
132. Colin Powell, December 22, 2003.
133. Stephen J. Hadley, October 18, 2003.
134. Dr. Condoleezza Rice, January 31, 2004.
135. Colin Powell, December 22, 2003.
136. Ibid.

137. Alberto R. Gonzales, September 12, 2003.

138. Donald H. Rumsfeld, February 21, 2003.

139. Stephen J. Hadley, October 18, 2003.

140. Alberto R. Gonzales, September 12, 2003.

141. Stephen J. Hadley, October 18, 2003.

142. Margaret Spellings, November 12, 2003.

143. Dr. Condoleezza Rice, January 31, 2004.

144. Richard J. Kerr, November 15, 2003.

145. Tomlinson G. Rauscher, August 30, 2003.

146. Donald Etra, August 9, 2003.

147. Donald Etra, August 15, 2003.

148. Clay Johnson III, September 26, 2003.

149. Rex W. Cowdry, M.D., September 6, 2003.

150. Alberto R. Gonzales, September 12, 2003.

151. Collister "Terry" Johnson, Jr., October 16, 2003.

152. *Houston Chronicle*, February 25, 2001, page A1.

153. Collister "Terry" Johnson, Jr., October 16, 2003.

154. Logan Walters, February 7, 2004.

155. Clay Johnson III, September 26, 2003.

156. Karen P. Hughes, February 2, 2004.

157. Carl M. Cannon, December 1, 2003.

158. Judy Keen, December 15, 2003.

159. Minutaglio, *First Son*, page 278.

160. Karen P. Hughes, February 2, 2003.

161. Clay Johnson III, January 12, 2004.

162. Dan Bartlett, December 5, 2003.

163. Ibid.

164. Andrew H. Card, Jr., September 15, 2003.

165. Collister "Terry" Johnson, Jr., October 16, 2003.

166. *Washington Post*, July 25, 1999, page A1.

167. Andrew H. Card, Jr., September 15, 2003.

168. Margaret Spellings, November 12, 2003.

169. Clay Johnson III, January 26, 2004.

170. Margaret Spellings, November 12, 2003.

171. Dan Bartlett, December 5, 2003.

172. Ibid.

173. Dr. Condoleezza Rice, January 31, 2004.

174. Ibid.

175. Margaret Spellings, October 9, 2003.
176. Karl Rove, December 5, 2003.
177. Ibid.
178. Karl Rove, January 12, 2004.
179. Clay Johnson III, January 2, 2004.
180. Stephen Friedman, December 12, 2003.
181. *Washington Post*, November 26, 2003, page A1.
182. Dr. Condoleezza Rice, January 31, 2004.
183. Alberto R. Gonzales, September 12, 2003.
184. Dr. G. Reid Lyon, January 27, 2004.
185. *Newsweek*, August 7, 2000, page 32.
186. Charles E. "Chuck" Taylor, June 28, 2003.
187. Collister "Terry" Johnson, Jr., October 16, 2003.

Bibliography

Bruni, Frank. *Ambling into History: The Unlikely Odyssey of George Bush*. New York: HarperCollins, 2002; Perennial edition.

Bush, Barbara. *A Memoir*. New York: Charles Scribner's Sons, 1994.

Bush, George W. *A Charge to Keep: My Journey to the White House*. New York: William Morrow, 1999; Perennial edition.

Frum, David. *The Right Man: The Surprise Presidency of George W. Bush*. New York: Random House, 2003.

Hughes, Karen. *Ten Minutes from Normal*. New York: Viking, 2004.

Kessler, Ronald. *The CIA at War: Inside the Secret Campaign Against Terror*. New York: St. Martin's Press, 2003.

———. *The Bureau: The Secret History of the FBI*. New York: St. Martin's Press, 2002.

———. *Inside the White House: The Hidden Lives of the Modern Presidents and the Secrets of the World's Most Powerful Institution*. New York: Pocket Books, 1995.

Minutaglio, Bill. *First Son: George W. Bush and the Bush Family Dynasty*. New York: Random House, 1999; Three Rivers Press edition.

Moore, James, and Wayne Slater. *Bush's Brain: How Karl Rove Made George W. Bush Presidential*. Hoboken, N.J.: John Wiley & Sons, 2003.

Sammon, Bill. *Fighting Back: The War on Terrorism—from Inside the Bush White House*. Washington, D.C.: Regnery Publishing, 2002.

Walsh, Kenneth T. *Air Force One: A History of the Presidents and Their Planes*. New York: Hyperion, 2003.

Woodward, Bob. *Bush at War*. New York: Simon & Schuster, 2002.

Index